THE ARK'S CARGO

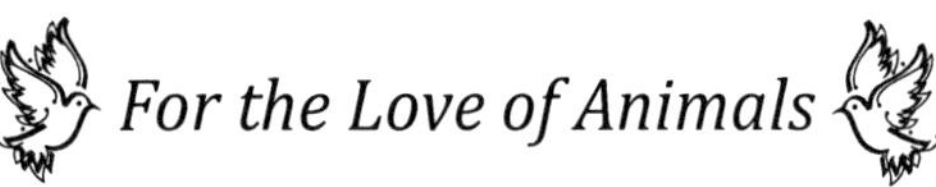

For the Love of Animals

WILLIAM W. BUISCH, DVM

Order this book online at www.trafford.com
or email orders@trafford.com

Most Trafford titles are also available at major online book retailers.

Printed in the United States of America.

ISBN: 978-1-4669-7771-6 (sc)
ISBN: 978-1-4669-7770-9 (hc)
ISBN: 978-1-4669-7769-3 (e)

Library of Congress Control Number: 2013901166

Trafford rev. 01/18/2013

www.trafford.com

North America & international
toll-free: 1 888 232 4444 (USA & Canada)
fax: 812 355 4082

Dedication to My Family

This book is dedicated to my family
with special recognition
of my four "forever young kids"
who fill my life with
"Love and Joy"!

Amory Nan Cariadus
Julie Ann Moreland
Richard William Buisch
Anna Mae Pierce

CONTENTS

ACKNOWLEDGEMENTS

This book could not have been completed without the most capable assistance of the following special individuals in my life who have provided countless hours in reviewing and providing editorial comments to assure this writing would be completed in the best manner possible. They include: Ms. Sabrina Brem, Mr. Daniel Martin, Mrs. Helen Terrell, and Mrs. Gladys Wells. I would also thank Dr. Andrew Goodwin, PhD., a specialist in aquatic diseases and Mr. Sebastian Belle, Executive Director, Maine Aquaculture Association, for their review of Chapter 19—Fishing for Salmon and Carp. Their thoughts and comments were most welcomed and appreciated.

In addition I am indebted to the following individuals who have played such a special role in my life's work as an International Veterinarian. They include: Mr. John B. Adams, Dr. Pedro Acha, Dr. John Acree, Dr. J. Lee Alley, Dr. Joan Arnoldi, Dr. John K. Atwell, Dr. Lowell Barnes, Dr. Charles W. Beard, Dr. Richard E. Breitmeyer, Dr. Corrie C. Brown, Dr. Jones W. Bryan, Dr. Thomas Bunn, Mr. Alan R. Christian, Dr. John R.

Clifford, Dr. Max E. Coats, Dr. Francisco Collazo-Mattei, Dr. Michael T. Collins, Dr. Arthur Davis, Dr. W. Ron DeHaven, Mrs. Joanne DesRoachers, Dr. Linda A. Detwiler, Dr. Roger Drummond, Dr. Robert J. Eckroade, Mr. Greg Evens; Dr. Peter J. Fernandez, Dr. Gerald Fichtner, Mr. Bob Frost, Dr. Granville Frye, Dr. Robert Geyer, Dr. E. Paul J. Gibbs, Dr. Chester A. Gibson, Dr. Michael Gilsdorf, Dr. Andrew E. Goodwin, Attorney John Golden, Dr. Temple Grandin, Dr. Christopher M. Groocock, Dr. Arthur Hall, Mr. Neil Hammerschmidt, Dr. William L. Hartman, Dr. Stephan Hasler, Mr. Max Hepner, Dr. Billy R. Heron, Dr. Bob R. Hillman, Dr. Sam D. Holland, Dr. Thomas J. Holt, Mrs. Margaret Huggins, Dr. John P. Huntley, Dr. John L. Hyde, Dr. Billy Johnson, Dr. Daryl Johnson, Mr. Robert Jones, Mr. Myron Jones, Ms. Margaret Kelly, Mr. Ed Ketchum, Dr. Daniel King, Dr. Harold King, Dr. Lonnie J. King, Mr. John Kinsella, Dr. Ralph P. Knowles, Jr., Dr. Elizabeth A. Lautner, Ms. Amy W. Mann, Ms. Linda Mansfield, Dr. Maxwell A. Lea, Mr. Bill LeRoyer, Dr. Donald H. Lein, Mrs. Sue Lendrum, Dr. Jim Logan, Mr. Larry D. Mark, Mr. Raul Marroquin, Dr. Bret D. Marsh, Ms. Barbara M. Martin, Dr. David T. Marshall, Dr. Thomas McKenna, Mr. Terry Medley, Dr. Charles E. Messengill, Dr. Norvan Meyer, Dr. William Moulton, Dr. Lee M. Myers, Mr. Carl Nagle, Dr. James E. Novy, Dr. Richard E. Pacer, Ms. Roxanne

Payne, Dr. Jim Pierson, Dr. George Pearson, Dr. Benjamin S. Pomeroy, Dr. John R. Ragan, Dr. Valerie E. Ragan, Dr. James A. Roth, Mr. Andrew R. Rhorer, Dr. Mo D. Salman, Dr. Beverly Schmitt, Dr. Dale F. Schwindaman, Dr. John Seacat, Dr. E.C. "Buck" Sharman, Mr. Larry Slagle, Dr. Bill Smith, Mr. Paul Smith, Mr. Oyvind Snopestad, Dr. Judith R. Stabel, Dr. Susan M. Stehman, Dr. Terry Taylor, Dr. H. Leon Thacker, Dr. Charles O. Thoen, Mr. Otto Torenson, Dr. Alfonso Torres, Dr. A. Wesley Towers, Dr. Susan C. Trock, Dr. Bill Utterback, Dr. G. Gale Wagner, Dr. Sherrilyn H. Wainwright, Dr. Thomas E. Walton, Dr. Gary M. Weber, Dr. Stephen E. Weber, Dr. Scott J. Wells, Dr. Norman G. Willis, Dr. Saul T. Wilson, Dr. Nora E. Wineland, Ms. Diana L. Whipple, Dr. Robert H. Whitlock, Dr. Taylor Woods, Dr. John H. Wyss, and Dr. Earnest W. Zirkle.

In addition there are many others who have crossed my path in life and while not mentioned by name; have contributed so much. To all of you my thanks and gratitude.

PREFACE

What is there in the story of Noah's Ark that could possibly created the beginnings of a passionate career in Haiti, the Jungles of Panama, or on the Road to Timbuktu?

The story of Noah's Ark has been told numerous times throughout history. As a child I remember my parents and grandparents recounting the story as if it had just occurred. There always seemed to be a bit of drama in their voice and you could see in their smile that they really enjoyed telling the story as the eyes of their children and grandchildren sparkled with awe and wonder.

My grandmother was my favorite story teller and she would often begin this story by emphasizing the love of God and the beauty of the world he created. She would note how important it was for us to enjoy His creation and all living things. She would stress the beauty of the flowers on the hillside, the pleasure of walking in the countryside, and the joy of fishing down by the river or even bringing in the cows in the cool of the evening from the south forty pastures. Yes, even Buttons, our family dog, was special to us all.

Well, it seems, as my grandmother's version of the story goes; long, long ago, there were a lot of people bickering and not treating each other very well. As far as God was concerned (and my grandmother agreed) the people at that time were mean and nasty! They were not good to each other and were not good to God who had created this wonderful place to live in.

So, what happened? According to her, God wanted to start over with a family that was known to be loving and good to those around them. So he asked Noah and his family (good people) to build a boat, an Ark, large enough to carry two of every kind of animal living here on this earth.

This include livestock such as cows, horses, pigs, sheep and goats; wild beasts such as lions, tigers, elephants, and giraffes; as well as all kinds of birds and reptiles that crawled on the ground. God also asked Noah to load the Ark with enough food to feed all of the animals and for his family as well.

Finally the day came when Noah finished building this gigantic boat, the Ark. He loaded it with two (a male and a female) of each kind of animal existing at that time.

Once all of the animals and Noah's family were on board, it started to rain.

It rained, and it rained, and then rained some more. It was way more rain than they had ever seen and the wind blew like it had never blown before. For forty days and nights, the rain would not cease. Soon the land was covered with water, even above the highest mountain tops.

Now, my grandmother was a soft spoken woman, and yet at this point in the story, she would use her hands and voice to give us the true feeling of this terrible storm. She would shake her fists and use as deep a voice as she could shouting, "Boom, Boom, Boom!"

To add to the drama of the event, she would turn any lights within reach on and off. While her antics of lightning and thunder might be ludicrous to some, I can assure you they would scare the BeGemmies out of each and every one of us.

As the story continued, those of us listening to her would hold each other tight and of course the youngest kids, who didn't understand what was going on, would suck their thumbs and have this look of befuddlement in their eyes. I wouldn't be surprised if they were wondering what in the world was going on and why we were so riled up?

The last part of grandmother's Bible story was always the best. After the rain had stopped, the flood waters started to recede. Before long, a beautiful white dove, a dove that Noah had released earlier in the week, appeared in the sky carrying an olive branch in its beak. Seeing this gave Noah the assurance he needed that dry land was nearby and that they would soon be able to offload the animals, starting a new life together.

Then grandma would pause and smile broadly, noting that God decided to celebrate their successful voyage by placing a colorful rainbow in the sky. It was a great big rainbow that stretched completely from one side of the sky to the other. It was gorgeous and captured the beauty of many different colors. It was a spectacular sight indeed.

Yes, it was an exciting story and often each of the kids would want to participate, sharing of their own experiences; how many rainbows they had seen, how they looked, and especially how each of their rainbows was the best and most beautiful rainbows ever seen.

Often my grandmother would end the story noting that for every year since that time, the number of people in Noah's family and the number of animals on this earth have grown larger and larger.

In fact, each of us, you and me, today are part of this family, Noah's family. We can be proud of that because Noah was a member of God's family and so that means we are part of God's family too.

Then, after a moment of silence, in her own grandmotherly way, she would smile and stretch out her arms to each and every one of us saying, "You know God loves you!!! And so do I!!! And that includes You, You, and You!!!

Now as I look back to those wonderful years, I am thrilled to be able to recount the exciting adventures I have personally had since that time as an International Veterinarian. The tremendous opportunity of working with many of God's animals has and continues to fill my Heart with Joy!

It is therefore with great pleasure that I share with you some of these stories and the remarkable efforts being taken by many nations to foster improved animal health worldwide.

And finally, it is my hope that through these chapters you will have a renewed appreciation of the world we live in and the delicate balances that must be maintained to preserve life and to sustain it abundantly!

CHAPTER 1

What a Beginning!!!

What is there about adversity that prepares one to face the challenges of an International Veterinarian? Why do we have to face such challenges at a young age? Even a sense of homelessness at one point brought out the frailty of life as well as the rewards of persistence and dedication to the task at hand.

It was 1962 and my first experience away from my family. I was on my way to attend college in Manhattan, Kansas and it seemed like a long way from my home in Rochester, New York.

Now, as is often the case, I had more than enough advice to help me in the process of deciding where to go for my education. The best example of what I had to deal with is that of my Father's Aunt Grace. She made it known that she had traveled to Kansas in the 1920's and as a result knew the area well.

In her opinion it was a big mistake to even consider going to that part of the country for an education. She noted that life in Kansas was not easy and that in many respects the area might be considered not up with the times when compared to what we were used to in New York. Even a little rain would make the roads impassable and in some cases would put your car up to its axles in a quagmire of mud. And then with great emphasis, she would add that at times you could be stranded, unable to move your vehicle for days.

Nevertheless, as a grown adult (19 years old), I had already made up my mind; was sure that the roads had to have improved since the 1920s; and was determined that Kansas State University was where I wanted to be.

I can still remember the day my parents left me off at the curb next to my dorm. My room was on the first floor right under the cement seats of the Kansas State University "Wildcats" football stadium. Six students were assigned to my room number 127 and as you might imagine, I didn't know a single one of them. While the rest of my roommates were from Kansas, I was the foreigner. I was from New York and as a result, I got all the usual New Yorker questions:

- What was a New Yorker doing in this part of the world?
- Did I have all my Papers in order? Did I have a Passport?

- Did I understand the importance of them checking my credentials to assure that it would be acceptable for me to be in their midst?
- Why did I speak so funny? Could I ever learn to talk right?
- Have I ever seen a Jackalope? (I later found out that this was a mythical half rabbit/half antelope.)
- How could they trust me with all the gangsters and mobsters living in New York?

This was all done in jest and I assumed they were just having fun, and yet it didn't help my nervousness at this time without any family support system nearby. To be honest, I am sure part of my nervousness was due to the fact that for the first time in my life I didn't know anyone within hundreds of miles and as a result didn't trust a single soul.

While you may consider this a little bit weird, I was most likely the only one at the University who had a lot to learn about trust and obviously I was not ready to learn this concept at that time or any time in the near future!

All of my belongings were under lock and key. Somehow I was able to fit them all in my trunk and as I think about it, that trunk wasn't as big as some might think. I wasn't about to unpack my trunk. There was no way that I would even begin to consider putting my clothes in the closet as everyone else had done. After all, the closet assigned to me did not have a lock on it.

Furthermore, my distrusting attitude was well established and in part related to the fact that I came from a rather poor family and knew I couldn't afford to lose my clothes. Back home in New York we always locked everything and I was not about to change my ways now!

Fortunately for me, it only took a few months before I truly appreciated my roommates and the wonderful sense of humor they had. At that point I started picking up the Kansas ways of doing things and appreciated the freedom and trust their way of life allowed. And, oh yes, before long all my clothes were stored in the closet, just like everyone else.

On my second day at Kansas State University, I knew I had to go to the nearby Basketball Coliseum to register for the classes I wished to take. It was a huge building and it took me quite a while to find where I needed to be, which line was for new students, and which line was appropriate for out of state students.

Not only that, but the myriad of forms that needed to be filled out and the seemingly endless questions sure complicated the process and at times caused somewhat of a panic as I struggled through the initial stages of truly being on my own. You might say it was almost overwhelming, and yes, I was shy, very shy. It was clearly very difficult for me to ask questions of anyone.

Nevertheless, I so wanted to be successful in college, to show everyone that I was of strong family stock, and as some might say that at the age of 19, I was a "Macho Man". In fact the ego in my head made it loud and clear, "Don't Screw Up!"

It was at that point that I met my advisor. He was a man of tall stature; assigned to help me identify my Major Course of Study as well as the classes I needed to take that semester.

When asked by my advisor what I wished to major in I boldly announced in as deep a masculine voice as I could muster, "I have decided that I wish to Major in Pre-Veterinary Medicine and to Minor in Music with the Church Organ as my instrument of choice.

Wow, I couldn't believe what happened next. My advisor, with his imposing stature, promptly stood up and pounded on the table for all to hear and shouted saying, "Young man, you had better make up your mind! You can't do both! They are different areas of study; each is very difficult; and it is time you got your act together! If you want to go to this school, you had better decide right now which Major it will be. What about it! I don't have time for such nonsense!"

Then to add insult to the injury he had already inflicted, he added, "Your grades in High School weren't all that great and you should feel lucky to even be here! Do you understand? So, what will it be?"

With that scenario, it didn't take me but a fraction of a second to respond in as calm and as deep a voice as I could muster, "Yes sir, please register me in the Pre-Veterinary Medicine Curriculum as a Major. That is what I really want to be! Yes, a Veterinarian!"

"Good," he said as he calmed down and proceeded with the enrollment process.

You can be sure that from that moment on, I was as quiet as a mouse. Only occasionally I would answer, "Yes Sir, Yes Sir, that will be fine," as he outlined the courses I would need for the year. It was all part of the learning process and as I gained more confidence through the years, it was one of the few times I can ever remember being treated in such a rough manner.

Fortunately I was able to continue my interest in music and soon became the church organist at the local Methodist Church. While I never accepted money for playing the organ at Sunday Morning Worship Services, my attitude on accepting money at weddings was quite different.

As you might agree, weddings are always fun to attend and as you might guess, in college towns, love is often an important part of the culture. As some might say, "Love Blooms" and as a result there are always plenty of weddings to attend. For me, attending and providing the music for these wonderful events truly helped pay my way through college and at times provided the unexpected bonus of a little extra pocket money that was always gratefully received.

With that, I must admit, however, that I would often let the devil get a hold of me and when the bridal couple would ask me what I charged, I would respond with my standard answer, "You can pay me whatever you think it is worth. I enjoy playing the church organ and I am honored to be asked to provide the music for this special occasion."

And you know what? They would always pay me more, much more than I would have ever expected! Since my parent's income could only pay for bare essentials, the income obtained as an organist at weddings was most helpful.

This was especially true when I combined that income with the other two jobs I had. They were the positions of a classroom custodian and that of a telephone operator in my dorm.

The telephone operator job was great in that I always worked at night (after midnight). This was a quiet time of day (very few telephone calls); giving me plenty of time to study and write the numerous papers college professors so delight in assigning on a regular basis.

In all, I must say that my experience at Kansas State University was outstanding. The professors provided me with an education that has paid back dividends over and over again. The technical training and the art of dealing with difficult situations, in a positive way, have been so useful to me through the years. I will always thank the Administration and the Professors at Kansas State University for their professionalism and quality of instruction. The sharing of their expertise put all of us as students on a solid foundation and prepared us for a future of success.

Soon it was the summer of 1965 and I had just received a letter from the Dean of the College of Veterinary Medicine congratulating me on being accepted as an alternate for one of the two alternate positions for the Veterinary Class starting in the fall of that year. You can imagine how disappointed I was. Alternate, an alternate position, what good is an alternate position?

After three years of successful study in Pre-Veterinary Medicine, I wanted to be in the class, not an alternate that would get in if someone already accepted in the class decided to drop out. Who would ever drop out after all the rigors of getting accepted? I was angry to say the least! So, I decided to visit the Office of the Dean of the Veterinary School and see what he might suggest.

The Dean was very generous and even though he had a busy schedule, invited me into his office and again congratulated me on being accepted as an alternate for the next class starting in the fall.

I shared with him my disappointment and my conclusion that no one would drop out after trying so hard to get in.

He acknowledged that was most likely true and reminded me that over eight hundred students, most of them highly qualified had applied that year and that I should feel great to have been accepted as an alternate with only eighty students selected for the Veterinary Class that year.

So I asked what he would recommend that I do during this next year if a class slot did not open up. He thought for a moment and then suggested that I might consider taking more courses to strengthen my preparation for the Veterinary Curriculum.

I thought for a minute while looking down at the floor. (Who knows why we look at the floor. Obviously the floor doesn't know the answer.) Then, I graciously looked his way; thanked him for his advice; and indicated that rather than pursuing more course work at this time, I would most likely seek the possibility of finding a job with a Kansas Veterinarian specializing in Large Animal Medicine. Hopefully this would be helpful as I gained as much practical experience as possible.

He agreed that would be a wonderful way to proceed and wished me much success, further indicating that he would encourage me to apply again next year if a class position did not open up this time around. I thanked him for his time, and with a big smile noted that I would keep in close contact with him.

That night, I discussed this with my friend, Frank Harrison. He suggested that he could take me to Salina, Kansas during the Summer Recess and that I might try to find a job there. I thought about it for a few days and then decided I would accept his offer and as a result, since I had no car or other mode of transportation, knew I must find a way to get around. Basically I needed wheels and to me a motorcycle would fill the purpose just fine.

About a week later, I asked Frank to take me to the local Motorcycle Dealer; I looked over the various models and decided, considering the funds I had saved, which model would best meet my needs. The motorcycle I selected and had to have, was a Super Powered (sure 50 mph top speed with the wind to your back) and definitely the Sportiest Machine you could ever dream of (more like a moped) Super Sport Honda.

When the dealer asked if I had ever driven a motorcycle before or would I need any help in understanding its operation, my stupid male ego jumped right in and I said without hesitation, "I really don't need any help, but thanks anyway."

After the dealer had returned well into the service area and out of sight, I turned the key on and using the kick starter, had the engine running in no time. How easy could this be? Next I settled in my seat comfortably and as in the movies used my foot to press the shift lever into gear.

At first I had trouble figuring out where the clutch was. But, once I got that figured out, I was on my way. And having ridden a bicycle many times before, this wasn't bad at all! But then, who would have believed, right in front of me was a stop sign! What do I do now? Yep, you are so right! Panic set in! I didn't know where the brake was! I swerved to miss the stop sign, dodged the cars screeching their braking tires while maneuvering to avoid colliding right into me and my precious new cycle.

Wow, the next thing I knew; could it be? Oh, yes, against all odds, I had safely made it across the road!

And then, Oh, No! There I was, again, facing danger; speedily projecting my brand new sporty machine right into a woods or let's call it from my minds perspective, a gigantic forest with no way out! The trees in front of me were just too much to handle and I knew; not only that I was losing control, but had lost control before I had even left the dealer's lot.

Thankfully, however, in some miraculous way, I was able to find neutral while in the same instant scrambling for the brake pedal that was so needed at this time in my life. You should have seen me. I had the shakes like you wouldn't believe and rightfully so. You bet, I was one lucky dude and at the same time I learned a valuable lesson or two. First of all, I must admit that the most important lesson I learned was that honesty pays, it always pays. Secondly, as I am sure was obvious, letting the male ego take control of my life was stupid, unbefitting to anyone with the least amount of common sense/rational thinking, an unbelievable, crazy, stupid thing to do!

Once the summer recess began, Frank and I loaded up his red Volkswagen Bug with all of our belongings, a trunk's worth for me and slightly more for him. Neither of us really felt impoverished. We knew that some days would be better than others. We always lived on the edge and it didn't matter if we had to ration our food, we just felt this was the way college kids lived and found joy in the simple things of life.

Once the car was loaded, Frank, in his Volkswagen, and I, on my Super Sport Motorcycle were on our way to Salina, Kansas. It was a beautiful day and route Interstate

40 from Manhattan, Kansas to Salina, Kansas was a smooth ride and as pleasant as could be. The sky was a deep blue and a few puffs of white clouds drifted overhead. The temperature was warm and the light nylon jacket I was wearing was billowing in the breeze.

It made me feel as free as a bird. I would weave back and forth on the road singing some of my favorite songs. I didn't even care if an occasional bug smashed onto my helmet as long as I didn't have them in my teeth or sliding down my throat as has been described by some of my fellow bikers. Time went fast and soon we were in the great city of Salina.

It was then that I opened up my wallet and realized just how limited my funds were. (So what ever happened to preplanning?) All I could find was a twenty dollar bill and a little pocket change. I suddenly felt very much alone, especially with the knowledge that Frank had to leave shortly for his home in Wichita, Kansas.

I said to myself, with a hope that the God I worshiped might be listening: "I think I am homeless and with the little amount of money I have, I am scared! Yes, I am really scared! I need your help! Do you think you could spare a little time?" You could tell I was really discouraged.

When I finally looked up, lo and behold (good religious words) there on the corner of the street was a public telephone and a telephone directory. So, I ran over to the telephone and started looking through the telephone directory for anything that might be helpful. And what did I behold? Yes, a listing for the local Agriculture County Agent's Office.

Why is this important? Well, when I was a small fry, living on the family farm in Lyons, New York, it seemed the County Agent was always the one to call when we had questions for which we could find no answer. He was always friendly and was noted for his helpfulness when folks needed assistance. So that did it! I would call the County Agent's Office and ask for his advice.

The phone rang three or four times and it seemed like an eternity. Soon a soft voice answered and said, "County Agent's office. May I help you?" Just her voice alone seemed to calm (at least somewhat) my nerves and I asked if the County Agent was in.

It must have been my lucky day. He was in and she indicated she would put him on right away. As you can imagine, this call was quite difficult and I was definitely nervous knowing that I was homeless and did not like the idea of having no other support system near-by.

I told the County Agent my name and explained my circumstances. Basically, I needed a job, and would he by any chance know of any jobs available at this time? He paused and then without hesitation said, "Son, would you be interested in working on a farm?" Since it was wheat harvest time, he occasionally had inquires and always tried to help farmers find the help they needed. Of course I answered in the affirmative.

"Well, then," he said. "I just received a call from a Mr. Frank Zeman, at (Telephone number) asking if there was anyone available to help him during the Harvest Season." I was so excited and replied, "Oh, sir that would be great! I will give Mr. Zeman a call right now and thank you so much, you have been so helpful. I really appreciate this."

As you can imagine, I couldn't wait to call Mr. Zeman. My hopes were very high and I said a short prayer, thanking God for this opportunity and asking God, if at all possible, to help me make a good impression.

Mr. Zeman answered the phone and my heart was going a mile a minute. I introduced myself and discussed the conversation I had with the County Agent, and then asked if he had found anyone yet to help him during this year's wheat harvest? If not, I was available and would truly like to work for him.

With that, Mr. Zeman (Mr. "Z") noted that he had not hired anyone at this point and asked me what I knew about combines and harvesting wheat. My heart dropped, "I'm sorry, but I know nothing about combines and harvesting wheat." What a surprise when he answered, "Good, when can you start?" "Early tomorrow morning," I responded. "Good, then we will see you at 8am tomorrow morning, is that all right?"

Then, with a lump in my throat I said, "Sir, may I ask you another question? "You see, I don't have a place to stay and I wondered if you might have a barn or shed that I might sleep in so that I could be out of the weather should it rain or storm outside."

Mr. "Z" asked me to hold just a minute and then after a brief pause said, "Bill, I discussed this with my wife and she said you could sleep on a cot we have stored here at the house. We would be willing to set it up in the basement right under the furnace ducts. Now, you need to understand that if it rains; our basement leaks and there will be water on the basement floor. If that is all right with you, you are welcome to stay at our home. I thanked him profusely and he said, "Well, then, come right over and we will get you set up." He then proceeded to give me his address and directions on how to get there.

Then, with still another lump in my throat I said, "There is one more thing, sir, I have no money for food and wonder if

I could be paid on a daily basis for the first few weeks."

Again Mr. "Z" put me on hold and this time it seemed to last forever. Finally he came back and said, "This is the deal, you come to work for me, you work seven days a week, you receive a cot to sleep on in the basement, three meals a day cooked by my wife and we will pay you one dollar per hour. If you can agree to that you can come right over." I immediately agreed and rejoiced like you wouldn't believe. It seemed like a miracle and in many ways I believe it was.

Frank Harrison, my college roommate and I rode over to Mr. Zeman's (Mr. "Z's") home, met Mr. "Z", the wheat farmer; Dorothy, his wife; and Barbara, their beautiful daughter. Then Frank Harrison and I said our good-byes and my life harvesting wheat began.

The next morning I rose early, had a big delicious breakfast prepared by Mrs. Zeman and soon was in Mr. "Z's" pickup truck on the way to one of his farms. On this particular farm, Mr. "Z" had several head of cattle and a couple horses, a large wheat field and a small field of corn.

Soon my training began. Mr. "Z" taught me the importance of properly maintaining a wheat combine, a machine that cuts the stalks of wheat and then thrashes the wheat removing the grain from the stalks. Daily maintenance and care was needed to keep this gigantic machine running smoothly. The process involved a visual inspection as well as checking the oil level and greasing the various spigots that were located all over the machine.

It was then about 10 am in the morning and time to start harvesting the wheat. Prior to that time, generally speaking, the wheat cannot be harvested because it is too wet. Apparently the morning dew can create a moisture problem and one must wait until the morning sun and wind have dried the grain to the proper moisture content before it is considered acceptable for storage and shipping.

So, I jumped on the combine with Mr. "Z" and in no time we were in the field harvesting this year's wheat crop. I watched closely as Mr. "Z" operated the combine never dreaming that he would ask me to take over after only a couple hours riding with him.

Soon, he turned to me and asked with a serious face, if I thought I could operate the combine. I indicated that I was watching him closely and was learning as fast as I could, but didn't know if I really had it down to where I could actually do it. He then said, "Well, here, you sit where I was sitting and let's see what you can do." I was nervous as could be; I started out slowly and finished one round of the field.

We were almost back to where we left the truck, when Mr. "Z" looked at me and said, "Bill, I need to go to town to get some parts for my John Deere Tractor and will be back in just a little bit. You will do fine." I hesitated and then shouted out, "Bur Sir, are you sure I can do this? I don't want to do something wrong and damage your machine." Mr. "Z" again calmly indicated that I would do fine as he jumped off the combine and motioned for me to go on.

Well, it really shook me up and all I could think of was what an expensive machine this was. I could imagine all sorts of difficulties including hitting a rock, smashing into the truck while trying to unload the wheat harvested, or even not being able to stop the combine while going through the bordering fence, etc., etc.

So it was with great caution that I ever so slowly started to move forward. At first I moved very slowly and took as much time as necessary to avoid any potential problems. Then, as I gained confidence, I would advance a little faster and at last, yes, at last it even began to feel somewhat comfortable. True, I was still a bit nervous. But, by the middle of the afternoon, I was settled in and at times actually enjoyed the experience; the feeling of the wind in my face, the miles of golden grain swaying in the breeze, and the feeling of being free and enjoying the beauty of God's creation.

About 5 o'clock in the afternoon, I saw Mr. "Z's" truck in the distance heading down the road. Was I ever glad to see him coming. As I stopped to unload another load of grain freshly harvested, he pulled up beside me. He was smiling and indicated we had done enough and that it was time to go home. He had someone else driving each truckload of wheat into the storage elevator in town and so we called it a day.

As we were leaving the field, I spoke up and indicated I was surprised that he left me in the field alone driving this expensive piece of machinery (the combine). "What if something went wrong?" Mr. "Z" just gave me a quick glance and with an even bigger smile on his face, said; "Well, Bill, you did great and I knew you would." With that, I said, "Sure, but what if something went wrong. It could have been a mess."

Mr. "Z" again smiled and calmly responded, "Bill, see that little hill off in the distance?" I looked at him a little puzzled. "Ah, huh." "Well, I was sitting in my truck with these field binoculars, parked right there on top of the hill watching everything that was going on and you did just fine. I knew you were ready and just wanted to build up your confidence so you could do it on your own." With that, I realized and shared a smile as I thanked him for his confidence and appreciation for all that he was doing for me.

On the way into town, we passed a pool hall and with a glance in that direction, Mr. "Z" asked if I had ever played pool. I indicated that I hadn't and he said, "Well then, I guess it is about time you learned." With that he swerved the truck around into a parking lot right next to the entrance.

After renting a table, I asked Mr. "Z" if he played pool a lot. He replied, "On Occasion." I said, "Well then, you must be good at the game!" He looked at me with a wide grin and said, "OOOOOOoooooo, I do ok."

Then after he explained the object of the game and carefully placed the balls on the table in a triangle formation, he asked me to take the first shot with my cue stick to break the balls apart. I still didn't know what he meant, so he further explained what I needed to do. So, I leaned up against the pool table, took aim and hit the white ball with my cue stick; pleased as punch that I hit the balls in the triangle formation straight on. The balls went in every direction and as one can imagine, not a single ball went into any of the six pockets around the edge.

So, now it was Mr. "Z's" turn. He calmly took aim and one by one kicked and spun each of his balls into the various pockets and won the game. I never had another shot. I looked at him and we both started to laugh. With that, I said, "Right, so you just do ok, only play once in a while. I'd like to see you when you are really good." We both left with grins on our faces and it was the start of a wonderful summer.

Later in the year, I was allowed to ride their horses and even spent a few nights camping out near the pasture land where the cattle roam. In such instances, I would take a bath in the cattle watering trough before snuggling in my sleeping bag and gradually falling asleep under the stars. It was so peaceful and the quiet sounds of the evening were truly special, especially considering how I missed the simple luxury of country living.

Often the only sounds I would hear were those of the coyotes calling in the night. Sometimes they sounded so close that one might even imagine or sense the possibility of feeling one of them breathing down their neck. I wonder who would be more surprised, the coyote or myself. It was a delightful summer I will long remember.

During that year I also worked at the Town and Country Animal Hospital for a Dr. John Seacat and a Dr. Daniel King (Dr. "K"), Veterinarians living and working in Salina, Kansas. They had a mixed large animal (cows, pigs, horses) and small animal (dogs, cats) practice. They were bright individuals and I received a lot of valuable experience working under these two capable practitioners.

They worked the local Livestock Market, often called a Sale Barn in addition to all of their other duties and that gave me a totally new perspective of the Livestock Industry. I used to love going to the Livestock Market and hearing the auctioneers with the thrill in their voices rattling off the various bids and/or offers frequently given by the nod of a head or a flip of a hand. The auctioneers were very good and were able to sell a lot of animals in a very short period of time.

The veterinary work at the Market/Sale Barn was intense. The number of animals that needed to be inspected, blood tests that needed to be performed, and vaccinations that needed to be completed were at times overwhelming. Then there were the castrations of young bulls, dehorning procedures and other functions of the Veterinarian's Office that needed to be done. All of this was necessary to assure the health of the animals going to slaughter or to new homes (farms for breeding purposes or further growth, as was often the case with young pigs being fed out and sent to market at a later age).

The market was a busy place and the lunch room was always packed, attracting customers with the smell of a home-cooked meal and the conversations of a friendly clientele, each of whom had numerous stories to tell of interest to one and all.

As you might imagine, a day in the life of a Veterinarian is packed with activities from daybreak to sunset and then some. As a case in point, I remember one evening receiving a call from Dr. "K" at about 2 am in the morning. He needed my assistance for a dystocia (a difficult birth) in a mother cow, located on a farm just outside of town. We met at the clinic and after loading a few things in the trunk, were on our way.

Unfortunately, I soon realized that the livestock owner we were visiting was not a regular client. In fact, according to Dr. "K", the owner of this cow always called on another Veterinary Practitioner during the day and would only call him if there was a middle of the night emergency. Dr. "K" was rightfully so not happy and emphasized that we would do what was necessary, but by the same token, once the work was completed, we would leave as soon as possible.

Well, I was not prepared for what happened next. For as we drove through the front gate, there stood a man I knew and knew quite well. He was an active member of the local church I attended and as such I could not keep my mouth shut. Obviously, this was a very difficult situation for me. I was happy to see him and quickly rattled off a friendly greeting. Before long we were discussing a wide variety of topics while Dr. "K" and I went about our business.

On the way back to the clinic it was clear that Dr. "K" was a bit puzzled. But, fortunately after explaining the situation, we both laughed and noted it was probably best that we didn't show our displeasure as might have been the case.

Other situations that bring a smile to my face include the time a pet skunk was brought in for a rabies shot. According to the owner, this particular skunk had already been de-scented or more specifically the scent glands had been surgically removed. However, when the needle on the syringe was inserted into the skunk's rear leg, the skunk let us have it and sprayed the room with an odiferous smell that lingered for too long in spite of our efforts to clean the room with a variety of products.

Another client of interest was that of a lady who had a beautiful, well cared for female Labrador Retriever. She would bring this Bitch (adult female dog) into our office at least once a month for an exam. This particular owner must have had a fascination with the dog's breasts because she always insisted that we examine Missy's "Dinner Buckets" (Breasts) and was always worried that something might happen to them whereby she wouldn't be able to support the birth and raising of puppies in the future. We didn't know why this owner had this obsession, but we always would oblige her request and try to reassure her that what she was observing was quite normal and that Missy was just fine and doing quite well.

On another occasion, a young man came in with a German Shepherd for boarding and indicated he was going on a vacation and would return in two weeks. What we didn't know was that this particular dog was a trained attack dog and about midweek of the first week, this dog suddenly turned on me, growling ferociously, rushing forward as it used all its strength to attack me with its mouth wide open trying to reach my throat. Luckily I had a lot of experience handling dogs and knew immediately what to do; thereby restraining the dog and quickly putting him back into his kennel.

When the owner came in to pick up his dog, I was still upset and let him know how I felt about the situation he had put me in. I shared with him that in the future, he must forewarn us. Then we would know how to handle the dog and eliminate the serious risk he had put us in at this time. He apologized and indicated he didn't tell us because he was afraid we would not take the dog in for boarding. I was still quite stern with him, but noted that we do board all kinds of animals, and with the proper knowledge and communication, we are able to avoid giving signals to the dog that might be inappropriate. With the use of the appropriate equipment, we could assure the safety of all involved.

And then, my favorite was Farmer Allen. Often he would come in just to talk. He was a kind, friendly gentleman and was known throughout the community for his generosity. He was well to do and yet the way he dressed and the way he talked; one might think he was from the other side of the tracks or in other words, a very poor individual, an impoverished man. In reality, his biggest problem each year appeared to be that of deciding to which charity in town he should donate his annual gift of $10,000 to $20,000.

Well, on one occasion, he rushed into the office and exclaimed, "Doc, I got to tell you. In the future when I do business with you, it will be cash only! You know why?" Of course, we had no idea why. So, with a chuckle in his voice, he proceeded, "Well, you know that Bull that always charged you every time you came into the farm gate? Well, let me tell you, he won't be charging anymore. You know why?"

"Hmmm, no, sorry."

"Well, I took away his credit card!!!" "Har, Har, Har, Har." And with that I believe I have said enough about my life in Salina, Kansas.

The year passed quickly and soon I had my application in for another attempt at being accepted into the Kansas State University, College of Veterinary Medicine. I will always remember the day the University Professors interviewed me this time around. We had five professors interviewing each of the candidates and each one interviewed one candidate at a time, each in a separate office. Each interview lasted 15 minutes and then a bell would ring signaling the time to move to the next room and the next interview session.

This year I was amazed at the interview process; no difficult questions and a casual conversation asking what I had been doing during the year I was out of school. One professor even used the entire time making calls on his telephone. When the bell rang, he asked if I had any questions and I responded, "Do I have your support in being accepted for the Veterinary Class beginning this fall?" His only response was a smile and the words, "Get Out Of Here!" "You know I can't divulge that information now!" "Just keep up with what you are doing!"

After being accepted into the Veterinary Curriculum, time seemed to fly. Again, playing the church organ provided most of the funding I needed. Also, I took out a student loan and assisted my friend, Frank Harrison, in moving and re-covering Billiard Tables at Fort Riley as well as remodeling several apartments for a local landlord.

God was good to me and somehow whenever I ran out of money, I would receive a check from one of my jobs, just in time. Also, my summers were filled with work and through a thrifty way of life; I was able to make ends meet. As I have noted, the years went fast and before I knew it, I had graduated and was doing the work I love!

Chapter 2

Learning the Business

Academic wisdom alone doesn't always work. In reality, there is a need for experience. At times, this is quite different from our expectations.

Immediately upon graduation, I started working with the United States Department of Agriculture (USDA). Now, what was there that convinced me that I should join the Federal Government as a field veterinarian? Well, it all began during my third year of professional training at Kansas State University when I decided to work during the upcoming summer recess for the Department. What I found was a cadre of highly trained, technically sound individuals, whether they worked in the field of research and development or the field I so enjoyed, that of animal disease control and eradication. This organization was on the cutting edge and the excitement of seeing the benefits of their efforts to society, brought personal rewards beyond measure.

I was assigned as a member of a Task Force organized to coordinate the eradication of Hog Cholera (currently called Classical Swine Fever) in the State of Indiana. It was a pleasure working with the Diagnosticians and Epidemiologists as they used various tools and approaches to identify Hog Cholera infected swine. This, plus the opportunity to participate in the surveillance programs so critical to the disease eradication process made this an experience that convinced me this was where I belonged and this is what I wanted to do, no doubt about it!

One of my most memorable experiences was working with Dr. Sam Young. He was the first to have observed and identified what we commonly call the Shaker Pig Syndrome. From his experience, when Sows (Mother Pigs) were infected, their baby pigs would shiver as if they were chilled to the bone. He called this the "Shaker Pig Syndrome". What was amazing to me was that this was often the only clinical sign I would see. Then, when tissue samples (i.e. tonsil biopsies) were taken from their mothers, the sows; invariably the lab results would almost always indicate that this herd was infected with the Hog Cholera virus.

Now, once Hog Cholera was diagnosed in a herd of swine, an active surveillance program was immediately activated throughout the area. This required identifying the location of every single hog within a ten mile circumference and was important in that any swine not accounted for could be a potential reservoir of disease, spreading millions of infectious virus particles from one premise to another. The inability, on our part, to identify the presence of that one hog, could possibly negate all of our efforts to eliminate the disease in that area and as a result nationwide.

Immediately after finding a swine herd infected, the pigs on that farm had to be destroyed and buried. This was necessary in that there was no known cure and if we attempted to provide supportive treatment (intravenous fluids, blood transfers, antibiotics to control secondary infections, etc) as is routinely done in human medicine, the costs would have been astronomical and therefore prohibitive, especially in an agricultural setting.

As a result, each hog was humanely destroyed by injecting them with a quick acting euthanizing agent. The individual administering this drug always made sure that another person was assigned to watch their every move. The reason for this extreme amount of care was that if there was an accidental self-injection by the person administering the drug, immediate care had to be taken by another person to resuscitate the person mistakenly receiving the drug. The drug used at that time inhibited breathing and if the person assigned to keep close watch on them could immediately provide artificial respiration, the individual would recover and according to our supervisors, have no permanent damage.

Oh joy, for one thing, I have never heard of anyone actually having had this experience and secondly, you can be sure, I never wanted to be the first to have the pleasure of having, in my opinion, the trauma of this experience. If the person assigned to faithfully watch, forgets to keep a watchful eye and an accidental self-injection of this paralyzing drug occurs; well, so much for a life well lived.

Now, the Animal Health Technicians we worked with were highly trained and had an in-depth understanding of the behavior of swine both as individual animals and in groups. They worked hard, long hours and would work as long as necessary to assure the disease eradication program was a success. There is one experience that I will long remember and each time it comes to mind a smile suddenly appears on my face. In this case, after a long, arduous morning of work, all of us (about six men) sat down for a spell to rest our fatigued bodies and to gulp a few swigs of water. By now each and every one of us was covered with perspiration and as hot as the noon day sun. And yet, this brief respite from the task at hand was, "Oh, Oh Soooo Refreshing"!

We sat along a chain linked fence and really didn't even feel like saying very much. And yet we were feeling good in that our accomplishment that day had brought us one step closer to eradicating this costly, debilitating disease. Well, as tired as we were at that time, the owner's hunting dog, Felix decided to mark his territory and cool us off. He was on the other side of the fence and having noted the distinct odor of hogs all over our bodies; he decided to mark his territory by raising his hind leg and one by one sprayed each of our backsides with a fresh stream of his ever fragrant, freshly eliminated dog urine. It was something to behold! And the funniest part was the realization that each of us was so tired we couldn't move an inch while all of this was happening and remarked to our disbelief how good the wetness felt on our backs at this time. From that point on, it was clear that when a group of individuals truly believes in doing something worthwhile, it is amazing what they will put up with to accomplish the task at hand.

Later in my career, I had the fortune of attending a training program for the purpose of being certified as a Foreign Animal Disease Diagnostician. The course was held at a Research and Diagnostic Center on Plum Island, New York. It had a reputation of being one of the best Foreign Animal

Disease Research and Diagnostic Facilities in the world.

Each of the laboratories at this facility had different levels of security depending on the steps needed to prevent the escape of disease. As one entered the inner sanctum, each scientist, technician, and/or animal handler had to disrobe and change into laboratory clothing before entering. This was repeated over and over again as they progressed into the higher levels of bio-security.

Accordingly, as you left each level of bio-security to the next lower level, the process was reversed with the addition of a complete shower between each change of clothes. Then, before an individual could leave the secured area, he or she had to completely strip down (yes, in gender specific locker rooms), taking off all of their clothes, scrubbing their hands, cleaning their finger nails, coughing up any phlegm in their throat; spitting it out, showering thoroughly and then . . . .

Yes, and then, for the so called thrill of our life, each of us had the wonderful opportunity of running down a long narrow corridor with numerous shower nozzles, in good working order, projected on each side. This rite of passage was for the sole purpose of thoroughly soaking each and every one of us with a disinfectant spray before we were allowed to finally enter into an area considered clean. As one entered this passageway sensors would turn the showers on, spraying each individual with a very cold . . . . Yes, I said, **"a very cold, disinfectant spray!"** All I can say is that each of us knew when someone was running down that passage, in that everyone including myself would scream at the top of our lungs all the way to the end. It only took a few seconds and we were soon in a warm room, ready to change into our street clothes, exiting the secured facility and bound for the boat waiting in the harbor ready to take us back to the mainland.

After I finished College, it was clear that I was ready to start my career with the United States Department of Agriculture. I loved the multitude of activities encountered. This included testing a wide variety of farm animals for diseases of concern; completing health inspections and inspections of facilities at zoos, laboratories, animal exhibits as well as the traveling animal acts (circuses, etc.) passing through our geographical areas of responsibility.

I can still remember the joy of my children when I received a call from the National Zoo Director on the very day their first Panda Bear cub was born. He asked if I would like to bring my children down and, of course, I was delighted. The look of wonder on my two girl's faces, Amory and Julie as they viewed this tiny bundle of joy snuggled up in a small incubator truly thrilled my very being as a father who loved his children dearly.

On another occasion, the owner of an animal act asked if my kids would like to come to his home to see his animals. Again, as you can imagine, it was an opportunity I couldn't refuse. I can still remember the warm greeting we received as we entered their simple and yet immaculate home. In no time, we were sitting comfortably in his living room and before long, to my amazement one of his chimpanzees came meandering in, jumped up and down a few times and then quietly sat down close to the dining room door. He put his arms up in the air, gave a big chimpanzee smile, made a few chimp sounds and then bounced off for the kitchen where the owner's wife was probably giving him a snack or two as his reward.

This all happened so fast that I totally forgot how strong chimpanzees can be and didn't even think of the danger it could have posed for my family. Luckily, all went well and as could be expected, this was all the kids could talk about for weeks to come.

One activity that was quite meaningful to me was that of working with Tennessee Walkers, a breed of horses known for their smooth ride. At that time, some of the trainers were determined to cause the Tennessee Walkers to extend their front legs forward to a much greater extent than was normal for their gait. Unfortunately, in such cases, the gait was artificially created using cruel procedures that made the lower portion of their legs extremely sore. The trainers would apply blistering agents such as mustard to the pastern (area just above the hoof), thereby making the area very sore to the touch. Then a heavy collar would be attached thereby severely irritating the pastern area each time the horse took a step. The result was a horse throwing and extending (kicking) its front feet forward creating a showy (in this case artificial) gait so desired in the show ring.

In my opinion it is criminal to cause pain and suffering in a horse just to win a horse show. The use of such techniques saddens me especially when you consider that the Tennessee Walker has a showy gait on its own terms and as such is a pleasure to watch. My purpose at these shows was to examine the horses being shown and to determine if any illegal substances were being used.

On one occasion, while attending a local horse show, I remember noticing a horse I didn't recognize. After asking a few questions, I realized this horse had just arrived and was in the process of being prepared to enter the competition. I approached the trainer and indicated I would like to examine his horse. I directed my attention to the horse's front legs and especially around the pastern areas just above the upper edge of the hoof. Unfortunately the pastern area was extremely sensitive to touch. Furthermore, the areas were both blistered and had a greasy feel. The horse even shed a few tears in that a light touch to these areas inflicted severe pain as the horse flinched, rapidly withdrawing its leg from my grasp. Seeing this, I seized one of my sterile gauze patches with a forceps and wiped the affected areas so that the greasy substance would adhere. I then placed the gauze into a sterile container and sent it to the Toxicology Unit of our National Laboratories in Ames, Iowa for analysis.

I obtained information as to the name of the horse, what events it was signed up to perform in, who the trainer was, as well as the name and address of the owner. I advised the trainer that I believed the horse to have been sored and that this was caused by the use of a blistering agent. In addition, I noted that a substance had been applied to the pastern areas and that this substance had a greasy feel. To explain this, the trainer indicated that the horse has been under veterinary care and that the greasy feel was due to the application of a salve used to help in the healing process.

As soon as I learned the name and address of their Veterinarian, I packed up my gear and headed for the Veterinarian's Office.

Upon arrival, the Veterinarian agreed that this horse was under his care. However, he had not been called to that stable for several months and had not prescribed any salve for this horse. I asked him if he would sign an affidavit (investigative form) outlining what he had said and he agreed to do so. About a week later I received the results from the National Laboratories. They indicated that the greasy substance was a mustard blistering agent, verifying the horse was sored. Unfortunately for the horse, it was a pitiful, painful, experience the Horse Protection Act (law) was trying to prevent. Shortly, thereafter, the owner, who turned out to be a United States Federal District Judge, was found guilty and required to pay the maximum penalty of $2,000.00.

All I can say is that I had a wide variety of experiences from that of working with animals in the elimination of Diseases such as Brucellosis and Tuberculosis; to testing animal feed for Salmonella bacteria; to assuring that animals were treated humanely. I was also involved in the export of animals to other countries as well as serving as a Foreign Animal Disease Diagnostician, making sure that some of the world's most devastating diseases didn't become established in our hemisphere.

Not only was I concerned about the health of domestic food animals; but, I was also concerned with the health of Exotic Animals such as elephants, bongos, lions, zebras, etc. It was a fascinating beginning. I loved my work and soon I was ready to take on the new adventures that were not only a challenge to me, but also filled my spirit with immeasurable joy and satisfaction.

CHAPTER 3

Just a Lot of Bull

Then, there is the challenge of working overseas. Our view of reality can be quite different when providing leadership for the very first time. This adds new excitement while working in a Swiss Bull Stud/Semen Collection Station providing the first Simmental Cattle Genetics to the United States.

Sometimes it is surprising as to what one can become involved in as a Federal Government employee. For example, on one occasion I was asked to supervise the activities at a Simmental and Brown Swiss (two different breeds of cattle) Semen Collection Station located in Utzendorf, a town near Bern, Switzerland. Since this was the first attempt at importing Simmental genetics into the United States, I was to certify that all of the semen being collected was from healthy bulls and followed the specifications of the protocol established.

To begin with, there was an experience, a remarkably new experience that occurred during my first week in Switzerland. The hotel I stayed in was a classy hotel with the latest amenities. Nevertheless, I was not prepared for what occurred the morning after I arrived. To start with, before retiring in the evening, I had asked for a wakeup call at 7:00 am. Then promptly at the appointed hour the next morning, there was a gentle knock at my door. And what did I observe as I barely opened my eyes from a deep slumber, but a fantastically beautiful young lady, a lady smiling from ear to ear as she unlocked my door; briskly entering the room; and placing a small pitcher of coffee and another small pitcher of warm milk along with a Danish on the night stand right next to the head of my bed.

Now you might be asking why she was flashing such a broad exuberant smile. Well let me try to explain. As a young, single, American bred male, it was a moment of surprise and mixed emotion. Not only was I ever so pleased to see this beautiful young lady and delighted to have this type of wakeup service so unheard of in the United States; but, unfortunately, I was embarrassed to no end! This was due not only to my puritan, prudent upbringing, but also; unfortunately I was embarrassed by the state of undress I was in. You see, since the room was much warmer than I was used to, there I was spread out on top of the covers in a deep slumber, naked as a

J-Bird. Upon realizing the predicament I was in, I did what any young buck raised in a strict upbringing of Mennonite ancestry would do. I grabbed anything and everything I could find to cover me up and tried to act calm and collected while feeling all the nervousness and embarrassment of a young man not sure what in the world was going on or what was considered appropriate behavior in a circumstance like this.

Nevertheless, in spite of these unusual circumstances, my first week was still filled with anticipation and wonder. In this instance, I was temporarily assigned to sit in for Dr. Robert Moody, the U. S. Director, so he and his wife could take a much needed vacation. Dr. Moody was highly respected and most helpful in clarifying the responsibilities I would have as a member of the Semen Collection Station's Director's Office. In this instance, the Director's Office was run by two Co-Directors; one representing the United States Government and the other representing the Government of Switzerland.

The Swiss Director was a young Veterinarian by the name of Dr. Stephan Hasler. He was a gentleman and a scholar and as a result, later moved up quickly in their organizational chain of command. I will always remember him as a bright young man with a gift of being able to appropriately address issues of importance to the success of this Center and business adventure.

During the next week, my first week on my own, I was a bit shaky and unsure as to how to meet my responsibilities without being in the face of everyone assigned to this station. At first I was hovering over the Swiss employees whether it was in the semen collection process, the dilution process, or the testing, packaging, freezing and shipping process.

Before long, I noticed a lot of fussing and the repeated use of a phrase by the Technical Staff. It seemed to have a tone of frustration and it was always in one of their four native languages, Swiss German. After hearing this phrase over and over again, I grabbed my Swiss German/English Dictionary and tried to decipher what they were saying. Soon I figured it out and it made perfect sense. You see, they had just about had it with my constant presence rechecking everything they were doing and as a result of their frustration, they were saying, "Why doesn't he trust us?"

I then realized that I had better reconsider what my responsibilities were and what level of technical oversight was necessary. This taught me a great lesson I have carried with me since that time. It was clear that they were technically competent, and as Swiss citizens were proud of their high standards, exceeding by far the standards other countries imposed on them. They were proud of this fact and for anyone to question their integrity was downright insulting. I also realized that I couldn't be there 24 hours a day and that I truly had to have a certain level of trust in them.

It became clear that my primary responsibility was to assure to the American people that this importation was safe and that the animals the semen was collected from were healthy and free of disease. Once I clarified my role and accordingly adjusted my approach to the technical staff, I noticed and sensed a major improvement in our working relationship.

My visit to Berne, the Capital of Switzerland, was enhanced by one of the animal handlers who took the time to show me some of the historical sites nearby. This included an old Roman Coliseum, old churches, and the beautiful medieval structures throughout the capital city. It was interesting to note that through the ages, the city has required that the medieval exteriors be maintained while the interiors could be altered as needed to keep up with modern times. There was a certain charm as one walked through the city and in many instances, one could see enchanting vistas filled with the beauty of God's creation. The old, narrow, cobblestone and medieval stone structures stimulated the senses and each trip down one of the streets filled one with awe and wonder.

It soon became evident that this was a special place indeed and before you realized it, you would want to experience everything about this magical city that you could. For instance, being in part a connoisseur of fine cuisine, a food hound so to speak, I soon wanted to experience the local cuisine and especially that which might be classified as authentic original Swiss cuisine. Luckily, in no time, I found just the place.

I was directed to a certain side street with a neighborhood tavern on one corner. I was informed that the restaurant could be found on the second floor of this tavern and that there would be no indication of the presence of a restaurant at this site. It was a popular site for locals and everyone who needed to know was aware of its presence and in most instances provided a clientele that kept the facility filled with satisfied customers.

Those who suggested visiting this restaurant assured me that I was in for a real treat and that I would cherish the experience for years to come. To get there, I was to enter the front door and walk up the stairs at the rear of the tavern. At the top of the stairs, I would be met by the owner of the restaurant and would be seated at one of three long tables along with the other guests who had been seated earlier. Well, I did as was suggested and was ever so grateful for the experience I was about to receive. The owner promptly seated me with a delightful group of people. Even though I was a foreigner, and I didn't speak their language, the evening was still one of the most enjoyable I have ever had.

A menu was provided and of course, I had no idea what to make of it. I didn't have the first notion as to what it was all about. Nevertheless, through pointing to their food, then pointing to an item on the menu and yes, much talking and laughing amongst ourselves, I was able, with their colorful help, to select several courses that were, oh, so special. The flavors, textures, and presentations were outstanding. What an experience

It was fascinating to watch the exchange between each and every one of them. I could tell they were having a great time figuring out the perfect selections for my consideration. For example, one might point to something and then place their fingers on their lips with a kiss as if to say, mmmmm, this choice is the best! When it appeared that a majority of them agreed on a selection, I would nod in approval and we would move on to the next course. I can still remember the joy it brought to each of them. They would all smile; clap their hands while nodding in approval, and some even cheering at the top of their voices. This continued for the most part at least until the first course was presented. Then all eyes were on me. There seemed to be a hush as they waited for my reaction. The look in their eyes said it all. The big question at the moment and on the hearts of each and every one of them was, "Did we make the right choice?"

As you can imagine, the whole evening was an exciting adventure and it filled my heart with joy. The food was delicious and I am sure my reaction showed that at all times. This created a bond between all of us and it was with reluctance when I had to say my good-byes and leave this fantastic loving, kind, generous group of people. But that alone, to my surprise was not the only part of this experience that made this night so exceptionally special. You see, as I got up to leave, one of the couples came over to me and while putting their hands on my shoulder, said in perfect English, "Thank you for a wonderful evening. We are from the United States and tonight you made us all so proud. Do enjoy your stay here in Switzerland. The people here are truly wonderful people and we are sure your stay here will be just as special as they are." I could not ask for more. I was indeed honored and privileged to enjoy the company and culture of these loving, caring individuals who will always be special to me now and as long as I live.

While we are discussing restaurants, a couple of weeks later, I had a bit of a different experience. This time I heard of a great restaurant in the countryside. It was a small restaurant that had a country home like ambience. I decided it would be worthwhile to give it a try. By this time, I recognized a few words on the menu and as you might surmise, a little knowledge can sometimes be the start of your downfall. So, on this occasion, I decided to order some soup and as an entrée, fish. The owners of the restaurant were hospitable and the meal was served in the comfortable surroundings of this family's home. It included the warmth of a fireside hearth and the friendliness of those you would consider to be your best and most trusted acquaintances.

Now, when the soup arrived, I was indeed pleased. The soup was seafood and somewhat like a traditional chowder. The flavor was outstanding and my mouth exploded with a taste begging for more. The aroma and flavor were a perfect combination. Therefore, it made my day when the waitress asked if I would like some more. Nevertheless, after the third bowl, I started to wonder why she was so intent that I have more and then more, ad infinitum. After making it clear, I didn't care for any more; the main course arrived. To my surprise, what I had ordered was, in fact, not a so called, main course. Rather it was an appetizer. All I could do was laugh at myself as the waitress pointed to something more substantial. Again, as a result of the waitress's persistence and hospitality, I had the perfect ending to a meal that I will always remember and cherish.

On the way home that evening I had a chance to drive through the countryside. In Switzerland the countryside is something special to behold. The fields are well tended and the backdrop of the tall, majestic mountains fills one's mind with the warmth and touching music/stories told in the Sound of Music. It is both calming and soothing to see all the beauty and peace of the last rays of the sun setting in the west. And yet this was not to be the usual peaceful setting as I had hoped for. You see, it was time for a little excitement and in my mind it was more than I needed. For over the horizon, a battalion of troops was marching my way. Not only was there a battalion of troops, but I also found numerous tanks heading in my direction, more than I wished to count or consider.

All I could imagine was that for some reason we were in the middle of a combat zone and for all I knew with all the concern and the news in the papers about nuclear weapons, not only could we be in one of the combat zones, but also in the middle of a world war. How could this happen in such a peaceful country as Switzerland? Why was I the only one on the road with all the troops heading straight for me? As if by impulse, I quickly pulled off to the side of the road and parked right under the only tree I could find as if to hope that tree would provide enough camouflage to protect me from being found and any harm that they might wish to inflict on me. My heart was madly beating and luckily I was still young and fortunately for me, the panic was not about to do me in.

As in the movies it seemed like an eternity for the troops to arrive at my location. Was I ever relieved when the tanks and accompanying troops split and continued their march around me and the tree that was my only means of "protection". I was still shaking and had no idea what was going on. As soon as they disappeared over the horizon and as soon as I could think rational thoughts again, I slowly eased the car onto the road and continued without incident to my hotel.

As I explained my evening to the hotel clerk, she smiled and shared that all I had observed was just the weekend training maneuvers of the young men assigned to that unit. It appears that all young men must be part of their military and that weekend maneuvers keep them in a state of readiness should there ever be a conflict that needs their support. At last, I too could smile and as the strain of the evening dissipated, after my evening prayers of gratitude, I was more than ready for a good night's sleep.

Now, I must applaud the work of the Center's animal handlers. They were well trained and understood the behaviors and temperaments of each of these highly valued animals. Each had the unique ability to observe minor changes in behavior whether it was in one particular bull or possibly in a small subset of bulls. On one occasion they noted a concern when the bulls in general seemed to be favoring their feet as if something about their hooves was bothering them. After thoroughly checking each of their hooves and again reviewing the nutrients in their feed, I came to the conclusion that they probably were just not receiving enough exercise. So, I asked them to increase the time each bull was assigned to the exercise ring.

In this case, after increasing the period of exercise by about 20 minutes per day, all of the foot problems seemed to disappear. Once the bulls began this regiment, (believe it or not) they seemed to enjoy the extra exercise. Could it be that their male egos needed a little more attention?

All of us wanted to keep these animals in the best shape possible. We worked closely with each and every one of these bulls, so highly valued for their breeding potential.

As could be expected, an emotional bond quickly developed between the animals and their particular animal handler. The trust that had built up between them became quite evident. At such times, we had to remind ourselves of the strength and aggressive nature each of these animals possessed and the importance of taking the necessary precautions to assure our own personal safety.

By the same token, a kindred spirit was firmly established. The bulls wanted to be playful and yet had no idea just how dangerous their actions (for instance a quick turn of their head as if snuggling up to their handler) could be. This unfortunately happened to one of the handlers while I was there. Even the handler admitted that he was sure the bull meant no harm; but, rather was just trying to be playful. However, in this case, when the bull flung its head against the handler, it threw him high into the air against the wall of the building nearby. As a result this young man had the wind knocked out of him and saw the stars circling around his head, for some time, before he came to.

I can still see the look of fear as he stood in the doorway to my office and advised me of his immediate resignation. After relaying the experience he had just lived through, I truly understood and wished him the best for the future as well as asking if he needed an ambulance and/or a way to the hospital, which was promptly provided. We do thank God that all went well with his recovery.

Now, as I have explained, we were preparing semen from these Brown Swiss and Simmental Bulls for export to the United States. The semen was being shipped to an Artificial Insemination Company located in the Midwest. As such, this company wanted to market the genetics of these bulls to the best of their ability thereby maximizing their profits while improving the genetics of the national herd. So they hired a gentleman from Calgary well known for his photographs of various purebred breeds of cattle to help them in their marketing process. I did make it clear, however, that we were in a quarantined facility and that we had certain requirements that the photographer had to comply with. This would include showers, following our restrictions as to the distance the photographer must maintain from the animals, etc.

About a week later, the photographer arrived. He understood our restrictions and honored our every request. He was a pleasure to work with. It was interesting; however, the steps he took to assure quality photos were taken. He would study each animal in depth, and then ask our animal handlers to move each individual bull to different locations etc. to apparently gain the best light and angle before setting his camera. In some instances he would ask that we dig out some of the soil for the front legs to stand in. Apparently this along with the angle of the camera and the turning of the bulls head, Ooooh, so slightly, one way or another improved the image greatly.

I was truly amazed at the care and time he took for each animal. The only thing I could imagine was that these steps helped show a more massive neck on some of the animals, or a straighter back, and/ or in some cases either more or more even muscling. I would never have thought of all those tricks of the trade. And I must say the animal handlers were most patient and cooperative, assuring the photographer got the photographs he needed.

Finally a couple weeks later, I received the brochure advertising the semen available from these bulls. To be honest, I could hardly recognize any of them. They all looked perfect. Yes, I am sure they were the actual pictures of each animal. But, oh the lengths some people go to sell their products. I guess my grandfather had it right when he insisted on seeing the bull that would sire each of his dams (cows). To him this was critical to improving the progeny of his herd and I must say he was quite successful at that, as you might say in my own humble opinion.

Soon, my detail to Switzerland was over. However, before I left this beautiful land, I did take in a live production of the story of William Tell. For those of you unfamiliar with the history of Switzerland, there is the belief that William Tell was in many ways the one that brought the people together to create the beginning of the Swiss Confederation.

This event was presented in an open air theater at Interlocken, Switzerland. I was fortunate to have a seat next to the center aisle. The play was delightful and the acting was superb. However, little did I know that the cast included live cattle! Not only were there live cattle, but they were being herded down the aisle right next to me. Close enough to smell their breath and feel the brush of their bellies and swish of their tails.

As you can imagine, this was disturbing in that I was instructed in no uncertain terms that I, in no way, was to be in contact with any other livestock. What was I to do, especially when I realized cattle would be passing in close proximity? My first clue was when I heard the familiar sound of cattle bells traditionally fastened around the necks of Swiss Cattle grazing in the countryside. I was panic stricken. What could I do? Stand up and try to stop the show as I fled? Scream by the order of the U.S. Government that this cannot occur?—Oh—Sure!!—

To be honest, I sat there in a severe sweat. This was probably due to anxiety. I tried to calm down and accept my fate. I called the office as soon as I arrived at the hotel, had my clothes laundered and took a shower for as long as I could stand it while blowing my nose and cleaning under my finger nails repeatedly. I am thankful that my skin remained flexible and that I didn't look like a dried up prune. Luckily, the office agreed that the best plan would be to avoid the Bulls at the Center, explain the circumstances to Dr. Moody when he arrived in a couple days and return home knowing I could be pleased with a job well done.

This was the start of an International Career in which I learned that in spite of the best made plans, there can always be unplanned circumstances to deal with. They can be devastating or they can be a challenge depending on how adept you are at being open to alternative approaches to achieving the same objective and achieving it successfully.

Along that line of thinking, I will always remember the words of one of the speakers at a joint Massachusetts Institute of Technology/Harvard Seminar I attended. "Some folks will look at a cup and say it is half full. Others will say it is half empty. However, those who successfully encourage everyone around them to take advantage of the opportunities the same cup has to offer will jointly fill the cup to overflowing."

Recognizing the talents of others and that every day is a learning experience were important lessons to be learned. I will always cherish my time in Switzerland knowing that serving others to the best of our ability can often be the key to achieving success over failure. And finally, honesty and integrity rank high in the world of business and with God, you can be assured that amazing things can and will be accomplished.

CHAPTER 4

Noah's Ark???

Marriage and a Norwegian Assignment add a new dimension to that of International Service. Challenging the Veterinary Authorities as well as facing storms in the North Atlantic, while transporting the first Charolais Cattle to the United States, provided more than enough drama to thrill us all.

The time was early evening and the sky was clear. The moon was bright and was surrounded by a spectacular display of stars glimmering in the night. What a perfect time to ask the woman I loved for her hand in marriage. I was nervous with excitement, relatively confident that she would accept and as many a man can probably relate, praying that all would go well. It was Friday evening, the November air was crisp and my hopes and expectations were high. When I arrived at her home, her two children, Amory (6 years old) and Julie (4 years old), rushed to greet me with their arms wide open and smiles that would warm anyone's heart. Joanne, the beautiful love of my life, smiled and as only she could, made me feel most welcome in their home.

After playing with the kids for a while, we turned on the phonograph (record player) and played their favorite bed time tunes. Since it was the early 1970's, they thought that "The Carpenters", Richard and Karen Carpenter, a brother/sister team, were the greatest. The music was soft and soothing and one would think that under those conditions their restless minds would settle down and within a relatively short period of time, they would be fast asleep. But, Oh, No, as was their custom, about ten to fifteen minutes later, each of them slowly walked into the living room with their hands over their eyes and a sheepish grin (as if they were afraid they might see something they shouldn't) asking, "Can we have something to drink?" Of course they knew that we would grant their request. After all this was a nightly ritual and as you know, family rituals, by all means, cannot be broken. And if the truth be known, Joanne and I as well would have been devastated thinking something was wrong if the ritual wasn't carried out as anticipated and right on schedule. As you can imagine these girls were pure joys to be with! Both Joanne and I thanked God for the delight of again tucking these precious children in bed and wishing them a good night's sleep. And as is usual in such circumstances, within no time they were both sound asleep.

How did my proposal for marriage work out? Well, all I can say is I was a very happy man that evening and couldn't sleep a wink. In fact it seemed like it took forever before the day came when the wedding vows were finally exchanged.

On asking the girls the next morning what they would think if I married their mother, Amory smiled and filled with enthusiasm immediately answered, "That would be great!" But I can still see Julie standing there with this questionable expression that seemed to last for an eternity. Finally she said with some hesitancy as she looked over at Amory, "well, mmm . . . , I don't know." As you might expect, at that very moment, I didn't know what to expect. But leave it to Amory, she knew what to do. She looked back at Julie and with a stern look suddenly became my greatest advocate. "You know he will be a good father" she exclaimed! Julie thought for another moment or two and then with her wonderful smile and a twinkle in her eye said, "Wow, a new father Hmmm . . . . Well . . . . OK!!!" That is all I needed to hear!

Well, soon the festive weekend arrived. Since the wedding guests were limited to a small select group of relatives and friends, we all gathered the night before the big event for dinner at a restaurant owned by a cousin of Joanne's parents. The restaurant was still festively decorated for the Christmas Season and a few touches were added to make the evening even more special for the occasion at hand. This also happened to be my soon to be daughter, Amory's birthday (December 31st), the best ever. The next day Joanne and I were happily married; Joanne's parents opened up their home and we were provided a memorable reception that was filled with love and warm wishes.

Now, before we continue, I must confess, I have left out one important piece of information. What I haven't told you is that shortly after our marriage on January 1st, I was being assigned to work in Norway. In fact, my reporting date was January 7th. Yes, at our young age, this was all quite exciting.

The plane trip from Baltimore, Maryland to Oslo, Norway was basically uneventful. Since all of this was a new experience for the girls, their minds were filled with all sorts of questions. I noted their excitement and felt it important to discuss the notion that we were going to a place that might be quite different from what they have seen and heard at home. The people will speak a language we will not understand, they may do things differently and their foods may not look and/or taste the same as we are used to. In any case, we will have a lot of fun and when we return home, we will be able to tell everyone about this, our trip to Norway.

Fortunately it wasn't long before we arrived. After checking in at our hotel, we were quite hungry and were pleased to find a restaurant on the main floor. I can still remember the Maitre'd as he led us to a table in their formally decorated dining room. Our table was in the center of the room and conveniently located near the kitchen entrance. The guests all seemed quite friendly and all my mind could think of was the fine linens, the fine china and the fragile long stemmed crystal glasses just waiting for a youngster to smash inadvertently, of course. I was a nervous wreck and that doesn't even consider the anxiety my new wife and children must have felt at that time. Joanne quickly moved the glasses to the center of the table and each of the girls just had this look of exhaustion and yet excitement considering all that was going on.

We took a few moments to look at the menu and were so relieved to see hamburger and chicken listed as entrees. My daughter, Julie and my new bride ordered chicken, Amory ordered hamburger and I ordered fish. All we could talk about was how good it would be to get some shut eye after an enjoyable meal. Little did we know what was about to happen next. After a small salad, our main entrees arrived. Joanne and

Julie's chicken and my fish came out first. They were all artfully prepared and smelled absolutely delicious. Then, out came Amory's hamburger. Oh, what a disaster! Before I could say anything, the waiter further aggravated the situation by breaking a raw egg and spreading it along with some pickle relish on what was obviously raw hamburger. My heart went out to Amory and I am sure all she could think of was "Oh, No, do I have to eat this?"

Almost immediately we had projectile vomit all over the table as well as everything else in close proximity. I can still see the look on Joanne's face as she said concisely and to the point, "Amory, Julie and I are leaving!!!" She didn't need to say more. It was understood. I was to take care of this mess, the humiliation, and the explanation, if there was any.

The next day, after a good night's rest, we were ready to do a little sightseeing. It was a beautiful day and after a hearty breakfast, we thoroughly enjoyed a walk to Frogner Parken, a park not too far from the Hotel we were staying in. This park is well known and tells the story of mankind from birth to death through the placement of a circle of statues beautifully hand carved by Gustav Vigeland. In the middle of this circle is a magnificent carving of what I would call the staff of life . . . Some indicate it represents a scene from the biblical story of the flood that came shortly after Noah finished the building of his Ark. The anguish on the carved faces of the multitude of individuals struggling and competing for the highest point on earth is something I will never forget. Apparently it took almost 14 years for this series of carvings to be completed.

This was a beautifully created piece of artwork. It was very moving to say the least. After enjoying the artwork on a personal level it soon became apparent that my appreciation was nothing compared to the interest Amory and Julie seemed to have in this project. They went from statue to statue and just gazed upward at each figure as if they were mesmerized by the beauty of each carving. This was all quite remarkable and I celebrated to think that as demonstrated here, creative pieces of art could truly speak to all, regardless of age or wisdom or culture.

But, oh, no, little did I know the thoughts going through their young little heads. For you see, as was unbeknownst to me, they saw it quite differently and as a result viewed the artwork from yet another perspective. With my inability to recognize what my children saw in this beautiful piece of artwork; I never dreamed that in fact their minds were not appreciating the lifelike carvings representing the different stages of life (birth through death). Rather, it appears that this was the first time they had seen artwork depicted in the nude and from their standpoint, so many at one time. I am sure this experience gave them a new appreciation for art and from my point of view; I still remember the many interesting questions that followed.

For those of you who have traveled to Norway, you are well aware that the country is filled with a rich history from the days of the Vikings to the modern day. It is also filled with the latest technological advances and the peace and joy of a nation filled with the important matters of family, community, etc. We, as a family were fortunate to be able to visit many areas of historical interest. Our favorites were the Viking Museum and the National Folk Museum.

The Viking Museum had several exhibits showing pieces of Viking Ships or as I remember, there was at least one that was basically still intact. This Museum provided a history of their rich heritage and the importance of their presence in civilization.

Then, the National Folk Museum further clarified the development of this heritage and greatly enriched our understanding of the impact their nation has had on life in general and the future development of the world as we know it today. It was especially interesting to see the evolution and use of wood structures in this part of the world.

One of the points of interest I especially enjoyed was the development of the Stave Kirke/Stave Church. Structurally, it was of a design that prevented the main framework/posts from deteriorating/rotting away. They were tall structures and one wondered how they ever built such tall and sturdy structures, especially in a climate that some might consider to be a harsh environment. The interiors were very dark and I will always remember the comment made by my daughter Amory upon entering the Gol Stave Kirke at this museum in Bygdog, Oslo, Norway. In a very quiet voice she exclaimed, "Boy, it sure is dark in here. You can't see anything. I wonder if anyone else is in here." With that we were all surprised as we heard a young lady's voice say, "Welcome to the National Folk Museum and this ancient Stave Church probably built around the 1300s." Yes, we had someone who was able to give us a brief history of the Stave Kirke and for that we were grateful.

Now you may be asking, why was I in Norway, and what did I plan on doing while I was there. In this instance, I was in Norway to process the very first shipment of Charolais Cattle (25 head) for export to the United States. This importation was very important to the future of the Livestock Industry in the United States.

The Charolais are known for their massive muscling and improved daily gains thus adding to the efficiency of production of our national herd, while providing more of the tasty steaks and other cuts of meat, so in demand by the American Public.

Since Norway was free of major diseases of concern, we agreed to allow these highly valued animals passage to the United State if certain precautions were being taken. It was, therefore, my responsibility to assure that all of the necessary tests, etc., as required, were properly completed. I am happy to report that we found a perfect isolated location for the quarantine of these animals as well as a source of feed that was promptly delivered upon the arrival of the cattle and the beginning of the thirty day quarantine period. I was pleased that all was going well.

Fortunately my lovely wife had a lot of courage and spirit and on her own found a beautiful cottage that fit our budget perfectly. It was located in the countryside with plenty of hills and valleys perfect for our family excursions each evening, cross country skiing under the twinkling stars and soft lit moon light.

Now, remember we were comfortably situated in what I would call the North Woods. In other words, we were in an area where the winter sun is barely at the level of the horizon and often just a few rays of light will appear. Furthermore, this glimmer of light only occurs between the hours of 10 am in the morning and 2 pm in the afternoon. Otherwise, it is dark and the only source of available light is that of the moon. It is no wonder that the Norwegian people love color and have the most beautiful homes I have seen anywhere. Their wall hangings are always bright and cheerful and as most of us have seen; their handmade wool sweaters are always so colorful, made to warm the heart and soul of the lucky one wearing this artfully created piece of work.

Oh, yes, it is also important that I mention that my wife and I, as newly-weds, thoroughly enjoyed the beauty of the Norwegian landscape as well as the romantic effect of the ever present moon light on our lives.

After living there only a few days, we soon realized why so many Norwegians seem to prefer cross country skiing to work, school, etc. You see, their standard mode of operation was to only plow the snow on their roads between the hours of 8 am and 5 pm, Monday thru Friday. In other words, watch out, if you intend to drive at night or on weekends. From my perspective, driving could be quite a challenge, especially on those curvy mountain roads that didn't seem to have any markings or guard-rails. For me, it was embarrassing in that you could almost count on me going into a ditch on the way to the Quarantine Station every weekend. I know my Norwegian friends were not happy, having to get their tractor out to pull me out of a snow bank, especially when it happened two or more days in a row. This was unnecessarily troublesome and so it didn't surprise me when they would continually press me to use my cross country skis.

And again, as on every occasion, I would apologize and then humble myself noting that unfortunately I knew my limitations and was sure I didn't have the strength and endurance to ski that far. Nevertheless, I am sure it was difficult for them to understand and I felt bad that even their parents and grandparents could easily ski such distances and did so, on a regular basis.

Well, it was a joy living in our little cottage nestled back from the main road. Each night after dinner, all four of us would put on our cross country skis and head for the hills. It was a delight skiing under the moonlight and I will always have fond memories of the joy seeing my girls conquering one hill after another. Soon they learned to ski quite well and would love to make a difficult turn and then stop to watch Joanne and I tumble in the snow as we lost our balance or hit a bump we couldn't handle. I am sure that made their day and pleased them to no end. The smiles on their faces said it all. Then, after returning back home to our little cottage; we were always ready for a snack, bedtime stories and a night of peaceful sleep.

Now, I say peaceful sleep. But let me explain. There is one thing I don't understand to this day. As you recall, Joanne and I are newlyweds. Yes, I know, I have said that many times. So, when we found single beds in the cottage, we, of course, would immediately move two of them together, so we could snuggle up, especially on those cold winter nights. Well, lo and behold, it amazed us and to this day we cannot figure out why, every Thursday after the cleaning lady left, we would find our beds separated and against the opposite walls. I don't know what the cleaning lady was thinking, but, I am sure she must have been aggravated to have to move those beds every time she came to clean. I, for one, know, at least, from my perspective, it aggravated me to no end to have to move them back together every Thursday evening.

Well, let's get back to the purpose of our being in Norway and the processing of the cattle destined for America. Once the cattle arrived at the quarantine station, health inspections were completed on a daily basis. Then, about three weeks later, it was time to complete the mandatory tests required for the importation of these 25 head of cattle into the United States.

One of the required tests was for the purpose of trying to isolate the Foot-and-Mouth Disease virus should it be present. This was done by taking a scraping of the surface cells of the esophagus and pharynx of each animal being exported. A Probang instrument was used to collect just a few of these cells. It is a rod/handle about two feet long with a cup (slightly larger than a quarter wide and 2-3 inches deep) attached. The mouth of the bull or cow was held open by a mouth speculum with one hand, while the other hand placed the Probang down the animal's throat with the distal end of the Probang (bottom of the cup) entering first. Then a gentle (I am sure the cattle were not in the least bit thrilled with this experience!)up and down stroke would secure all the endothelial cells from the esophagus/ pharynx needed for the test sample to be complete. In addition blood was collected to detect the possibility of different disease viruses that might be present. All of these samples were then shipped to our Foreign Animal Disease Diagnostic Laboratory at Plum Island, New York for completion of the diagnostic tests needed.

While the required tests are helpful in identifying whether the animals were or had been affected with a specific disease of concern, I found the daily examination of each animal and the taking of a rectal temperature reading to be most helpful in providing me with the additional certainty necessary to certify their freedom of disease.

Even though Norway is officially free of tuberculosis (Mycobacterium bovis), we also required the completion of a cervical intradermal test for that disease. This involved shaving a small area on the animal's neck, measuring the skin thickness at that site, and injecting a small amount of Tuberculin into the skin. We again measured the skin's thickness at that site 72 hours later. If the skin thickened and the measurement increased a certain amount, we would read the test as positive and the animal would be refused entry into the United States. Well, it was just my luck; three of the animals reacted positively to this test and thus had to be removed from quarantine.

Now, how was I going to explain this to the Norwegian Exporter and more importantly, to the Chief Veterinary Official of Norway? What can I say when the Norwegian Government has officially established that their country has been free of Tuberculosis (Mycobacterium bovis) for many years? Thank goodness, the Norwegian Officials understood that this test was not a definitive test. Nevertheless, in our testing protocol, we wanted to eliminate all possibilities of infection or issues of cross reactions that might create issues for us now and in the future.

In this instance we asked that the three animals be removed from the quarantined herd being considered for export. In addition, we asked that all of the remaining animals stay in quarantine for an additional 60 days. Then, at that time, we planned to retest them with the same Test. If they remained negative (as they should), and all other tests previously submitted were negative, they could then be shipped to the United States for the completion of their U. S. Quarantine procedures at the Clifton, New Jersey Quarantine Station (this station no longer exists).

This gave our family additional time to better understand the culture and lifestyle of the Norwegian people and added much joy to our lives. This included the pleasure of observing our children, Amory and Julie playing with the neighbor's children. They would build tunnels and forts in the snow banks and play all sorts of games. Within a few weeks, they were able to communicate and it would always surprise me when they would refer to one of the other children telling them one thing or another. To this day it still amazes me how quickly young children are able to pick up a foreign language, especially without a teacher or dictionary.

One weekend in Norway will remain in my memory for a long time. With all the beauty of winter, there is always the special time of enjoying the snow as a family. This particular weekend we all agreed we needed to build a snowman. Somehow the discussion soon turned to the realization that it wasn't fair that we only built snowmen and never even considered snow-women. So, we were going to be the first family to build a snow-woman. Then, with all of the excitement, it appears we must have overdone the finer qualities of a woman's anatomy (yes, the breasts—most likely my doing) because it wasn't long before we heard that the neighborhood thought our beautiful piece of art work was probably really not appropriate. So, as you can imagine, we did the right thing and quickly demolished this creative work of art and yet kept it etched in our minds forever.

Fortunately, with the additional 60 days of quarantine completed, all of the remaining animals in quarantine were negative on the Tuberculin Cervical Skin Retest. By the middle of May, the **Norwegian Exporter, Otto Torenson; the Farm Manager, Oyvind Snopestad;** and I were busily preparing the animals for their journey to America. In addition arrangements were made for my family; Joanne, Amory, and Julie to fly to the United States. Since my wife was pregnant and the children were still small, we as a family felt it was best that they not travel on a cargo ship with all of the possible unknowns and in my mind, possible risks of such passage. Yes, you did understand correctly. I did mention that my wife, Joanne was with child. It was from my point of view a relatively easy pregnancy. Now, Joanne may disagree and what can I say, I have never had the experience. It was all worthwhile, though, in that a few months later, our son, Richard, was born, a special plus to our marriage, and from that point on I have always had the joy of pointing out from time to time that this is my son, Richard; made in Norway.

As time grew closer to our departure, I advised the Exporter, Mr. Otto Torenson that I would like to inspect the trucks the night before our departure. I wanted to be sure the trucks transporting the animals were free of manure or other materials that might interfere with our efforts to prevent the exposure of these cattle to any disease agents that other animal manure might contain. Unfortunately when the trucks arrived in the early evening hours, there was evidence that the trucks had not been cleaned to my satisfaction. I discussed my concerns with the exporter and indicated that the trucks were not acceptable in the condition they were presently in. It was obvious, however, that the exporter thought I was excessively picky and exclaimed, "Apparently the only form of transportation that will be acceptable to you, is to transport them in school buses and in school buses with the seats removed". Clearly he was not a happy man!

Early the next morning, I arrived at the quarantine station just in time to see several TV camera men, newspaper reporters, and other media personnel arriving on the scene. I had no idea this would be such a newsworthy event. After advising them on the distance restrictions necessary to prevent any interruption in the day's activities, I was horrified to observe several yellow school buses coming up the lane. Now, I was truly worried as anyone would be. I could see the TV and Newspaper images being signaled all across the United States. Was this simple export going to become an international incident? Was I going to be the laughing stock at home and abroad? Would I have a job when I returned home? Could I do anything to avoid the disastrous reporting that was surely going to happen as a result of this event? My brain went into high gear and I knew I had been had.

After facing this mountain of worry, I decided anything I could say at this point would only make things worse. So, I just got busy helping the farm manager, Mr. Snopestad, load the animals on the buses and followed the buses to the cargo ship in my rented Ford Escort. Sure enough, all of the media personalities had already found their way to our ship and were strategically located to get the best pictorial shots available.

The cattle were offloaded into cargo containers that were altered to provide the environment needed to house them for their 12 day journey across the North Atlantic. They all had halters on and were lead off the back of the school buses onto a steep incline. They were frisky and anxious to leave this strange environment. I was on the edge of my seat during the entire off loading and worried that some of the cattle might fall, break a leg or have other injuries. The look in their eyes was a look of terror and the way many of them jumped, twisted and turned upon exiting was on the verge of giving me heart failure for sure. Finally they were all safely placed in the containers and the crane operators slowly lifted them up to the ship's deck where they were to remain for the entire trip. After checking each of them carefully, it was a great relief to find them in fine shape and settling down quite well. It was only a short time later that we were on the open seas and on our way to their new home.

Life on a cargo ship was a new experience for me. The daily activities were routine. However, I will always remember one occasion, when the captain informed me that they were having a training event that afternoon at about 2 pm to be sure that all of us would be able to exit the ship safely should an emergency exist. He encouraged me to fall in line on deck behind the rest of the crew when the alarm sounded and follow the procedures being implemented by each of the crew members in front of me. The Captain could tell I was nervous and he assured me that everything would be fine. All I would need to do is follow his direction as is required of all crew members. After all, he was the Captain. Noting the smile on his face, I said: "Yes Sir," and promptly gave him a salute. We both smiled and with that I returned to my afternoon chores.

At two o'clock, as promised, the alarm went off and the entire crew met on deck. They were in a long line passing by several long boxes containing sufficient life preservers to accommodate us all. The Captain stood to one side with a serious look on his face as the lifeboats were lowered and each crew member prepared to disembark.

Little was I prepared for the terror that struck me as I witnessed the way each crew member exited the ship and lowered themselves into the safety of their particular lifeboat! All I could remember were the orders the Captain had spoken to me earlier that day. Here I was witnessing each crew member one by one running as fast as they could and leaping from the deck with their hands out stretched reaching for the ropes used to lower the lifeboats. Once they had a grip on the rope, they would wrap their legs around the rope, and slide down the rope with ease into the safety of the lifeboat.

I was petrified! There was no way that I would be able to grab the rope, let alone arrive safely the thirty or so feet below in the lifeboat. My life was in the hands of the Captain and I couldn't believe he would make me do this. The fragility of life became very real to me and my only hope was in the prayers of youth and that God might somehow eliminate this experience of terror so encompassing my very being. Oh yes, I can't emphasize enough the relief and gratitude I felt as with only a couple crew members left in front of me, the Captain yelled, "Buisch, come over here! I don't think you are quite ready to do that!" All I could say was, "Yes Sir! Thank you, sir!!"

Of course the Captain and all of the Officers were greatly amused at my antics and obvious panic during the exercise and I must say that I found it amusing especially after realizing that they were just having some fun and we all felt a special bond and closeness when I demonstrated that I too had a sense of humor and joined in the laughter as they recounted the events of that day.

It was in the early morning of the third day at sea, when I was abruptly awakened. I couldn't believe it! I was being thrown from my bunk across the room hitting the far wall and landing on the floor. It was about 3 am and I was more than a bit roughed up and dazed when I suddenly realized that something just was not right. I remember hearing a lot of thunder. I felt confused and noticed that after a period of relative quiet, I would hear a definite knocking sound; Bam!! Bam!! Bam!!! What in the world was going on? Was I dreaming? Oh, No, it can't be! Yes, we were in rough seas and yes, I was continually tossed about in the room.

Finally, I was able to open my door and briefly stepped out into the hallway. At that same instance, the Captain was leaving his cabin. He took one look at me and barked, "Get back in your cabin and do not leave your cabin and for heaven's sake don't . . . , promise me you will not go outside!" I quickly agreed and hustled back into my room.

I must say the images that created terror in my heart that night will remain with me for a long time. As I looked out my small port window, it became evident that we were in the middle of a violent storm like I had never seen. The waves were gigantic. I had no idea how large they were. From my perspective, surely with fear etched all over my face, they were as big as the biggest skyscrapers I had ever seen. What occurred next just blew my mind away. For you see, the next thing I observed was that it appeared we were submerged by each wave as it passed over us.

Well after about an hour of this and being confined to my room my anxiety increased. I was beginning to panic. Was I going to live through this event? Had the crew abandoned ship? Was I the only one left? I just had to know! O, what should I do? So, after much deliberation (15 minutes max), I stuck my head outside my door. I looked around. No one seemed to be present. After a few more minutes, my curiosity got the best of me and I walked into the hallway with my arms outstretched bracing myself as I walked. I peeked out onto the deck. Just as I had thought, the gigantic waves were submerging the ship and submerging the ship repeatedly.

And then, to my astonishment, I couldn't believe what I was seeing. The crew was doing that which I thought was impossible! Such Courage! Such Dedication! You see, the cables holding the containers were on occasion breaking one by one. There was the possibility of losing everything on deck. And yet, the crew was actively working in this mess and without flinching, would run out on the deck when the ship bounced to the surface; would quickly attach one end of a new cable to the container holding the precious cargo; attach the other end of the cable to the deck floor; and then return, just in time, to the safety of the interior of the ship. Their timing was perfect and they moved with a determination and commitment, I have never seen, often at great risk to their own personal safety. Here I was, fearing for my life, almost totally incapacitated, while these men were worried about saving the cargo, the very cargo that included the twenty plus Cows and Bulls.

Fortunately the storm soon settled down and the rest of the trip was uneventful. I enjoyed the many delicious meals with the Captain and his Officers, I finished reading all of the books I had brought with me, and enjoyed the many conversations I had with Mr. Oyvind Snopestad, the Farm Manager as well as with the Crew.

After twelve days at sea, we were at the New York Port of Entry and the Longshoremen were boarding the ship. I quickly found the Captain and advised him that we were not to unload any cargo until my counterpart from the United States Quarantine Station arrived and the cattle had been off loaded. The Captain looked at me and with a smile advised, "That is none of my business. I brought the cargo to the United States and now it is the responsibility of your government for any actions necessary at this point. I don't off load the cargo. Your longshoremen do that."

So, with as much courage as I could muster, I shouted as loud as I could, "As a representative of the United States Department of Agriculture; you are to immediately cease unloading the ship until my counterpart arrives. At that point he will off load the cattle and then give you permission to resume off-loading the cargo destined for this Port of Entry." To tell you the truth, I couldn't believe what happened. All of the Longshoremen, big muscular men, looked up at me and without a moment's hesitation found a place to sit down and waited for further directions. I was amazed. What if my counterpart doesn't show? Who is going to pay these folks for the time they are not permitted to work? Am I not the responsible official?

Well, fortunately, it was only a few minutes before my counterpart arrived. He brought with him several trucks and a crew sufficient to off load the cattle in a quick and efficient manner. Boy was I ever pleased to see him. We were fortunate in that on this trip all of the animals arrived safely except for one that had a broken back as a result of the horrific storm we endured.

As you can tell, I loved our trip to Norway. It was an experience of a lifetime, the people were friendly and the time we had as a family was a series of memorable events that I shall cherish forever.

CHAPTER 5

The Dismal Swamp

The Dismal Swamp provided further growth to a young rookie veterinarian. While filling life with wonderful memories, there was one event I shall never forget.

It was my first temporary assignment and as such was an adventure I was looking forward to. In this assignment I would be working in an Emergency Task Force assigned to eliminate Hog Cholera in the State of North Carolina. The circumstances and conditions were different and truly unique in a variety of ways. For starters, parts of the area affected with this disease were located in a swamp. In fact, the area of North Carolina in which we worked, has often been referred to as The Great Dismal Swamp. This wet swamp land is prevalent along the Atlantic Coast from Norfolk, Virginia to Elizabeth City, North Carolina and beyond. It is an area rich in bio-diversity and is an excellent example of the symbiotic relationships so important to the future health of our planet's animal and plant life (a subject/book for another time).

In this case, the Headquarters for our Task Force was on the outskirts of Elizabeth City, North Carolina. I can still remember the night I arrived. There was an air of excitement and everyone was as friendly as could be. I was amazed at the camaraderie and enthusiasm so evident in everyone I met. To me it was a wonderful way to be welcomed into the workings of such an elite group of individuals. What? Did I say Welcomed? Did I think this was a Welcoming Party? Whoaaaa . . . . No way! It definitely was not about me or the other 100 plus individuals who had just arrived from all over the country that memorable evening. No, absolutely not! Rather, as we were soon to find out, it was a party planned a week or more in advance by and for the 100 plus individuals we were replacing and this was a party planned with a lot of excitement and anticipation, a celebration of the time they had together and more importantly the fact that they were finally going home. No wonder they were so happy to see all of us arrive.

After a good night's rest, we were up early and before long, assigned to work in various areas of responsibility and specialty, whether it was surveillance, diagnostics, epidemiology, or whatever was needed at that particular moment. Again,

I was pleased to have been assigned to the diagnostic section. It was a great experience; sharpening my skills in observation, communication (asking the right questions), the use of current technology, etc.

One skill I no doubt had little or no experience in and yet in this situation was the most important; was that of empathy for the individuals and families affected. Almost immediately the value of obtaining and having this skill became evident. Fortunately for me, within a rather short period of time, I came to the realization that little, very little could be accomplished until we, as a Task Force and as individuals, had at least some understanding of the turmoil and agony so evident in the lives of those negatively affected by this terrible tragedy.

It was plain as day! You could see it everywhere! Just think about it! How could any of them even begin to cooperate and provide support to this massive undertaking unless we (obviously as total strangers) first recognized the impact of this disease on their livelihood as well as the very fiber of their lives personally? The message was there, clearly there! To have a lifetime invested in building a solid business framework; to carefully develop the breeding characteristics of their swine herd through careful management of genetics; and then to observe a disease destroy all of their efforts; was a tragic event to say the least.

For me, this was a shocker! At times it was more than I could stand! The pain and agony on the faces and expressions of those who had to live through this ordeal were incredible. For each of them the situation was often unbearable. Little did they imagine that at this time they would have this burden to bear, let alone the unknown and foreboding challenges of the future? You can be sure the circumstances and conditions they faced were unexpected, unwanted and in most cases devastating to all they had hoped and wished for. It was a scenario you wouldn't want to wish on anyone!

The sheer strength, fortitude and resilience of these producers reminded me of the words of Mother Teresa as spoken at one point in her life. They are words of hope and encouragement. They can make a difference in each of our lives. They are truly words of wisdom as she so remarkably understood. They are not only words, but when they are put into action; they are a reservoir of strength that can be used to overcome any and all adversity that should pass our way. Think about it! Her words of encouragement were as follows:

- **People are often unreasonable, illogical and self-centered; forgive them anyway.**
- **If you are kind, people may accuse you of selfish, ulterior motives; be kind anyway.**
- **If you are successful, you will win some false friends and some true enemies; succeed anyway.**
- **If you are honest and frank, people may cheat you; be honest and frank anyway.**
- **What you spend years building, someone could destroy overnight; build anyway.**
- **If you find serenity and happiness, they may be jealous; be happy anyway.**
- **The good you do today, people will often forget tomorrow; do good anyway.**
- **Give the world the best you have, and it may never be enough; give the world the best you've got anyway.**
- **You see, in the final analysis, it is between you and God; it was never between you and them anyway.**

About two weeks after I arrived at the Task Force; I received a telephone call from my father. It was always good to hear from him. However, this time I was surprised to hear what he had to say. First of all, he wondered how things were going and how I enjoyed working in North Carolina. Of course, I was elated and shared the joy I had working with the talented people from all over the country and also shared with him how humbling and yet worthwhile our work was as seen from the perspective of the producers.

What came next, I was not prepared for. Dad asked if I would mind if he came down for a couple weeks and observed what I was doing. He noted that he had no idea what a veterinarian did. As such, it was quite embarrassing especially considering that his son (Me!) was now a member of that profession and frankly when people asked what kind of work I did, he wanted to have some idea, at least more than what he could obtain at the local library. It appears that even with his upbringing on a farm, he had no idea what a veterinarian did. Apparently his dad took care of all of the health problems and when the local veterinarian came on the scene; dad was always assigned to some other task elsewhere on the farm.

After checking with my boss, I found out his visit would be just fine and in fact many of the Task Force members from out of state had their wives or husbands there with them; helping out with a wide variety of Task Force duties that needed to be done. This was most accommodating and as you might expect; fostered good will, especially for those assigned for extended periods of time. Within a few days, my dad arrived and it was a special time for us both. I must admit, however, that it did seem a little strange having my dad hold pigs as I took tonsil biopsies (yes, even veterinarians find tonsils of interest) or blood for diagnostic purposes. And yet we both so enjoyed our time together and had many exciting memories to reflect on for years to come.

For my second tour of duty to this particular Task Force, I was given an assignment that was both challenging and yet rewarding at the same time. In this instance, I was asked to serve one month as the Acting Laboratory Director at the North Carolina State Veterinary Diagnostic Laboratory in Edenton, North Carolina. The Director, who normally managed the daily operation of this facility, had put in long hours continually for many months and needed a break. Apparently the presence of the Task Force had raised the level of awareness and need for laboratory support in all animal disease situations and as such the workload had increased quite substantially.

So, what could I say? After all, don't we, in the veterinary profession, as in other professions, need to be there for each other? Isn't that part of life? And so, again, what could I say? Of course, even with my limited experience and some apprehension, my answer was in the affirmative; willing and ready to dig in, so to speak, and do the best that I could! After affirming that I would be glad to help, the butterflies in my stomach began to act up. Did I have any idea what I was getting in to? Yes, I was a recent graduate of Veterinary Medicine. But, really, what did I know about being a Director of a Laboratory, especially one as important as this one running in conjunction with a major Disease Eradication Program?

I suddenly felt humbled and went into the Laboratory relying heavily on the expertise of the talented staff that had committed their lives to this important work, and had worked for years at this great institution. I was fortunate in that the technicians and other professionals were most helpful and accommodating. I learned a lot from them and will always cherish the time spent with them. Soon the month had passed and yet the friendships developed will long be remembered. We worked seven days a week and the hours ranged from early in the morning to late in the evening. It seemed as though there was always more that needed to be done and yet with this extraordinary staff, we somehow were able to keep our heads above water.

On one occasion, about the third week into my assignment, I, unfortunately, had a head cold that was bothering me and in some ways driving me crazy. About 2 pm in the afternoon, it seemed to have gotten worse. In fact, I felt so bad that I decided to take off and get some rest. The staff encouraged me to do so and indicated they would be able to carry on, which I was sure they could do. Upon arriving at the motel, I immediately headed to my room; took a couple aspirin, a decongestant, and an expectorant. I had just about had it with the irritation of a nasty head cold and was ready to hit the sack and get some rest. After about thirty minutes of tossing and turning, I started thinking about what a beautiful day it was and that I might be better off resting in the heat of the day by the swimming pool. Oh, yeah!

Well, as luck would have it, the staff at the Laboratory called the Director at his home, and he was so worried that he came over to the motel to see how I was doing. What can I say; how do I explain; is there an excuse when the Director finds me in the late afternoon on a bright summer's day lounged out in my swimming suit on the deck of the motel's Olympic swimming pool? All I can say, he was most cordial, probably too cordial and simply stated he was worried about my welfare and hoped I would feel better soon. You can bet, I was up bright and early the next morning with no concern for my physical wellbeing and as a result was the very first one to arrive at the front steps of this fine facility. Of course everyone had already heard about what happened; in fact, the very details of what had happened; and of course, they had a lot of fun, rightfully so, teasing me about it for the rest of my stay.

I must say that the experience with these fine individuals was truly worthwhile and provided many lessons well learned. Then, within a couple months, the last case of this horrific disease, Hog Cholera was uncovered and there has never been a single recurrence of this disease in North Carolina since that time.

The logistics of a Task Force operation can be quite extensive and often require as many as two hundred to three hundred people with a wide variety of expertise to assist in the eradication effort. Even the State Police and Guardsmen are called on to enforce the movement restrictions and to assure no, not one instance of an infected pig, pig product or virus contaminated piece of equipment moves out of the area so quarantined. It is a massive undertaking and yet the dedication, trust, and commitment of the various Task Force members as well as the affected producers and allied industries are impressive to behold. Without that trust and commitment by everyone involved, you can be sure we could not have accomplished eradication. And for that, we can be truly thankful.

Now, why have I gone through all of this detail? Well, you see, Dr. Saul Wilson, who was probably my most important mentor and I were among the last to direct the final eradication efforts. As a result, it seemed important to share some of the complexities involved in any disease control/eradication effort. As you read the brief summaries of the many adventures I faced from this point on, I just want to emphasize that in no case is the success of these programs due to the efforts of any one person. Rather, they are the direct result of a shared vision and commitment of numerous individuals who have a passion for improving animal health and the health and welfare of mankind.

In closing, I would like to recount a disease investigation I thoroughly enjoyed. The local Practicing Veterinarian had just called and indicated that he was concerned that a swine herd he had visited might be infected with the Hog Cholera virus. He asked if I, as a specialist in the diagnostics for Hog Cholera, could pay a visit to the farm and let him know what I thought.

Well, at the time of my arrival at the farm, the owner and his son were riding up the farm lane on their green, John Deere tractor. The tractor's engine was loud and I am sure they didn't think I could hear a word they were saying. You see, they were having a good time and between themselves were making fun of me, considering the fact that I, as a Federal worker, was coming to their farm. If I remember the phrasing of their conversation correctly, it went something like this:

> **"Here comes the Fed! Here comes the Fed! He's come to diagnose Hog Cholereee!"**

> **"Here comes the Fed! Here comes the Fed! He's come to diagnose Hog Cholereee!"**

And then of course, they would laugh and again repeat the phrases in perfect unison. Well, as you can imagine, there was no way I could hold back. And so, after they turned the ignition key off, I shouted out:

> **"Here comes the Fed! Here comes the Fed! And I've come to diagnose Hog Choleree!!!!"**

Of course we all had a good laugh and fortunately their swine herd was not infected with Hog Cholera. But rather it was infected with Erysipelas, another disease of swine that clinically can resemble the clinical signs of Hog Cholera, the disease we were trying to eradicate. In this case and especially with the presence of Hog Cholera infected swine herds near-by, I applaud the actions of this Veterinarian for his concern and for rapidly bringing it to our attention. It was through the eyes and ears of the local Veterinary Practitioners and their professional interest in the success of this program, that we were able to declare on January 1, 1978 that the United States was finally, yes, finally free of this disease that for far too long had terrorized our valued swine industries.

We, in the United States, are fortunate to have eradicated numerous diseases of economic importance. This has not come easily and yet it has been repeatedly accomplished! How? Well, basically we can thank our forefathers and the leadership that was home grown in our valued Livestock Industries. From the mid 1800s, with our nation in its infancy and few if any diagnostic tools, these courageous men forged ahead to control and eliminate disease. This took a formable commitment in that disease control programs at that time were often based on clinical signs alone. They recognized the need for controlling animal diseases and fostered the notion that disease costs. They understood the principle that eliminating livestock disease would benefit not only the producers, but the consumers as well.

And thanks to them, we have a readily available source of protein, a source of protein that is not only reasonably priced, but also safe for human consumption, and yes, for our enjoyment! To our forefathers we say thank you! Thank you for your foresight and thank you for your commitment to disease control, the health of our livestock industries and the health of our nation as a whole!

CHAPTER 6

A Hen Pecked Life

Directing Task Force Activities has its share of challenges and disruptions, especially when the morning paper indicates that these activities are a "Total Failure".

It was the beginning of March, and for some, the worst of winter was over. The days were getting longer and if you lived in the south, you might think, if not hoped that spring was just around the corner. It was that time of year when sunny bright days could warm the very core of your being and yet, as well, the long dark chilly nights could send a shiver up your spine. It was the season of ever changing weather patterns that are so difficult to plan around. It was the ideal time for colds and the sniffles. And what made it worse was that such colds and sniffles would spread rapidly from one individual to another.

Now, as you probably know, it is no different in the animal kingdom as a whole. For example, should the flu get a foot hold in a large population of swine or birds, it is just a short period of time before the disease has rapidly spread. In nature, it is a well-known fact that the Flu/Avian Influenza virus is often an uninvited guest of our wild bird populations. In fact, it is often found in a wide variety of birds and especially in migratory water fowl as they migrate across the United States.

Fortunately, this is usually of little or no consequence to the wild bird populations as a whole. First of all, birds in the wild usually have plenty of fresh air around them and secondly they normally only spread the Flu virus when they are in concentrated populations such as farm ponds or small waterways.

Then, if we consider birds, anatomically, as a set of lungs with two legs, two wings and a beak, we will understand that if they are infected, they are usually acutely ill, greatly fatigued and disabled to the point that it is unlikely they will be able to actively mingle with and/or spread the Flu/Avian Influenza disease to other birds, especially in the wild.

Furthermore, we find that domestic poultry in the United States are rarely, if ever, infected with the flu. They are usually confined to a building and have no way of being in contact with wild birds. As a result, they don't have to deal with the same disease problems as associated with their kin folks in the wild.

Unfortunately, however, there are times when they can be exposed as was the case of an outbreak of Avian Flu/Influenza in the early 1980s in Virginia, Delaware, and Pennsylvania. In that instance, the flu virus was thought to have been introduced into the poultry houses by the farm workers. You see, the farm in Pennsylvania, where this disease first appeared, had a farm pond and unfortunately migrating water fowl loved to frequent the pond area. After capturing a few of these migratory birds and running tests for Avian Influenza, we found them to be infected with exactly the same type of Avian Influenza as found in the infected poultry house, thereby giving substantial proof that the migratory water fowl had to be the source of infection.

Apparently the farm workers enjoyed walking around the pond during their lunch breaks and as a result picked up some of the contaminated duck feces on the bottom of their boots. As you can imagine, when they returned to their work inside the poultry buildings, they must have introduced the virus by leaving some of the infectious material/virus throughout the buildings/cages/areas where poultry were housed.

Once poultry in a commercial poultry house are exposed to the virus and become infected, the disease spreads rapidly. This is especially true since the birds are in an enclosed area and housed in close proximity. Each infected bird becomes another virus factory and with each labored breath effectively contaminates the surrounding air with a multitude of live, highly infectious, viral particles. Even with the use of fans to assure the adequate flow of air throughout each of the buildings, one sometimes wonders if in the case of the presence of virus factory birds; whether the fans are a deterrent or rather may in fact facilitate the more rapid spread of the Avian Influenza virus laden dust particles throughout the building.

For infected broilers (birds raised for meat production) and turkeys, the crates and containers used to haul the birds to slaughter are also found to be heavily contaminated with the virus and if the crates are used again (without being properly cleaned and sanitized), the disease can and will spread. Furthermore, scientific studies have found that contaminated dust particles on the surface of table eggs and fertile eggs (used in chicken hatcheries) spread the disease rapidly from premises to premises. If the egg flats used to transport the eggs from one place to another are not cleaned and disinfected between each use, they can become an effective conveyance/ vehicle for spreading the disease.

The disease virus has even been found in processing plants where each egg is washed and sanitized for human consumption (table eggs). In such cases, we could isolate the infective virus everywhere in the rooms where the eggs were being processed. This included the equipment, the ceiling, the floors, the walls, and even the air. As a result of these findings, immediately after identifying that an egg processing plant had received eggs from a known infected premises, we would have to shut the plant down and insist upon a thorough cleaning and disinfection of the entire premises before it could again begin the processing of table eggs for human consumption. From what I have said, I am sure you can understand why.

Another piece of wisdom we learned during this particular disease outbreak was that the potential for short distance spread of infective virus by air is very real. In one research study, it was found that we could isolate virus from the air as far from a building of infect birds as 50 yards, but no further. This information was a key factor in further understanding how this disease spread (epidemiology). You see, prior to this we often had no clue, in many instances, as to how the disease spread from one place to another. Often people would say, when they visited a neighbor, that they parked away from the buildings housing the infected poultry and as a result should not have their poultry flock tested because they were never exposed.

With this new information we now knew that if they were within 50 yards and especially if their car or truck was parked in a direct line to the poultry building's exhaust fan, there was a good chance that their vehicle was contaminated with the nasty virus. Again, this could often be the information needed to tie the spread from premises A to premises B. It could also be the mechanism for spreading the disease by trucks delivering feed; poultry company trucks, farm tractors, etc.

Well, now, let me tell you a little bit more about this particular disease outbreak. It first came to our attention in rural Pennsylvania. Suddenly several poultry producers noticed massive die offs in their individual poultry flocks. Often 30 to 50 per cent or more of the birds in a particular flock would die within a 2 to 3 day period of time. Yes you are right! This is a no brainer! You don't have to be a veterinarian to know this is a serious health problem.

Once laboratory specimens were submitted from the affected birds to our National Veterinary Services Laboratories in Ames, Iowa, it was short order before we received word that these excessive death losses were caused by an Avian Influenza virus. Then within 3 to 4 days we received additional word that the virus had been typed and that it was a strong lethal H5N1 virus. In fact, historically, it would have been identified as Fowl Plague.

To understand how we arrived at that finding, I would like to explain a little further. As part of our National Laboratory procedures, once the virus is isolated, eight disease free chickens are inoculated with the isolated infectious virus. If three or four of the chickens die within four days of the date they were inoculated, we say the virus is Highly Pathogenic Avian Influenza.

This conclusion immediately activates our Nation's State—Federal—Industry response teams. At this time they were called Regional Emergency Animal Disease Eradication Organization (READEO) Teams. These emergency response teams were ready to begin their response effort with the key members of the team on site within 24 hours. Then additional team members from throughout the country began arriving in large numbers to assist in these emergency response efforts. Upon arrival, each member received onsite training, especially in the area of bio-security (the personal precautions that need to be in force by each of the team members to prevent disease spread).

They would receive information on the specific characteristics of how the disease they were fighting spreads. In this case, our lead trainer, Dr. Kay Wheeler, would ask whether the change of coveralls and the washing of boots were sufficient to stop the spread of disease from one premises to another. The answer was often a surprise to those in attendance. In their minds they would believe that such activities plus the washing of hands would have been sufficient.

Well, at that point, Dr. Wheeler would point out that the Avian Influenza virus is smaller than the smoke generated by a cigarette. He or one of the recruits who smoked would then take a drag on a cigarette and exhale; blowing the smoke through a pair of coveralls as used in farming operations. You could hear the OOooos and Ahhs from the participants as they observed how easily the smoke passed through. This quickly convinced them of the importance of not going onto another premises after they had been on a premises thought to be diseased and especially if they thought the flock might be infected with the Avian Influenza virus.

Not only did we prohibit them, in such instances, from going on another premises that day, but we also asked that they wash and disinfect their car or truck and asked that their coveralls be bagged and taken to be washed in hot water before they were used again. We also asked that the clothes they were wearing under their coveralls be laundered and that they take a shower and wait at least 24 hours before visiting another premises.

Another point of interest; is the finding that, as is often the case, we have been able to isolate the Avian Influenza virus from the throats of individuals who have been around infected poultry. In fact we have routinely been able to isolate the virus up to about 24 hours after the individuals have been exposed. And what is most interesting is that none of them are sick or show any clinical signs of illness. This has always raised the question in my mind when doctors have indicated that there is a public health concern because they have isolated the virus from humans in various countries and/or in local situations.

To me the question is whether these individuals had poultry or duck ponds near their home. Even if someone dies and the authorities claim they isolated the virus from them; did these individuals live in close proximity to poultry or migratory birds as is the custom in many parts of the world? Was their death truly caused by the Avian Influenza virus or was there some other cause that was not detected? As such, were these individuals actually infected and acting as virus factories with their tissues/cells replicating the virus or were their throats just a good medium for temporarily preserving the life of the virus that may have been present in or near their homes?

The panic created in 2009 and 2010 with the issuance of H5N1 vaccine in my opinion was definitely overblown. It is unfortunate that fear is such a great seller in our media today. One often wonders how much actual experience some of our so called experts have actually had in the field with the disease in question?

In the 2009-2010 example, it was my understanding that for the virus to become a human health hazard it would have required something like six points of mutation at six different points on the viral genome. Although I am not a virologist, it is my understanding that all of these mutations occurring in the right combination; was highly unlikely. In my opinion the concerns raised were way over-blown and not within the realm of reality.

In fact, what is even more amazing is the understanding that the Flu cases in the United States referred to in the early 1900s that caused high death loss in human beings (the plague) were actually introduced to people directly by wild birds and not domesticated poultry. I don't believe there have been any human introductions in the United States from domestically raised poultry except for possibly one case reported prior to the 2009-2010 outbreak where one human being supposedly died from the disease and that was in my mind questionable understanding the studies we have recently completed.

Remember, when we have an outbreak of Highly Pathogenic Avian Influenza, we have hundreds of individuals on site working with these infected populations of poultry to quickly and effectively eradicate the disease from those populations. If there was a serious risk of this disease mutating and causing death in human populations, we would not put our people at risk.

Now, let's return to the outbreak of disease I was involved in the early 1980s. As I have indicated the first cases were diagnosed in Pennsylvania and were classified as Highly Pathogenic Avian Influenza (Fowl Plague). Shortly thereafter the disease was diagnosed in Virginia. However, this time the disease was of low virulence and not very strong. In fact the clinical signs were relatively minor and caused only minor illness in the bird affected. As such, the cases in Virginia were not determined to be Highly Pathogenic Avian Influenza as had been diagnosed in Pennsylvania.

The Virginia Poultry Industry was outraged! They wanted their flocks to receive the same attention by State and Federal Officials and wanted the disease eradicated before it could mutate and cause serious problems to their Industry!

I can still remember a meeting called by Senator John Warner, in Richmond, Virginia. It was agreed, the State and Federal Officials would first discuss the problem and then the meeting would be opened to the press waiting outside. Senator Warner was a highly respected individual and helpful in keying in on the important issues needing to be addressed. He was able to make us all feel at ease. So, I was sure the press conference would go smoothly and felt the meeting was worthwhile. Little did I know what was to transpire under the glare of the local TV cameras and the numerous microphones pressed up to our table.

The Lieutenant Governor began, outlining the seriousness of this disease, as well as the steps taken by the State, to control disease spread. Then it was Senator Warner's turn. I can still see him in his usual statesman approach as he spoke words of praise for all that had been done by the State of Virginia. He recognized the seriousness of this disease and the negative impact it was having on their poultry industry.

And then, with the most stern, glaring look I have ever seen, he looked straight into my eyes and with anger in his voice as he slowly rose from his chair, said with clear sincerity and disgust, "Dr. Buisch, when we consider all that the State of Virginia has done to control this devastating poultry disease, where has the Federal Government been all of this time? You work for the United States Department of Agriculture and you are responsible for the control and eradication of such diseases and where were you?" Then, with his clutched fists hitting the table, he said with renewed emphasis, "What has your agency been doing all this time? Don't you care what happens to the Virginia Poultry Industry? When are you going to get with it and realize this is a serious problem?"

You can be sure; I would rather have been anywhere else on this planet than in front of the cameras with the Lieutenant Governor and Senator John Warner. What fun they were going to have on the five o'clock news! Well, I simply looked at Senator Warner and calmly (with the sweat pouring off the palms of my hands and my knees shaking to the bone) responded that we were also concerned with the situation and had sent diagnosticians and epidemiologists to Virginia to assess the situation. I assured him, even though the State had primary responsibility, we were ready to respond with a Cooperative State, Federal, Industry effort, especially considering the connection to the Pennsylvania cases already receiving federal support.

Actually as bad as this scenario looked, it was what was needed to politically support the State asking for Federal assistance. The Virginia Commissioner of Agriculture and the Federal Secretary of Agriculture had already agreed to the terms of a cooperative effort and within 24 hours we had a team on site ready to roll.

About a month later, I received word from my boss, Dr. E. C. Sharman, that there were some issues in regard to our unity of purpose in Virginia. He asked me to drive down with him the next day (Friday) and to take on the position as the Federal Director of Operations. Well, it was good that we drove down together in that it gave us some time to discuss the various issues of concern and to agree on not only the approach that might be most effective, but also to arrive at some conclusions as to why the use of vaccine at this point would be more problematic than helpful.

The change of leadership was a shock to everyone (there was no forewarning) and I was fortunate to have at least the weekend to settle in before the shock waves reverberated in the Task Force and the local community. The first thing I did was to meet with my State Counterpart and asked for his indulgence in allowing us to be located in the same office with our desks adjoining. I assured him my only purpose was to reinforce that we were working together.

Secondly, we called in our Administrative Officer, Myron Jones, one of the brightest, astoundingly accomplished logistics geniuses I have ever worked with. We asked that he find a new location that would allow all of our Task Force operations to be housed at one location and that all communications and computer support be unified so that we were all working from the same page so to speak. It was amazing; Mr. Jones had the State Director and myself in the same office within the hour and all of us in one location within a week's time. Unbelievable and yet true!

Then, the State Director and I decided to personally visit each of the poultry producers who seemed to be the greatest critics of our approach in this joint disease eradication campaign. On one premise, the owner was livid that we were asking for the impossible in their cleaning and disinfection efforts. I asked him if he could take us to one of his poultry houses so I could better understand his concern. Fortunately, one of our Sanitation Specialists was currently present in this particular building that had just completed the cleaning process. He expressed his concerns and pointed out the presence of substantial white discoloration on the floors and walls. He noted, in his opinion, this was sufficient evidence that the house needed further cleaning.

The Poultry Producer got all excited and exclaimed that these buildings were old and that it was unreasonable to request any further cleaning. Well, I looked at them both and without cracking a smile promptly sat down on the floor where there was some of this whitish discoloration and slid my heinie/buttocks back and forth as well as sliding some distance forward. You see what made this look ridiculously funny was the fact that it was Sunday afternoon and I had just come from church and was wearing my best black pin stripped suit. Everyone looked on in astonishment. When I got up and brushed myself off, the evidence was there for all to see. There was not one bit of material, dirt or discoloration on the back of my pants and I looked at the Specialist/Inspector and said, "It looks like they did a fine job and with the application of a disinfectant followed by thirty days of time, I can't see how any virus could survive." As you can imagine, that became the standard.

On Monday morning we had our first meeting with the industry and the questions flew. But it was soon evident that the industry members who were the biggest critics were now on our side. The discussions we had and the changes in procedures assured them we were listening to their concerns and were on the right track. It was a wonderful feeling to recognize that we now had their support.

There was one concern, however, that bothered the industry representatives and that was that while we had some outstanding epidemiologists (individuals who study how and why diseases spread); none of them were recognized professionally as poultry experts. As a result, the poultry producers had trouble accepting their recommendations. In their minds the Poultry Industry was a different can of worms, so to speak. So I made a call to Dr. Bill Utterback in Sacramento, California, an individual highly regarded for his understanding of epidemiology, especially in regards to the poultry Industry. I can still remember the conversation we had. After explaining how much we needed his expertise, asking him if he would catch the next plane to Virginia, and asking him to head the Epidemiological Section, there was a long pause.

Then, after much thought, he responded with, "Bill, to be frank, I don't think I am the person you need. You know that you and I have differed at times and frankly we sometimes just don't see eye to eye!" "That is true', I exclaimed. "But that is the very reason it is important that you be here. The last thing we need is a "Yes Man". We need you to challenge us, especially when it is important to saving and supporting our valued Poultry Industries. You can and will make the difference we need! I will forever be grateful. Please come!" My heart almost skipped a beat with the joy of hearing his quick response, "Bill, I will be glad to come. I will be on the next plane East for sure." "Oh, thank you, thank you, Dr. Utterback! You are a good friend indeed!"

It was amazing what Dr. Utterback was able to do. He along with Dr. Daryl Johnson, a Poultry Specialist from Georgia made all the difference in the world. The Poultry Industry listened intently to every word they uttered and would allow them unrestricted access to their entire operations, so valuing the recommendations made. I will never forget a remark made by one of the Poultry Industry Chief Executive Officers, a few months after the disease was eradicated. He said, "Dr. Buisch, while I might not admit this publically, even with this devastating disease, because of the valuable lessons we learned from this experience, we have increased our productivity by at least 5 per cent this year. We thank you and the outstanding State, Federal, Industry Team you had working with you." As you can imagine, that comment made it all worthwhile.

Well, after being on the scene for about six weeks, I was beginning to feel that we were on the downswing and that the effort would be a success. Well, so much for my thinking. I can still remember that particular day when I went, as was my custom, to the local restaurant for breakfast. The morning paper had just arrived. I sat down with my eggs, bacon and toast; was just beginning to plan the things that still needed attention; when . . . . Whoa, could that be, was I reading the headlines on the front page correctly? Oh, no, this can't be! There in giant, at least 1/2 inch high letters was the headline on the front page, a quote from a local veterinarian, **"Avian Influenza Task Force—A Total Failure"**.

I couldn't get to my office quick enough. I was a nervous wreck. Finally, our media expert, Max Heppner arrived and I showed him the paper and exclaimed, "So what do we do now!" Oh, Mr. Heppner (Max as he liked to be called) was an outstanding journalist and knew right away what needed to be done. He simply looked at me with a look of understanding and sympathy and asked, "So, Dr. Buisch, who do you know that would be considered the world authority on avian influenza? And how can I get a hold of him or her?"

It didn't take but a minute as I exclaimed, "Dr. Robert Webster, of course, Dr. Webster at St. Jude's Hospital is the world's expert and we have asked for his counsel on many an occasion." "Well then, good!" he replied, "I will contact him immediately and see if we can use some of his quotes as a counter in tomorrow's paper." Well, you would think I could rest easy with that. But, no, I had to have an anxiety attack that brings on the Tums for relief after an hour or two. As I mentioned, the bad news was on page one with large headlines. And as for our rebuttal; it was on page eight; hardly noticed except for those who were looking for a response.

As would be my luck, or was it the workings of the Almighty, the church service I attended was packed the following Sunday and with whom should I be seated by the ushers, but the very Chief Executive Officer of the Company for whom this veterinarian worked. All we did was acknowledge each other's presence. Then, after this week's humbling experience, all I could do was bow my head. Whether it was to avoid looking my friend, the Chief Executive Officer in the face or to truly ask for God's grace and guidance, especially in this most troubling situation, I truly do not know nor remember.

Well, after a brief lunch and changing my clothes, I took the afternoon off (as I recommended to all of our employees) and walked the Appalachian Trail which was located nearby. Oh did I ever need that break! God seemed to reassure me that everything would be fine; especially with the birds singing; the squirrels playing; and the fragrance of the multiple patches of flowers here and there. Life was good!

Later that week, I was not sure what to expect when the Veterinarian, so quoted, showed up at my office door. He asked if he could come in and I motioned my hand for him to enter as if we had been friends for life. Then it all came out. He had come to apologize and felt bad that his comments had created so much difficulty for us. This meant a lot to me and I thanked him for coming in and sharing this with me (which must have been most difficult). He indicated that other industry members and some of the public were upset with his comments and he was truly sorry it came out the way it did. I, of course, could relate in that the media will often exaggerate as to what is said and I have often wondered how what I have said could have been interpreted in the context as written or presented on the TV or Radio in so many of my so called famous (or in my interpretation, in-famous) sound bites.

Another feature that made this experience interesting was that we were in the middle of an Amish/Mennonite farming community. As you can imagine, their philosophy of life and their belief system in some ways is quite different from those of us brought up under different cultures and circumstances. One belief they obviously firmly held to was the biblical concept that you give unto Caesar (the government) what is Caesar's and you give unto God what is God's. Another concept was that if one of your brethren is possibly wrong, you bring two or three of the believers to talk with them and hopefully help them make the right decision.

In this case we had an owner whose poultry were unfortunately found to be infected with the Avian Influenza virus of concern. The owner was very passionate about his birds and did not believe the birds were infected. They did not have a high death loss as seen in the most severe cases. He had become quite attached to his birds and had a lot of pride in how he cared for them. It was upsetting to him; especially when you consider that he was not seeing a high death loss. Finally after meeting with other church members, he did agree to the government buying his birds, humanely destroying and then burying his birds. Even though he cooperated fully, this is another example of the tragic impact such a disease has on so many individuals.

Well, as a result of this interaction, I was fortunate in being able to talk with one of the Mennonite individuals about an area of interest for me personally. You see, my grandmother's family was apparently of Pennsylvania Mennonite heritage. Therefore, I was truly interested in learning more about their faith and belief traditions. As such, I asked if there was any possibility that someone outside of the Mennonite religious faith could attend one of their church services on Sunday morning. You bet, my spirits were high and I was overjoyed when they indicated that their church services are always open to everyone and if I was interested I would most definitely be welcomed to come.

Upon asking where the church was located, they indicated that the best way to find the church would be to drive to the center of town (Dayton, Virginia) at about quarter to ten on Sunday morning. At that time I would find a lot of horse and buggies leaving town. All I would need to do was to follow them out into the countryside to their church. So, sure enough, at about quarter to ten on a bright Sunday morning several of my friends and I drove to the center of Dayton in my blue Ford Escort and lo and behold, there were dozens of Mennonites leaving town with their beautiful spirited horses and buggies heading for church. Soon we were in the country and heading down a narrow lane to a plain white building with 150 or so horses and buggies and soon to be one blue Ford Escort parked/tied up outside. The people were friendly and warmly welcomed us to their Sunday Morning Mennonite Worship Service.

As we entered the church, it was clear that all the women, young girls and babies sat on the rows of benches on the left side of the room and all the men and young boys sat on the benches on the right side of the room. Everyone was dressed the same with the women/girls in simple blue dresses with white collars and the men/boys in plain black suits. The men/boys had removed their summer straw hats upon entering the building and their hats were then hung on the neatly arranged pegs found on the right wall of the men's seating area.

Everyone was quiet and the reverence for the God they worshiped was most evident. The room was spacious and the front of the room had a plain raised platform just a couple feet higher than the rest of the room. The room for their worship encompassed the whole floor of the building and as I remember it, windows were only found along the side walls.

Soon their Service began as they all started singing a hymn of praise/adoration and then another and another. The music was without instrumentation and yet it was the most beautiful music I have ever heard (angelic) and it was sung in parts without any hymnals, music sheets, or projection screens as is often seen in churches today. You could hear the melody and yet the blended beauty of those singing soprano, bass, tenor or alto (or for that matter maybe other levels unknown to the rest of us) was something to behold. The holiness of the human voices in this setting with all of the associated majesty, reverence and awe; is beyond my ability to adequately describe.

As the Worship Service continued, a young man, obviously their Pastor came forward without any notes and an open Bible in his hand. He talked from his heart and gave the message often referencing specific Bible verses after praying for God's guidance and direction. Obviously the message was directed to those of us from outside their community. He spent a lot of time discussing some of their specific beliefs as well as the importance of trusting God's judgment/ decision-making/direction in our lives.

He noted that a Pastor of the Mennonite Church is a Pastor for life. The Pastor works the land and contributes to the good of the community with his physical labor as does all of the rest of the community. He pointed out that when a Pastor dies, the next Pastor is chosen by God. Apparently anyone in their community can nominate a man they believe would be a Godly person to lead as their Pastor in the future. Then at a specially called meeting for the purpose of selecting the next Pastor, a row of books equal in number to the number of nominees is placed in the front of the room by (if I remember correctly) their Bishop.

After a prayer asking for God's guidance and direction, each of the nominees come forward and pick up one of the books. After all of the books have been retrieved, the nominees could, at will and as often as they wished, exchange books with the other nominees until they were all satisfied they had the book God had chosen for them. At that point each of them would open the book they had in their possession. You see, each of the books had a piece of paper folded several times and randomly placed in it by the Bishop. Only one book had a piece of paper upon which was written the words directing them to be the new Pastor. This, of course, was of great interest to me. The thoughtfulness of their Pastor in helping us understand their trust in God was definitely appreciated.

Then after a closing prayer and another song, it was time for announcements. The one announcement that sticks in my mind is that reminding all of the women of the Tuesday gathering at one of their homes to make soap (truly, a cleansing event). I must say I will always value this special day we had in the life of the Mennonite Community and definitely felt God's presence as we worshiped together.

After the Service several of the men welcomed us and thanked us for coming. One of the gentlemen even asked if we would like to follow them to their home for some good Mennonite cooking. I thanked him; indicating it was very generous of him to invite us, but we would hate to impose on his wife like that at the last minute. He assured us it was no imposition and that every Sunday they have their entire family over, including at least 35 family members or more.

With that we agreed to take him up on this most generous offer of hospitality. He then nodded in approval; looking me in the eye and saying, "Sir, I may be wrong, but I do believe you might be interested in taking a buggy ride. Would you be interested in riding with me to my home?" I looked at him and smiled, "Yes Sir, it would be a great honor." During that short buggy ride to his home he asked me how I liked the Shenandoah Valley, how I liked my work, and even asked about the welfare of my family. When I noted that my wife and children did not come with me, he shook his head, and informed me that I was making a big mistake. He noted that family is most important and that God wants the family to be together at all times. He was right, of course and he insisted that I have them come down right away (unfortunately that did not happen).

Upon arriving at their home we all had a wonderful visit and soon we were called to the dinner table. I can still remember the prayer offered by this gentleman as the head of the family. I especially remember the humor included in the prayer when after saying Amen, he said, "And, Oh, Yes Lord, I do thank you for the Turkey we are eating today and for your protection in letting me capture this Turkey without all of the men in White Coats preventing me from providing the meal today." You see, the White Coats he was referring to were the White Coats our employees were wearing as coveralls in all of our Avian Influenza Task Force Operations.

During that wonderful dinner meal, the conversation was lively and as could be expected, they wanted me to try a little bit of every dish prepared. Again the men were separated from the rest of the family. The men all ate at one table, the women at another and the children at a third. I remember one time complimenting how delicious one of the prepared dishes was; I overheard one of the ladies at the next table saying, "What did he say?" Another replied, "Oh, he said he really liked the dish of corn and how it was prepared." Then a third young lady exclaimed with delight, "Oh, I prepared that; how nice of him to say that!"

As you can imagine, the food was delicious as tasty as could be. Just thinking about it makes my mouth water for sure. You would have loved it and if you have a chance and have not had any Amish or Mennonite cooking, just drive to the nearest Amish/ Mennonite Community and try some of their cooking in one of their fabulous Amish/ Mennonite Restaurants. You will be glad you did!

Well, not everything went well as planned and at one point I was called into the Governor's Office to discuss a concern they had with the way we were disposing of the depopulated Avian Influenza infected birds. Furthermore, they also indicated they were not happy with the way we were contaminating their waterways with the disinfectant we were using. To prepare for this meeting, I called the Company that made the disinfectant and explained the State's concern. I asked if they could send one of their experts to assist me at this meeting. In addition, I called our Department's Agricultural Research Service asking for someone to assist in discussing the design used in the construction of our burial pits.

The meeting was scheduled for 10 am and everyone was present, including the Lieutenant Governor, State Staff Members, and their constituents as well as those I had requested from the Federal perspective. The Lieutenant Governor began the meeting voicing her concerns relating to the disposal and disinfecting methodologies being used. The disinfectant concerns centered on the impact they might have on the environment. This included concerns for the fish and aquatic plant life as well as the purity of the water supply for human use. Then there were their concerns with the methodologies being used for burial. This included not only the contamination of soil, but also the concern that any leakage from the burial pits would further contaminate their under-ground wells as well as the streams and rivers so important to the communities they serve.

I expressed my appreciation for their concerns and thanked her for the opportunity to discuss these concerns with the hope that we could reach some agreement that would address their concerns as well as allow us to finish the Disease Eradication Program, so important to the future of their Poultry Industry as well as to our nation as a whole.

The Governor's Staff discussed the reasons for their concerns in some depth and strongly advocated that we immediately cease operations unless we could find another option for disposing of the birds. They also asked that we cease the requirement of using a disinfectant in the cleaning and disinfecting portion of our program. Their arguments were well prepared and most convincing. I then introduced our technical experts and asked them to share their thoughts in this regard.

The representative from our Agricultural Research Service emphasized that we have used individuals trained in proper burial techniques to assure the burial process was completed properly. Most importantly, the birds were buried at locations that would mitigate the chances of any contamination to the environment including that of preventing ground and surface water contamination. Secondly, our burial pits were designed to assure that the proper soils were added to the base, sides, and surface including proper compaction to further mitigate any leakage. Thirdly, vent pipes were installed to allow the proper ventilation of gases and to prevent the eruption of material to the surface. (Note, we still on occasion, unfortunately, had some eruptions and of course this always made the news.) And finally the birds were all biologic in nature and therefore their burial would be no different from other dead animals decomposing in nature with the only exception of the quantity.

As for the disinfectant issue, the company expert pointed out that this disinfectant had been approved by the United States Department of Agriculture. Furthermore, according to their research studies, the half-life of this disinfectant was short. Even if any of this product should reach groundwater, it would be highly diluted and of no consequence. They then reviewed the various studies completed and noted the State should not be concerned.

After much discussion, the Lieutenant Governor looked at me and startled me by saying, "Dr. Buisch, it is the State of Virginia's responsibility to protect the public water supply. As such, it is our determination that this Task Force Program poses a serious risk to our water supply and therefore must cease their operations in the State of Virginia immediately"

I couldn't believe what I had heard. I took a few moments to consider what she had said and then responded as calmly as I could. "Lieutenant Governor, I appreciate the opportunity to discuss this issue of such importance to your State and the Public you serve. I respect your decision and wish to express my concern for your Poultry Industry. The reason for my concern is that a slight variant of the type of Avian Influenza you have in Virginia has in Pennsylvania caused high death losses amounting to as much as 80 per cent or more of a flock so infected in a matter of just a few days. With the virus isolated here being of the same Hemagglutinin and Neuraminidase type as that in Pennsylvania; it is of great concern to the rest of our country and in fact is of great concern to most of the Countries we export Virginia poultry and poultry products to around the world."

"In addition, we are, in my opinion, in the final phases of eradicating this disease from the State of Virginia. It is unfortunate to stop the eradication process when we have come so far and are near the completion of our goal and mission. But, with your decision I must advise that we will stop all of the Task Force Operations and unfortunately for your valued and highly productive Poultry Industry, we will place a Federal Quarantine on the State of Virginia to protect the rest of our country's poultry populations and our valued export markets. No Virginia poultry, or poultry products, eggs nor meat will be allowed to leave the State of Virginia and I am sure the Avian Influenza virus will in one way or another destroy any possibility of the Virginia Poultry Industry surviving in the future. I am truly sorry for you, your valued turkey, broiler and egg industries, and the State of Virginia."

With that the Lieutenant Governor asked if she could confer with her staff privately for a few moments and then we would again gather before bringing the meeting to an end. About thirty minutes later, we reconvened and I am pleased to note that she reconsidered her decision and granted us full support with the encouragement that we finish the eradication program as soon as possible. She was a sharp lady and once she realized the potential seriousness of the Avian Influenza consequences to the livelihood of their Poultry Industry; her support did much to shorten the time until we were able as a State, Federal, Industry Task Force to successfully complete our mission and the Virginia Poultry Industry was able to resume business as usual.

It wasn't long, however, before I received some discouraging news from the United

States Department of Justice. They called to advise that the United States Department of Agriculture was being sued for damages by a Virginia Poultry Producer. They also advised that several of the Department's employees including myself were being sued personally for the decisions we had made. This was in reference to the decisions made in establishing the area federally quarantined in the State of Virginia. This quarantine prevented the interstate movement of poultry from the quarantined area due to the presence of flocks infected with Avian Influenza.

Even though the birds of the owner suing us were never infected with the Avian Influenza virus of concern; the State—Federal Quarantine, in effect, prevented them from selling and moving their birds, which were raised for breeding purposes, to potential buyers. As a result their business was severely affected with serious financial losses to them as a business as well as to their earnings as a family.

I can still remember the wife of the poultry producer getting on the stand and with tears in her eyes describing the terrible impact these restrictions had on them personally. The emotions were running high and I, myself, could feel their passionate plea and completely understood the terrible consequences such quarantine measures have on a family business. Their business had taken years to develop through painstaking devotion to honesty and perseverance; struggling to achieve a market that depended on them to deliver quality birds on a schedule arranged years in advance. While the quarantine was necessary to achieve eradication of this serious disease from the United States, that did not mean that all was well. The negative impact on the flocks within that area that never got the disease was unfortunately one that was the price of the benefit of the Eradication Program to the country as a whole.

Well, I can remember the day I first entered the courtroom just before the beginning of this important trial in Federal District Court (in downtown Washington, D.C.). The family filing suit was already there and having recognized me, quickly came over to say hello. As is the usual greeting we shook hands and they immediately indicated they were glad to see me and asked how I was doing? As you might expect, I responded that I have had better days. Not knowing that I was personally named by their lawyers, they looked confused and asked what was wrong and actually looked like they really cared about my welfare. I looked at them with what I am sure was a very sad face and shared that I was there because of their suit. It was the first time I had ever been sued personally and the thought of a $750,000 suit against me personally was a little more than I could bear.

Suddenly, they looked at each other and without saying anything more retreated to the front of the courtroom with their legal counsel. When I was asked to testify; I admitted that I was one of the individuals involved in the decision-making process of establishing the Federal Quarantine and its boundaries. I explained to the best of my ability the reason for the quarantine and the guidelines used in establishing the quarantine as it was established.

That night, I did not sleep very well. In fact, my brain was in overdrive as I thought of what a court decision in favor of the plaintiffs could do to me and my family. I knew that what little we had saved would be gone and that most of my future earnings would be gone as well.

The next morning it took several cups of coffee to get me going and for the first time, I really hated the thought of going to work. About 9:00 am, I got a call from our Attorney in the Department's Office of the General Counsel. My mind was overwhelmed with negative thoughts and all I could think of was: How could the Federal District Court make a decision so fast. I picked up the phone slowly and said, "Dr. Buisch, May I help you?" Well, it was our Attorney, as my secretary had indicated, and he was all excited. He said, "I just got a phone call from the Prosecuting Attorney and he indicated that his client asked that your name be removed from the list of defendants being sued." He added this was very unusual and he couldn't understand why they would do that and especially at this stage in the process. He indicated that when he asked for clarification, they just noted that they had their reasons and asked that he notify me as soon as possible.

Well, I can assure you that my rebound from the depths of Hell were at first unbelief and then after thinking about it, all I could do was celebrate and thank God for this miracle, for which I will forever be grateful.

Yes, my family and I did celebrate. However, knowing my full humanness and that I am not perfect (Oh, I wish I could do better); I immediately signed up for liability insurance and asked for one million dollars worth.

Now comes the best part! I can still remember the occasion, about six months later, when the Virginia Poultry Federation celebrated the successful eradication of this most formable disease. Numerous individuals were honored and I remember when they announced my name, I was greatly humbled and couldn't hold back the tears. The beauty of this experience was that we not only achieved the best we could for the Poultry Industry; but we also recognized and respected the outstanding knowledge and experience each of us as State, Federal, and Industry members contributed to the benefit of all.

CHAPTER 7

The Rose Garden

Promotion involves additional levels of responsibility. Basic human values can be greatly challenged. As such, how does one remain faithful to their beliefs?

Christmas was always a family event; a special time of joy and celebration; the celebration of Christ's birth. Every Christmas Eve, our family would go to watch with anticipation a Christmas Pageant presented by our local church. As proud parents, we were excited to see our four children participating and it didn't matter what their role might be; whether sheep, or cattle, or the bright star in the sky. The important fact was that they were up front and as far as we were concerned; they were the best performers around; no matter what role they played or how nervous they might be.

Then there was Christmas morning, and yes this was an important event. The children all rose at the first inkling of sunlight and we as parents put on a big smile and showed as much enthusiasm as we could after a long night of my wife preparing a feast for the next day and my trying to put their gifts together as quickly as possible. As you can imagine, that was often more difficult than it might sound. You see, as a typical male, putting toys together was my forte. And yet, for some reason, I just knew I could accomplish the task much more rapidly if I just threw the directions to the side and used my common sense to gather all the parts and assemble them in what I thought was the proper order. It seemed I never learned my lesson and year after year would eventually have to resort to the task of taking the toy completely apart; slowly reading the directions; asking my wife for assistance; and finally after a few small disagreements on how to complete the task; finish the task; and call it a night. As usual, this was more likely a late night task and as for the result, it was a difficult task to rise early in the morning with all the joy and excitement so evident in each child's face.

On this particular morning, there was more tension than usual between my wife, Joanne, and myself. It was a difficult time at work, and I was overwhelmed with what I felt needed to be done and done right now. It didn't matter whether it was the middle of February (usually a slower month) or Christmas Day. The office could not run without me (oh sure). And in this case, I was sure I had to be there; even though I alone would be showing up. Who else would work on Christmas Day? My reasoning was simple. There was an Emergency Animal Disease Situation in the Midwest. As the Director of Field Operations for our Emergency Programs Staff; I had to be there, no question about it!

My wife was angry and rightfully so. It was a blustery winter day and the snow was falling fast and furious. I can still remember the fury of the moment both in words and in the snowy, windy conditions outside. I left the house, jumped in my car, and as luck would have it, my car would not start. No way would it start!

My heart sank as I accepted my fate and meekly entered the house; explained the circumstances to my wife (who thought it served me right) and asked if I could have the keys to her car for my fateful journey to the office. Begrudgingly she handed them over and remarked that this was just another sign of how stupid my need to go to the office was. I nodded that she was probably right, but insisted that I had to go.

With that, I faced the cold winter weather and was on my way. It was not a pleasant scene. I was the only one on the road. Not even a snowplow had made it through. Nevertheless, I was as determined as ever and slowly maneuvered my way sliding as I traveled on the slick road from here to there. After all I had an important job. Yes, I needed to be there. Yes, the office needed me. My wife just didn't understand.

Oh, yes, the mind of a thirty year old male, who still thought he had it all together. (I remember asking my mother at age eighty-three, if she had it all together? After a couple moments she shook her head and said, "No way!" And then she added, "Bill, when you do, please let me know.") What a wonderful woman!

Well, as could be expected, I was within a couple miles of the office when all of a sudden my wife's car started acting up and as was my experience earlier that day, it just decided to up and die. This was too much! Even after several tries, there was no way I was going to get it started. In fact it must have been the battery in that soon the starter also decided to give up the ghost and remained silent. It was more than I could take; all of this aggravation in one day; and my day was just beginning. Was God trying to tell me something? Was the celebration of Christ's birthday more important than what I thought and knew had to be most important? Well, I guess so!

What made it even more difficult was that I did not have a phone and as a result, had the pleasure of walking in ankle deep snow the two miles to my office. But even that wasn't an easy task. For settling down in an office that didn't have the heat turned up was, oh, my, a special challenge. Yes, even though I was determined to work; I was chilled to the bone and am sure I had a few choice words to describe the events of this day and especially the chill of this blustery winter storm in full force just outside my office window.

At least, I thought I could still get a lot done; when all of a sudden the phone began to ring. Oh, good, I was needed. It was important that I was there. And then, oh, no! It was the building's security police. They wanted to know why in the world I was in the building on Christmas Day. Somehow the security system in place was able to locate the exact room I was in and I had better start explaining fast; who I was, what my password was, and of course I had to answer a series of other questions satisfactorily so they were sure I was who I said I was! Oh, dear, I hope the questions and answers I had given years earlier were simple. Hopefully I had the right answers. When I finished, whew, I passed. But adding insult to injury, he added, "This work had better be important. We are short on crew; I would never leave my family on Christ Day unless my boss ordered me to. Have a good day!"

Well, the next task was no fun. I knew what I had to do. I had to call my wife. All I could think of was that I had no way home and that I might have to spend the night in this forsaken building. As could be expected, my wife was still not happy, especially when I explained what had happened. Then the thought came to mind that we did have friends that lived just down the road from the office. Maybe, just maybe they would be willing to help. So, I gave them a call.

What a surprise! They couldn't believe they were getting a call from me, unless, of course it was to wish them a Merry Christmas, How nice . . . No, instead I was calling with the hope that John, oh what a good friend, would put on his winter coat, leave his family on Christmas morn, drive over with his battery cables in tow and drive me to my car. As you can imagine, John was not enthused and by no means wished to spend his day out in this weather. Nevertheless, after a lot of pleading, noting that I would owe him big time, he laughed and said, "Sure, I will be right over."

Then to add insult to injury, I realized that even with an Animal Health Emergency, everything was quiet not only in my office but also at the site of the emergency. No-one, not a single soul was called out. It was as it should have been; everyone with any sense was at home with their family. Finally, after all of this, we were able to get my car going. I was able to get home, John was able to make it back to his place, and I was able to partake of the delicious family meal so carefully prepared by my loving wife, Joanne.

A couple months later, our Agency's Deputy Administrator, Dr. John Atwell, asked if I would consider accepting the position of Assistant Director of International Programs for Veterinary Services. Oh, I couldn't believe it! How exciting! I would be working for Dr. Norvan Meyer. The opportunity to work with Dr. Meyer was an honor indeed. This was a program area I truly had a passion for, hoping I could be involved in for a long time.

Then the fun began. Within a couple weeks, I was asked to accompany Dr. Meyer to my first meeting of International Organizations in Panama City, Panama. I was thrilled! The subject matter was wide and varied. It was a pleasure to meet many of the movers and shakers in the field of Animal Health. There were country representatives as well as representatives from the Pan-American Health Organization, the Inter-American Institute for Co-operation on Agriculture, the United States Department of Agriculture, and the Regional International Animal Health Organization (OIRSA). It was clear that all of the participants were committed to jointly working in the improvement of Animal Health in the Americas.

Being my first meeting with these fine folks, I wanted to make a good impression.

They were remarkable individuals and seemed to have a good understanding of the political positions of each other as well as the wide variety of historical and cultural differences between each of their countries. Most of them were bi-lingual (Spanish and English). Fortunately the meeting was in English with only an occasional exchange in Spanish as might be needed.

At one point, the discussion became quite heated as there was a basic difference in how various members viewed the direction each of them should take in regard to an International Disease Control problem. Soon the discussion erupted with the representative from OIRSA, Dr. Pedro Acha, standing up and declaring it was time that he left the room. It was clear that they were at an impasse and that they all needed some time to reflect on the seriousness of this dilemma.

In this instance, I was sitting directly behind him, took his words seriously, and moved his chair to the side of the room in hopes of helping him make a quick exit. Oh, did I ever read him wrong! Apparently, all he was trying to do was to make a point on the seriousness of their discussion and that they needed to work on looking for alternative solutions. To further emphasize his point, he slapped his hand on the table and promptly sat down. Yes, he promptly sat down; sat down without a chair; and sat directly on the floor to the shock of everyone. And yes, especially me!

He did make his point and made it very clear! Everyone in the room knew him and loved him. They were, from my perspective, appalled that I would even think of doing such a thing. I may have been trying to be helpful, but obviously my actions were inappropriate. In fact, after that event, I had the reputation of being the one to watch out for in that you never knew when I might, Hmmm, pull the chair out from under you!

Well luckily Dr. Acha was not hurt, or at least that is what he claimed and we became good friends. Ever since that time, I have apologized numerous times. But I must say it brought us all closer together in that they all recognized it was not my intent to do harm. But, in my own way, I did create a scene that few would ever forget. In this instance, he won the support of everyone and was able to help find a solution that was both effective and timely.

Upon returning to the States, it became evident that International work required a lot of travel. For within a couple weeks I was asked to travel to the Philippines with a delegation of individuals from the Department. There were a total of seven individuals representing a wide variety of disciplines. The purpose of this trip was to identify areas in which our two countries could more effectively work together in agriculture.

Upon arriving we were escorted to our hotel and provided time to relax and rejuvenate before a week of intensive meetings were to begin. Then, early Monday morning we were taken to their Department of Agriculture headquarters and escorted to the Office of the Secretary of Agriculture. It was obvious that he was a very busy man and even though we were immediately admitted to his inner office, it was some time before he was free to talk with us directly. He was in the process of taking phone calls and it was evident that he had several he needed to complete before he could devote some time to welcoming us to his country.

Now, it is interesting to note that the telephone technology we were so fortunate to have available in the States was not available in the Philippines. Rather, it was very similar to the telephone systems I later observed in many countries of the world. In this case, there were several phone lines in his office and each one was connected to a separate phone. As such, there were several phone numbers one could dial to reach the Secretary's Office and yet the system of rotating calls that could be answered and forwarded was not in place.

In order to best utilize this system, the Secretary had three assistants, each with a separate phone to their car waiting for the

Secretary to take the call on their line. It was interesting to hear the variety of subject matters being discussed and as soon as he hung up, sure enough that phone would again start ringing. Then, as was their routine, the assistant having just handed his phone to the Secretary would answer the phone and hold it to his ear until the Secretary was available.

While most of the calls were concerning the importation of agricultural goods, or the national policy in regard to some aspect of the Secretary's work, it was at times surprising as to the detail some of the calls encompassed. This included obtaining information on construction materials to be used on some of their projects, building of roads, and most surprising to me the location of new rose bushes that were to be planted around their headquarters' building. Rose bushes, of all things!

To me this was micromanagement to the nth degree. While it might be considered as inefficient to have the Secretary making such decisions, in retrospect it obviously had its efficiencies. More specifically, there was no need for all the layers of government we seem to depend on. Either they could not afford such a luxury or ineffectiveness depending on your outlook.

Unfortunately, in our bureaucracy, multiple layers of government result in decisions being reversed and double reversed before a final decision is made. And then, as is often the case, the decisions will go up the chain of command to the one furthest from the impact of the action. As such, decisions are more likely to be technically wrong, based on political demands, resulting in big government screeching to a halt, and/or the addition of paperwork galore adding to the cost of doing business on a daily basis.

The week was filled with meetings. They were well organized and we learned a lot about agriculture and animal health from the perspective of the Philippine people and their government. They were already working with us in many aspects of interest to us both. Trade of goods and technology was off and running. Our visit was a continuation of the good relationships we already had in place. And numerous cooperative efforts and exchanges had already been established between their Veterinary School and the Veterinary Schools in the United States.

We visited several locations of significance to their life style and culture as well as of interest to our specific disciplines. And then in the evening hours we enjoyed the ambience and cuisine of their most popular restaurants and visited some of their out-door markets in search of country specific gifts and/or products that might be treasured on our return home.

On one occasion for which I shall never forget, we preceded dinner with a brief visit to a bar for some relaxation and some drinks. For some reason, the six men joining me on this trip wanted to have some fun, yes it was at my expense, for what reason I will never know, unless it was that I was new to the Department's so called upper ranks.

Nevertheless, it was clear to me that they had hired a lady to come on to me, walk over to me and sit on my lap, asking how I was and how I was enjoying my stay in the Philippines. Now I must admit she was a beautiful young lady. However, that did not change my feelings. I was not happy and not the least impressed.

I was happily married and in no way wanted to destroy a wonderful relationship I had in my home. In fact it upset me greatly and I am sure it showed on my face and in my being. Soon my colleagues were hardily laughing and to me it wasn't funny, no way! In fact I told her I was happily married and asked her to please leave me alone. Obviously she wasn't about to comply with my wishes in that my so called business companions/friends kept encouraging her on.

So, even though I had given up smoking, I asked one of my friends if I could have a cigarette. He obliged and lit it as I began to puff away. You see, at that point all kindness had left my body and I purposely blew all the smoke I could with every puff directly into her face. Soon it was obvious that she had enough of me. She made a few remarks saying I wasn't worth her time and effort and left! Finally, I had some peace and quiet. Well, that just brought the house down as my friends enjoyed every minute of this scenario as it unfolded. I quickly doused my cigarette and smiled saying thanks a lot. Of course every time I saw them in the future whether it was in a meeting or in the hallway, they would always smile and say, "Remember the Philippines?" And of course, I would always respond with a smile, "Yes, of course, how could I ever forget?" Now, you may be asking; did I ever tell my wife? Of course not! Who could?

Then there was a side issue that was brought to my attention by some of the people I was visiting with. While I have not personally observed this, it still angered me to consider that it might be a fact of life. At this time, there was still observable poverty and apparently some Philippine families lacked the resources to even put food on the table. In such instances, it was noted that there have been commercial fishing boat captains that have approached these families and offered to pay the family to allow them to take one of their sons as a member of their crew.

They would note that the boys would be well taken care of with clothing and three good meals a day as well as receiving monthly wages. What they failed to tell them is that the boys are like indentured servants having to pay for their food, shelter and clothing out of their monthly wages. Unfortunately their wages were always insufficient and they were always indebted to the Captain for the rest of their lives.

Furthermore, the young lads were required to swim at great depths corralling fish in the direction of the boat's fish nets. Unfortunately they were forced to swim to such depths that their ear drums would burst and they were deaf for the rest of their lives. We have all heard of human trafficking, but this is the first time I have ever heard of it in this form of abuse. Since then I have heard that this is apparently still occurring in not only the Philippines, but also in other parts of the world even with the apparent implementation of strict laws (that are difficult to enforce) to prohibit this practice.

Finally the week was coming to an end and it was time to pre sent our joint findings to their Secretary of Agriculture. We were all pleased with the accomplishments of our joint efforts and were sure the Secretary would be pleased. What I expected, however, was not to be.

The Philippine Secretary of Agriculture was not at all pleased with our findings, nor was he pleased with the cooperative efforts being planned. It was unfortunate in that we had tried to balance the program activities so that both the United States and the Philippines would achieve accomplishments that would be mutually beneficial. Unfortunately the Philippine Secretary of Agriculture did not see it that way and so vocalized his extreme disappointment.

You could hear a pin drop. Not one of his employees nor one of the United States Department of Agriculture employees said a word nor was about to.

I couldn't believe it. It angered me and as he was about to leave, I raised my voice and asked the Secretary if I could speak in that I respectfully differed and would like to have the opportunity to point out the distinct advantages to both of our governments accepting the cooperative efforts outlined during the week. Even though I could only speak to the Animal Health areas of the agreement, I was sure others in our group could speak to the plant, marketing and technical exchanges that would benefit us both. Fortunately he let me continue.

First of all, I felt we needed to work cooperatively in studying the health of wild Psittacine Birds, Parrots, native to their land. One of their islands had a rich abundance of parrots and would be ideal for such an in-depth study. Yes, it was their Federal Penitentiary/Prison, but the entire island was government owned and as a result the study could be conducted in the wild without any issues due to private ownership. The benefit of such studies would help us both have a better understanding of Newcastle Disease and especially Velogenic Viscerotropic Newcastle Disease of such importance to international trade. (Note: If you didn't know it, we in the medical field love to use our own vocabulary to make the public think we know something they don't.) (Velogenic basically means easily spread or strong.) (Viscerotropic means afflicting the internal organs of the body and especially the intestines.) This would indeed be of benefit to us both.

Secondly, there was the trade of Scientific Laboratory Personnel between our two countries. This would advance the exchange of technical information and would greatly improve the technical advancement of each of our National Laboratories.

Thirdly the importance of trade between our two countries could be advanced by the exchange in personnel relative to the quarantine procedures utilized by each country. This would foster greater understanding of our respective Animal Health concerns and as a result hopefully facilitate trade between our two great nations.

Well, luckily this broke the ice, and soon there was a dialog as both sides agreed to the importance of these cooperative efforts and the need to implement them in order to achieve numerous benefits for both sides. The Secretary listened intently, asked a few questions, and to our surprise, agreed to support our initiative and thanked us for the time we had devoted to putting this together.

While this was my first trip on my own without the presence and support of my boss, Dr. Norvan Meyer, it did build my confidence and gave me another appreciation of the world we live in. An important lesson noted at this point was that even though we may differ in many aspects as independent nations, we still have much in common. While we all face numerous difficulties, if we look closely, we will observe and cherish the commonalities in our desires and ambitions. These are the building blocks for our future. As such we can recognize this simple truth; there is always much we can do, even if and when we don't agree!

"ALONE WE CAN MAKE A DIFFERENCE."

"TOGETHER, WE CAN FIND THE GREATER GOOD."

"AND WITH THE GREATER GOOD WE CAN ACHIEVE THE IMPOSSIBLE!"

Another lesson well learned!

CHAPTER 8

Korea's Demilitarized Zone

At times, what we believe to be the truth can be viewed quite differently. Then, when documentation is collected near Korea's Demilitarized Zone, fear can become paramount.

Sometimes when you least expect it, your plans are put on hold and something new and exciting comes your way. This time I was asked to check on a problem involving the export of American cattle to Korea. The Koreans had just received our first shipment of Holstein cattle and were not happy. It was the beginning of a negotiated exportation of eight thousand head of cattle. So, Dr. John Acree, an export staff member and I were soon on our way to Korea. We wanted to be able to examine the cattle that were shipped and also wished to take blood samples so we could retest each animal for the specific diseases required by their government. In addition, we hoped to test each sample for genetic markers in order to identify if in fact they were the same animals as previously tested in the United States. Fortunately we still had blood samples from our previous collection in our laboratory in Ames, Iowa.

In preparation for the trip, we were advised that there was a rumor that the individual exporting the cattle had shot a couple individuals in the past. Whether this was intentional or accidental, they did not know, but wanted us to be careful. That was all I needed; a little suspense to add to the thrill and excitement already in place.

Upon arriving in Seoul, Korea, Dr. Acree and I got a good night's sleep, arrived early the next morning at the Embassy, and met with the Ambassador, as is the custom when on official government business. The Agricultural Attaché welcomed us and called the Ambassador's Office to advise that we had arrived. In this instance, the Ambassador was pleased with our prompt attention to this matter and emphasized how essential it was that we maintain good relations with our colleagues in Korea.

Then, after a quick lunch, we arrived at the Office of the Chief Veterinary Official. His aides and staff specialists, including an interpreter, were introduced to us and we were offered seats around a simple and yet elegant coffee table. Our discussions focused on the purpose of our visit and their concerns. The conversation was in the Korean language and the interpreter was helpful in assuring we understood everything that was being said.

Of special interest to me was the concept of "Saving Face". Everything was worded very carefully. In fact, their sentences were spoken in terms of possibilities. For example, their concerns were expressed as follows: "In regard to the cattle from the United States, we were fortunate in that the cattle arrived on schedule and were promptly off-loaded from the ship as arranged. We were looking forward to receiving cattle from your country, recognizing the outstanding characteristics and genetics your cattle are known for. I am sure you understand, as a member of the Veterinary Profession, that shipping cattle from the United States to Korea is hard on any animal. The stress of such trips can interfere with their health in many ways. In this instance we welcome your visit in that the cattle just don't seem to be responding the way they should. Hopefully, together we can figure out what is causing such difficulty. Again, thank you for arriving so promptly."

Now, wasn't that a wonderful way of putting it? Frankly after seeing the cattle, I would have probably been blunt and said it the way I saw it. The cattle were emaciated; breathing heavily; obviously in the poorest of condition. I would have questioned their health papers. Even their

Registry as Purebred Holsteins should have been questioned. These animals should have been shipped directly to slaughter, and then only for dog food. They were, in no way, worthy of export to another country.

Why did this upset me so? Well, it brought back memories of a shipment of dairy cattle I was responsible for processing for export several years previously. Most of the time, the health certificates and the Purebred Registry Certificates were in order. What especially annoyed me in that previous export was the fact that the exporter was in my mind falsifying Purebred Registry Certificates right in front of my eyes. You see the man exporting the cattle at that time was reading the individual ear tags on each animal as it went through the cattle chute. Subsequently, the exporter's personal secretary would enter that number in her computer and print out a so called Purebred Registry Certificate with the animal's description and ear tag number as the identifying marks. This certificate was then signed, as incredulous as it may seem, by the exporter's secretary as the Secretary of the Purebred Registry.

This upset me to no end. When I brought it to the attention of my boss, he indicated that I was only responsible for assuring that the animals at the time of export were still healthy as presented at that time. I had no jurisdiction for the documents relative to their Purebred Status. I couldn't believe it! Furthermore, it was upsetting when I read the Registry documents in more depth. In bold print the document listed the identification of the Dam (Cow) and Sire (Bull) giving the feeling that they were the actual parents of this animal. In addition, the certificate listed the average milk production of each of their offspring from this parentage and to me this was out and out lies. But then in very small print, just below the "Secretary's" signature it said, "This is being signed with the understanding that the animal listed is thought to be equal to or greater than that as presented." In other words it was a bunch of "Bull" of no value not even that of the paper it was written on.

I couldn't believe such fraud and abuse would occur and especially in a field of endeavor I so trusted and cherished. To my dismay, there was only one other time, while processing cattle exports, that I discovered misinformation being presented that in that instance was a cover up of genetic anomalies known to be present. How could we allow this to happen? In my opinion, our health certifications should include genetic abnormalities especially if the animals are to be used for breeding purposes. As we are all aware, genetic abnormalities can and do have an effect on the future breeding capability/capacity of the animals being exported.

To me, the greater the confidence of other countries have in the openness of our Animal Health Programs and the health issues we are facing in any location and/ or animal industry is important. We need to assure that the importing countries are receiving the best information available. Honesty increases the confidence another country has in what we have to offer and thereby assures that they will prefer and choose the livestock we have to offer over any others even if the cost of such livestock is higher than any others available. Quality management and quality animals (health and genetics) do make a difference and a marked difference in their marketability worldwide. Again, fortunately, in general, we can be proud of our livestock industries and should commend them for the quality and honest representation they adhere to.

Well, now, let's get back on track and back to my story concerning the cattle shipped to Korea. Soon it was clear there was a serious problem with these cattle that needed to be addressed. We needed their permission to observe the health of these animals and to have the opportunity to collect blood samples from each and every one of them. We also needed the availability of a cattle chute to confine the animals for our blood testing procedures and a crew of men to assist us as needed.

Again, in order to "Save Face", the discussion went on for some time. Of course, we must remember it took time for the interpreter to translate each and every sentence whether it originated in Korean or in English. Finally, it became clear that if we arrived at their Quarantine Station at a certain time on the following morning, there was a good possibility that the equipment and crew necessary for this endeavor would be available. The Director was sure to be there and most likely lunch would be available around noon. With that it was understood that we had reached an agreement and the meeting was over.

Then, the Chief Veterinary Officer (CVO) stood up, shook my hand, and said in perfect English, "Thank you for coming, Dr. Buisch! Would you like to have some tea?" Here, during this entire time, he and his colleagues knew the English language perfectly well and yet as it should be, the conversation in the formal meeting was in the Korean language and through an interpreter. The CVO and his staff were hospitable and after a warm reception and tea, we were on our way back to the hotel. Before dropping us off, the Agriculture Attaché apologized that he would not be available to accompany us to the Quarantine Station. He did note, however, that he would have a driver available to escort us to and from the facility. He felt good about our meeting and knew we would do fine on our own.

The next morning, after a good night's sleep, we were on our way. In route, we noted that the Quarantine Station was close to North Korea and the Demilitarized Zone dividing the two countries. At one point it was interesting to note that we were on a long wide road with a stop light at each end in the middle of nowhere. In addition we were surprised to note a line of blue lights along each side of this stretch of road. Since this appeared a bit unusual, we inquired as to the purpose of all these lights and why they were so placed? The Embassy driver just smiled and indicated that this section of the road was set up to be used as a landing strip for military aircraft. Actually, it was rarely used and then it was only used as a landing strip when an emergency situation might arise. Apparently the stop lights bring all traffic to a halt and allow the military planes to land. Amazing! Talk about efficiency, and dual use of facilities and in this case, roads. It is the only time I have observed such a road set up to be used by trucks, cars, and then of all things, military airplanes.

Well, the Director of the Quarantine Station greeted us warmly and after a short break for tea showed us around their facility. It was a large facility and housed several animal importations currently being processed for entry. As I have already explained, it was very disheartening to see the animals imported from the United States. They were in pitiful condition and were truly from my perspective totally unacceptable.

Soon, the animal handlers were ready to begin. They were well organized and able to quickly expedite the examination and sample collection process. Without the first inkling or understanding of English, it was amazing how quickly they picked up on our use of the English phrase, "O K". Before long, when we said "O K", the crew member assisting us at the chute would shout with a Korean accent, "O K". He would then release the animal, and I would hear throughout the stockyard one after another, to the far reaches of the facility, "O K". This was repeated for each animal as it was progressively moved forward and into the chute for examination.

Soon it was time for lunch and it was great to be able to share a meal with these fine folks. The crew was made up of young men and they were filled with enthusiasm and excitement in being able to help us in this regard. After completing a most enjoyable meal, one of the crew members approached me and with a big smile took a hold of my hand giving an indication that he would like to arm wrestle.

That, of course, sounded like it would be great fun. Obviously he was stronger than I and yet it was a challenge I could not turn down. I may have been fifteen years older, but what a thrill to arm wrestle at this time and place. What made it even more fun was the fact that my challenger respected my age and wanted to arm wrestle but also wanted to "Save Face", that is my reputation. He was much stronger as he slowly pushed my wrist down towards the table and then when my hand was within a couple inches of the table's surface, he would start to shake his arm as if it had lost all strength. After repeating this scenario four or five times, he pulled his arm away as if we were tied. Of course there was no tie. He was the victor. I shook his hand and made it clear as I raised his arm that he was the victor and everyone roared in approval.

After lunch we were back to work. That is, until we heard the most frightening sounds! "Ka—Boom"! "Ka-Boom"! "Ka-Boom"! Then, after a few seconds, another "Ka-Boom"! Now, I don't know what it would have sounded like to you. But to me, knowing the Quarantine Station was located close to the North Korean Border or as is the case, the Demilitarized Zone between North and South Korea, the sound I heard was not a welcome sound in any form or fashion! The sounds were un-nerving and to me sounded like we were in a war zone. I must have had a startled look as I shouted out to Dr. Acree, "Does that sound to you like it sounds to me?" I can still see that determined look on Dr. Acree's face as he shouted back, "Sure does, let's get this task done and get out of here!" There were no arguments from my standpoint and since we only had a couple more head to test, we were soon on the road back to our hotel.

That evening we received a call from our staff in Washington. We were advised that they had just finished talking with the exporter, advising him of the concerns the Koreans had. They noted that we were in Korea on site and were looking into the problem as raised by the Koreans. (Oh, joy now he knew we were in Korea and that was just dandy!)

Apparently the exporter blamed the condition of the cattle on the lack of proper feed upon their arrival. Dr. Acree and I could not agree. One, the feed they were receiving was the same for all of their cattle importations and secondly the feed we observed appeared to be of good quality. In addition, there was plenty of water and as such it appeared that the cattle were being fed and cared for quite well. Furthermore, another group of Holstein Dairy Cows of similar age had just arrived at the same time and this time they originated from

Canada. What a difference between the two groups of animals! Obviously the Canadian animals were of quality parentage and had been fed and cared for, since birth, in an outstanding manner. How could animals of the same age and supposedly same genetic quality look so different on arrival?

The next morning we visited the Agricultural Attaché as well as the Ambassador and soon we were on our flight to Los Angeles. Then, as a result of the rumors we had heard concerning the exporter's possible fascination with guns, our interest in safety remained high on our list. As a result, we decided that we would exit the plane separately. Dr. Acree would exit first heading for his plane taking him to Stormont Laboratories in Woodland, California (for genetic testing) and then, I would head for my plane a little bit later heading for Des Moines, Iowa. Once I arrived in Des Moines, it was only about an hour's drive north and I was in Ames, at the National Veterinary Services Laboratories (for the disease testing).

Upon arriving safely at home in Washington, D.C., we received the results of the Stormont Genetic Tests and learned that the blood tested prior to export was not from the same animals as those tested in Korea. This was interesting in that, in both cases, the cattle identified on the test forms were listed as being from the same animals with the same identical ear tag numbers. Unfortunately we found, instead, that the blood tested prior to export, although labeled as if it came from each individual animal, was actually from only a few of the animals. In other words someone had pooled the blood from disease test negative animals and split it into several individual test tubes as if it had been collected separately from each of the identified animals.

Also the tubes of blood that were collected in Korea and then tested in Ames, showed that several of the animals were positive to diseases that would have made them ineligible for export to Korea. This along with the clinical picture of emaciated cattle with labored breathing further gave evidence of fraud in the testing and preparation of the Health Certificates as well as the health of the animals exported. In our minds the Korean authorities were well justified in their concerns.

Within a couple months, we were in the courtroom with our staff of lawyers hoping to prove our case and to make the exporter liable for his actions. In my opinion we had a solid case. Our lawyers agreed and brought numerous documents to the courtroom to prove our case. In fact our lawyers had numerous boxes filled with files as evidence on their table and I was sure there was no way that we could lose. I wore my best pin striped black suit as did everyone else representing the Federal Government and we were ready!!!

My confidence was even more assured when I saw the defendant and his lawyer arrive. In this case, the exporter came dressed in blue denim coveralls and his attorney came in casual khaki pants and a long sleeved yellow shirt and no tie. The only thing in the defendant attorney's hand was an obviously blank yellow note pad. It appeared the defendant's lawyer was ill prepared, if prepared at all.

Soon the judge, in his black robe, was in his chair and the jury was allowed to enter the room. This, I must say, was not what I was prepared for. I mentioned that the defendant arrived in blue denim coveralls. But I was in no way prepared for what I was about to see as the jury entered. You see, every man in the jury was wearing blue denim coveralls as was the custom in this part of the world. I couldn't believe it! Even after our most convincing arguments on behalf of the Federal Government, it was clear that the defense lawyer took the approach that this poor man, the defendant, was only trying to do his job and he was shocked that the Feds would try to ruin his reputation when he had gone to so much trouble to do what was right. Their argument included the fact that the defendant had hired a veterinarian and paid good money to assure all the health requirements were met. He was indeed sorry that everything didn't go well, but he tried to do everything right.

Soon it was clear that we, in our pin stripped suits, were going to lose. Even though we had evidence that the exporter had taken the blood collected by the veterinarian to the Post Office to be sent to the laboratory, and had ample opportunity to switch the blood samples, we were not able to prove that he had done so and so from the defendants perspective we were going after a good man and basically we should be ashamed of ourselves! So it was no surprise when we learned that the verdict was not guilty. What was unfortunate about this whole case is that as a result of this tragic export, our reputation as a nation and as a governing body to assure that the animals exported met and exceeded the health requirements of the importing country, was destroyed and the remaining close to 8,000 animals negotiated for export was cancelled. It was years before any trust by the Korean Government could be reestablished.

Now, the veterinarian in this case had some serious problems as a direct result of this tragedy. His trust in the exporter directly delivering the blood samples he had collected on the farm to the Post Office, thus saving him an hour or two, resulted in an apparent fraudulent switch of blood samples along the way. Or if that is not the case and the Veterinarian was actually the one who pooled the blood as an accomplice to the fact, he was caught red handed. Either way, he could no longer do any federal work as a veterinarian, a difficult lesson to be learned.

CHAPTER 9

"Voodoo" Piggy Bank

The observed hunger and devastation to the masses will haunt me for years to come. Then to witness the populace striving for a better life was at times more than I could bear.

On January 12, 2010, Haiti, a small country in the Caribbean, was the recipient of a catastrophic 7.0 magnitude earthquake. Millions were homeless; thousands died. This was not the first traumatic event for them. After a period of hope and the building of their very first homes (previously cardboard and tree limbs provided the only protection they could aspire to); this blow was a reminder of the numerous times their hopes and dreams had been demolished in the past. From 1956 to 1986, their aspirations were destroyed over and over again by the tyrannical leadership of the Duvalier's. First there was Francois Duvalier, known as Papa Doc and then after his death, the presidency of Haiti was under the direction of his son, Jean-Claude Duvalier, known as Baby Doc. They knew little about governance and could care less. Their only aspiration, apparently, was to kill any who opposed them and to steal from the rest as much as possible.

It was under the "Baby Doc" Presidency that I was asked to determine if the Haitian people were ready for a joint United States, Canadian, Mexican, and Haitian Program, established to eradicate a serious disease of swine called, African Swine Fever. This was the first introduction of this disease in the Western Hemisphere and we wanted to get rid of this disease as soon as possible. There were no treatments known to control this terrible disease. It was urgent that this disease be eradicated before it spread to Central America, Panama, and/or North America. University of Minnesota Economists estimated the cost to the American people could be as much as five billion dollars; should the disease become established.

Well, I arrived in Port-au-Prince, the Capital of Haiti, early in the evening. The next morning I was taken to the Office of the Inter-American Institute for Cooperation on Agriculture (IICA), the organization responsible for coordinating this particular multi-national program activity. I was briefed on the current status of their program and the tremendous effort that had been made to inform the Haitians of the program goals and objectives. Their only concern was whether the population, as a whole, understood and accepted the fact that all of their swine would be killed (since there was no known cure for this disease) and that it might be a year or more before new pigs would be introduced and distributed.

Now, there is one point that should be emphasized. And that is the fact that if a family in rural Haiti owned pigs, they generally owned just one. Even if they had a pig, it was usually stunted in growth and very thin. Obviously it did not have the feed to reach its full growth potential. Nevertheless, their pig would somehow survive and then only by eating scraps and anything they could find in the wild. Frequently, the family pig was tended to by a young child, probably as malnourished as the pig. These pigs were the only savings account a family had. As such, they were often referred to as the family's piggy bank. They would only be sacrificed during special events such as weddings, funerals, etc. In essence, if a family owned a pig, they were considered to be well off. Oh, my, what a difference between their culture and ours.

After being assigned the Port-de-Paix area, I was introduced to my driver/language translator and was free to return to my hotel before starting the arduous day long trip early the next morning.

At the hotel I was surprised to see Dr. Ron Yoxheimer, a colleague of mine from

Pennsylvania. He was overjoyed to see me and yet, somehow, he didn't seem to be at all himself. In fact, in this instance, he was chuckling with occasional, hysterical, outbursts of laughter. He noted that it would only take a few days and he could guarantee that I, too, would never be the same. Then with a few more hysterical laughs he exclaimed that this is another world, a world where the unexpected is the routine and the value of life is rarely appreciated. The conditions under which the Haitian people had to live would, in his opinion, drive me close to the verge of needing the Psych Ward, if not completely make me crazy for life. This was not the Dr. Yoxheimer I knew.

He then shared what had just occurred in a section of the Capital City of Port Au Prince frequently identified as the "Iron Market". This section of the city was considered to be the poorest part of town where people lived in cardboard shacks and odd pieces of wood. There was an open market and thus the name "Iron Market". Apparently, earlier that day, Dr. Yoxheimer observed a man forcibly handcuffed by one of Baby Doc's Tonton Macoute Militias. The man was apprehended for stealing from one of the vendors. Not only that, but he was then beaten with a club and forced to walk up the road to the Police Station. Upon arrival, he was further beaten and then, without warning, shot to death for the crime he had committed.

Dr. Yoxheimer broke into tears as he described what had happened and clearly it was time for him to return home. He was on the verge of a nervous breakdown and was already severely damaged by what he had seen and heard. This is what I would call "Instant Justice" and this story alone caused me great fear and worry.

The next morning, my driver arrived in his Jeep and we were on our way. The first thing I noticed was the evidence of wall to wall people. Furthermore, drivers always laid their hands on the horn without slowing down and drove through the streets as if no one was there. It amazed me how people were able to get out of their way. This lack of value for life bothered me and I continually insisted that we slow down.

At one point, I noticed a man lying along the side of the road. It was clear, he was in great pain. It appeared his forearm must have been broken. As we were approaching, his friends stuffed a cloth into his mouth; quickly grabbed the man's arm; and pulled with a jerking motion to realign the arm as the man screamed in pain. They straightened his arm as much as possible and a splint was applied. The scene gave me heartburn as I realized the living conditions and severe limitations they were faced with on a daily basis. No doctors, no sanitation, no shelter, etc. This was a pitiful form of life!

Soon, we approached a Militia Guard Post at the end of any resemblance of a road. When it appeared that my driver wasn't slowing down; I asked him why. He indicated the Militia was there to check papers and to control movements into various parts of the country. With that, he noted we didn't need to stop. I became very nervous considering the story Dr. Yoxheimer had shared the night before. I wanted no part of that "Instant Justice"! So, with a few expletives and screams with vulgar words I thought I had forgotten, I tried to relay my concern! Fortunately the driver knew exactly what I wanted and immediately applied the brakes.

The Officer checked my papers and before long, we were on our way. From this point on our directions were simple: follow the valley north; approaching the first hill divert to the right; on the next hill, go straight over the hill, etc. On one of the hills, it seemed to be very steep and the crossing of several boulders put me on edge, especially when I had to hang on tight and lean forward or to the extreme left or right. It was a ride that beat all amusement rides for sure.

Now, as in most adventures, there was one experience during this voyage that was unplanned and totally unexpected. As is often the case, such experiences usually occur at the most inconvenient times. In this case, I needed a rest room and right now! Unfortunately in rural Haiti, such conveniences do not exist and in most cases a bush or tree are about the only structures available to insure some privacy. In this case I was pleased to find a group of bushes in the middle of a small field that I thought would provide the privacy I needed. Also, as unusual as it might seem, especially in Haiti, I did not see a single soul anywhere in sight. So I asked the driver to stop; I took a roll of toilet paper out of my sack; and rushed over to the cover provided by these tall bushes. No sooner had I dropped my pants and started to move that which needed to be emptied from my intestines, when, "Whoa", what happened? Had the theater just let out? Or had the church service just ended? I couldn't believe what was happening. For before I could finish what I was doing, hundreds, if not thousands of Haitians came out of the woods, the forest, and gathered to observe what I was doing. I was embarrassed and all I could do was finish what I was doing, clean myself up with the toilet paper I had with me, pull my pants up and with an attempt at a smile, meekly walk between the crowd and hop back into the jeep. The only explanation I could think of was that this was probably the first time they had ever seen a white man and of course, a white man that was at that instance doing what I was doing. The driver noticed my embarrassment and noted that I shouldn't let it bother me and that it is the same for all of us. When we have to go, we have to go!

The next day we were in the Port-au-Paix area and talked with numerous gatherings of Haitians. In all cases, the people seemed to be supportive. The only factor that bothered me was the question of how reliable could the observed support actually be? My only read had to be favorable and yet if I was one of them and lived in such a tyrannical system of government would I dare say anything other than support for whatever the government wanted?

After finishing our discussions for the day, I was asked if I could stay a while longer to socialize. I assured them that it would be an honor and so they gave me a rustic chair to sit on and began talking with me about life in the United States. In the meantime a couple of individuals ran off and returned, smiling from ear to ear, as they presented me with a small patterned blue plate (probably the only plate on site) with three pieces of meat, the size of the last knuckle of my little finger and as tough as shoe leather. In addition there were four thin slices of potato and five slices of banana. This was accompanied by a matching small demitasse patterned blue cup of coffee. As I took my first bites from this plate and sipped coffee from the cup, my mind was filled with the thought that this was definitely the worst, the very worst meal I had ever had. The food looked dirty, it looked disgusting and it tasted worse than I could ever imagine.

Then, fortunately, my brain and emotions kicked into gear and I abruptly came to my senses. You see, it was then that I realized that no-one, yes no-one had anything to eat and in fact I was being given the very best that they had. In this part of the world if they got a handful of rice a day, they were probably well fed. Soon I couldn't control my emotions and the tears started flowing. As I looked around, the community at large had a look of concern and possible confusion as to why I was crying when, in fact, they were trying to show some hospitality, hoping to bring joy and make me feel welcome.

Even my driver had a look of concern. After a brief pause, he looked directly into my eyes, and gently grasped my hand while asking if anything was wrong? All I could say was that my tears were tears of joy. I was so deeply moved by their thoughtfulness and hospitality. It was an honor to be in their presence and to share this special time with each and every one of them. And then to top it off with the food and coffee made me feel so welcomed. I wanted them to know that **I would cherish this moment for**

years to come! They immediately broke out in cheers and you could tell this moment meant a great deal.

Even though by our standards they had nothing, they still showed a form of neighborliness that in today's world is rarely seen. As you might imagine, what they did for me on this occasion was definitely special; filling me with the emotions of humbleness and yet great worth in that for me, this was the richest and most meaningful gift I had ever received!

That night I can assure you I did not sleep a wink. All night long, all I could think of was the beauty of that event; the kindness and hospitality of that village's citizenry as well as the love and care shown to me who for all practical purposes was a stranger and foreigner to their soil. As such, I questioned my life, my value system and my love for the strangers and foreigners in my life? No-one in America has any idea the pain and suffering so many in this world are faced with and yet in this case, they were willing to give of what little they had to a complete stranger and for that it brought them unbelievably great joy! I cried through most of the night and to this day thank God for that experience and to recognize that even in the worst of hardships, Joy can still be found!

The next evening after our last community visit, the driver and I headed back to our vehicle. It was beginning to get dark and the driver wanted me to be careful in that there was a ditch just ahead. I responded, "No Problem" when I suddenly fell head over heels into the ditch and cut my right leg open on a protruding rock. The driver rushed to my aid and indicated that I had just fallen in a ditch that was used by the community for their disposal of human waste, their sewer system so to speak. Since we were right next to the ocean, I quickly immersed my legs in the salt water and pressed the wound to encourage as much bleeding as possible.

The following day, we headed straight for the Capital City of Port-au-Prince. This time the hotel I had previously stayed in, "The Caribe", was booked full and I had to stay at another hotel nearby. The next morning, I was advised that a man was murdered a couple days previously in the very hotel I was staying in. What was even more unnerving was the room number within which the murder occurred. Unfortunately it was the room right next to the one I had just had a restful night's sleep. What can I say? So much for having the feeling of being safe and secure! I always knew life was fragile. But with the experiences of the previous few days, I had a whole new understanding of just how fragile life is and/or can be!

As a result of the National Survey, and the finding that the Media Campaign was successful, the Eradication Campaign began. The populace was most accommodating; bringing their swine to central points to be purchased and killed on the spot. The families received the payment allotted for their hogs and then were allowed to take the meat back to their homes for their consumption.

Soon it appeared that the last of the pigs had been bought and slaughtered. However, how could we know we had found every live pig existing in the country? Well, fortunately, we had worked for years with an organization at the University of Georgia called the Southeastern Cooperative Wildlife Diseases Study (SCWDS). They were known for their expertise in wildlife diseases and the capture of wildlife including pigs. As such, we asked their Director, Dr. Victor Nettles, and his wildlife team to assist us in this program activity. Within a few months they had found every live domesticated and/or wild pig in Haiti and were completing a three month period of intensive surveillance without finding another pig anywhere. The importance of finding every pig had to be our primary concern. Once we started repopulating the country with swine, if one pig remained undetected and it was infected, all of our efforts would be in vain and African Swine

Fever would still rein terror especially in those hogs being brought in as part of the swine repopulation effort.

So to make my life more complicated, the Program Directors asked that the United States help them determine when the Eradication Program was complete. Well this was a difficult decision to make. When do you know that the eradication effort is done and you as a multinational organization have done enough? Someone can always question whatever decision is made and especially if the decision is wrong. Of course, a lot of political pressure was made to bear. Many thought it was important to keep searching for pigs for a much longer period of time.

After discussing this with Dr. Nettles, we were in agreement that since this disease can be spread by Soft Ticks of the Ornithodoros species, we should try to collect these Ticks from as many areas as possible before we consider any program changes. In order to maximize the possibility of finding any ticks that might carry this disease, we concentrated our efforts in those areas known to have had infected hogs. After collecting the ticks, we sent them to our Laboratory on Plum Island, New York and asked them to test them for the presence of this viral agent. After extensive testing, they were not able to recover any African Swine Fever virus from any of the Ticks collected. We were frankly surprised! Then, considering the extensive search for live pigs already completed, we decided to recommend that the program discontinue looking for pigs and start the one year period in which the country would have no pigs before starting the repopulation effort.

The phones started ringing off the hook. There were several constituents who strongly differed with our assessment and pleaded that we rethink our findings. Nevertheless we held firm and I must say that even though I was confident in our conclusions, for several months I worried and knew my career would be over if another pig was found and especially if it was found to be infected with the African Swine Fever virus. Fortunately that did not occur. In August of 1984, Haiti was declared free of this devastating disease. Then, and only then, the repopulation with newly imported pigs was allowed to begin.

In preparation for this repopulation effort it was decided that the United States would try to help Haiti develop a basic animal health infrastructure. Without one, diseases could run rampart and several months or possibly years could pass before anyone would know that there was a problem. So often in the past, any assistance provided to Haiti was of no value in that once the program objectives had been reached, any and all future funding was discontinued. In the case of animal health and disease, we felt that we should do more! From our experience we knew that every country was different and that education was the key to success.

Also, we found that in too many cases, individuals with good intentions will go into a country and try to convince those they are working with to do the project their way and only their way. What we found, instead, was that you achieve greater success if you let the receiving country determine what is needed and try to help them achieve the next step in reaching their goals and objectives. And so, we asked the Haitians to come to the United States to pick out the pigs they would like to receive. We also built a Training Center in Port-au-Prince to train a cadre of individuals in animal health matters and assigned a Veterinarian to work with them. Further, we encouraged them to actively request any information that might be useful in improving the animal health and sanitation in their area of responsibility. This kind of dialogue created a passion for the work they were doing and proved to be most beneficial.

One concern, however, was that there were not enough black pigs in each shipment of pigs received. Apparently this is important to their social networks and the practices of their Voodoo Practitioners. Clearly, Voodoo was practiced widely and one could often hear their chanting and the sound of their drums late into the evening. On one occasion, an American Pork Producer and I were out in the countryside when we came upon a group of Haitians chanting under the leadership of one of their Voodoo Practitioners. The drummers were beating their drums; the participants were circling within the ring of fire; many were spellbound as if in a trance or passing out with their bodies going limp as the chanting and beating of their drums continued. Soon, the Pork Producer took a tight hold of my arm and exclaimed, "Bill, let's get out of here! This just doesn't seem like a safe place to be!" With that we hustled back to our Hotel! I always think of this with a smile on my face in that our Hotel was a small group of huts and within that grouping there was supposedly, so I was told, a Voodoo Practitioner. And yes, his sole purpose was to assure a safe, secure environment for all who chose to stay there.

Before long, the pigs for the repopulation effort were arriving and given to distribution centers throughout Haiti. While most of these centers were owned by a company called HAMCO, the requirements for distribution of these pigs was very clear in that fifty per cent of the offspring were to be distributed to the small peasant farmers in the region. From our observation, this seemed to be working quite well.

Soon the Training Center was in the process of being built and the building process, itself, was something to behold. The building was designed as one might typically expect. There were class rooms, a laboratory section for the completion of diagnostic tests and in another part of the building, a large examination room to be used for the restraint and examination of livestock (cows, pigs, etc.). At one point, we suggested that they might consider putting up a fence to contain any animals that might get loose as well as a gravel road to facilitate access into the facility. They accepted all of these suggestions and soon the facility was operational. While some may criticize the efforts we made in this regard (it is always easy to criticize), we feel that progress was made. It was important to be a positive influence and to encourage education and the continuum of personal improvement. We wanted to motivate and empower those with whom we were working to achieve a better life for themselves and those they cared about.

It always amazes me the will power and strength of character of those who live on such a meager existence. To give you an idea of what I mean, I would like to share with you my impressions of how the contracts, for the building of the fence and the road, were completed. As with most contracts, the contract for the chain linked fence was written with specific dimensions and patterns for completion. Nevertheless, I was totally caught by surprise when a truck with supplies and a crew of men arrived to install the fence as agreed upon. All they had on the truck bed were several rolls of wire, a shovel, and numerous wood posts cut to order. After the post holes were dug and the wood posts properly aligned and fully anchored, I was not ready for what occurred next. Contrary to my experience, the crew carefully and methodically constructed the chain-linked aspects of the fence weaving the long strands of wire by hand, wire over wire, until it met the specifications as outlined. The fencing did not arrive in a pre-manufactured state. Instead, the fencing was woven meticulously by hand on site. And as unbelievable as it may seem, the finished product looked just like the chain-linked fences available at Lowes or Home Depot, a sight to behold!

As for the completion of the gravel road, a truck arrived a few days later with several large boulders. This was followed by a crew arriving with chisels and hammers. Before I knew what was going on, this crew was chiseling these boulders down to the size of gravel as specified in that contract. I would never have dreamed that the contract specifications of our gravel road would be made to order and in such a manner. Obviously it gave employment to a lot of people and we soon had a fence and road that will always have a special meaning to those of us who witnessed their construction.

I must say my experiences in Haiti were way outside the range of any of my previous experiences. Even in the worst of times, these individuals were resilient and despite tragedy after tragedy, moved forward caring about the future of their families and the placement of others before themselves. As a people, they always seemed to have their priorities in the right place. The values and principles they live by, in many ways reflect the principles we are so willing to preach in our churches on Sunday morning. And yet, after the Haitian experience, we might raise the question and appropriately so, do we as Christians in America practice these virtues? Do we place others before ourselves as is so evident in the lives and society of the Haitian people, a society that is truly living on the edge?

As with so many of my adventures, the Haitian people will always have a special place in my heart. The recent tragedy of a level 7.0 magnitude earthquake was devastating. But, if we reach out and give as only they know how to give, we will soon learn the benefits of being a loving and caring people and in the end realize that we have gained much more than we could have ever thought of giving in return.

CHAPTER 10

"Heartwater"

A killer disease, Heartwater, is currently in the Caribbean. It is carried by a tick considered to be even more problematic. Then politics add another dimension.

In 1982, it came to my attention that there was a disease in the Caribbean Islands that if transmitted to the American Mainland, could cause serious damage to our valued Livestock Industries. It was a disease caused by Erlichia ruminatum, an organism that causes a leaking of the blood vessels, resulting in an accumulation of fluid in the lungs and around the heart. As such, it is commonly referred to as Heartwater.

The disease is spread by the Amblyoma variegatum tick, commonly called the Tropical Bont Tick. Current evidence indicates that Heartwater can survive in the Tick for many months. Then, considering that the tick prefers to feed on Cattle, the most problematic areas always seem to be where Cattle and the Tropical Bont Ticks are located in the same ecosystem.

For all intents and purposes, our cattle industries were frightened by the presence of the Tropical Bont Tick and Heartwater in that part of the world. It was even more troublesome when the Chief Veterinary Official of Uganda, Africa noted that Heartwater is a serious obstacle to cattle production in that it causes high morbidity and mortality wherever cattle are raised.

Heartwater in the Caribbean was already causing unacceptable consequences. Not only was the disease causing serious losses, but the presence of the Tick alone, with its unusually large, massive mouthparts, was causing losses in its own right. Unfortunately, as the tick broke the skin in order to obtain its blood meal, it frequently introduced serious bacterial diseases (i.e., Staphylococcus infections) into the animal's hide. Such infections would cover them with ugly abscesses creating skin problems clinically called dermatophilosis.

The Caribbean Island of Nevis, as a case in point, suffered the consequences of the introduction of the Tropical Bont Tick. Fortunately, the Tick was not harboring the Heartwater disease organism. So you would think that the cattle owners would rejoice in that they did not have to deal with Heartwater. But, oh no! The presence of the Tick alone was devastating in itself.

Their feeding for a blood meal created skin problems (dermatophilosis) in about 80% of the cattle on the island with about 90% of those so affected dying due to complications. As such, the Tick created enough havoc on its own. Then add to that the loss should there have been the introduction of Heartwater and you would have had an additional 60 to 80% dying because of that disease. That led many of us to believe that as far as the mainland of North and South America, this was a situation best fought on the islands of the Caribbean, rather than after it has gotten a foothold in the United States or Mexico, for instance.

So how do we treat the animals so affected? Well, antibiotics such as Tetracycline can be used and are effective in curing Heartwater infected animals. It is also helpful in curing Bacterial Infections caused by the bite of the Tropical Bont Tick. However, such treatments are costly and do not address the primary cause, the presence of this tick.

Now, there are pesticides that are effective in killing this tick as well as any other ticks that may be feeding on the cattle. In the United States dipping vats, similar to a swimming pool, filled with coumophas as a dipping agent, have been used for many years in the control of Fever Ticks in Texas. The cattle enter the vat of water mixed with the pesticide; swim across to the other side; and exit totally covered and dripping wet. On hot days this can be a most refreshing dip as they shake off the excess and enjoy the coolness of the gentle breeze that dries them off. While this all sounds easy enough, I must note that it is critical that the vat be properly manned and designed. Otherwise, the loss of animal life can be a problem. Another option, that has been used on occasion, is that of Pyrethrum sprays. This product, however, is usually reserved for animals of higher value, such as horses.

Even though these products work well, they are not considered useful in the Caribbean in that they would require periodic trucking of the animals to a central location or as an alternative, the movement of bulky expensive equipment to the premises of each owner. This would not work in that most of the owners do not consider the raising of cattle their primary occupation; they have a regular job elsewhere; and are only home during variable periods of time. So the scheduling and logistics would be unrealistic, a sure nightmare. And then, most of them own only one or two head. As such, the spooking of the cattle as a result of the catching and restraining as necessary for the periodic treatments, would be burdensome and frustrating for not only the owner and the cattle, but also for the person moving the equipment along narrow, twisting roads and alley ways.

So then, it was suggested that we might find a more workable solution if we used a pesticide from Bayer called, Baytical. This product had been used in Europe for many years and was typically used on farms that owned just a few head of cattle. The advantage of this product is that it is a pour-on. In other words, it is applied by pouring a small stream of the product from a bottle along the back of the animal from the head to the tail. This is just what we needed in that the application of the pesticide only needed to be done once every two weeks and could be done by the farmer without the assistance of other individuals. Moreover, it was received well by the animal. As such, these animals could be treated as part of the family and had no fear when the owners approached them as part of the application process.

After several weeks of discussions and consultations, the Inter-American Institute for Cooperation on Agriculture member organizations (including the Caribbean (CARICOM) Community, France, Mexico and the United States) decided that a meeting of all interested parties needed to be held. With that, we agreed that a meeting on the island of Barbados would be ideal. This would give us a chance to work on a possible agreement between each of our countries as well as to address the mechanics of eliminating this serious problem in the Caribbean. Oh, my, tell me about it! Are we talking about work, and going to work on the Island of Barbados? Give me a break! Is this truly work we are talking about? Or, as some might indicate, is it a vacation with some work attached?

Anyways, knowing that time flies when you are having fun, I was soon on my way to Barbados, arriving late in the afternoon. The first thing I wanted to do was change out of my stuffy bureaucratic pin stripped suit and into a pair of shorts and a light tee shirt. It was a beautiful day and the fresh seashore breezes gently welcomed me to the seashore and I was happy to have arrived.

Recognizing that this was my first trip to Barbados, I wanted to see as much of the island as possible. In addition, it felt good to get a little walking in at a somewhat brisk pace. I had only gone a short distance when I noticed an older gentleman apparently taken by my brisk walk and looping gait. The next thing I noticed was his pointing directly at me and then pointing to the curb next to him and nodding in the affirmative as if to indicate that I should stop and join him, as we jointly contemplated the events of the day and the future of this world.

As you might imagine, I was curious and stopped to see what he had in mind. He didn't say a word. Instead he just kept pointing to me and then to the space on the curb right next to him. By then my curiosity had gotten the best of me and I couldn't believe what I was doing. Yes, I was doing exactly what he wanted me to do. You got it! I sat down on the slightly raised curb and right next to him. After all this, you would think he had something to say. But, oh no, all he did was look straight forward and didn't say a word. I was beginning to wonder what this was all about. Just how long was I willing to sit there? Yes, he was a kind looking gentleman and for some reason I stayed put. We both just sat there and sat there, without saying a word.

Knowing my character and the fast paced world I lived in, I couldn't believe that here I was obeying a total stranger, sitting by him as if we were old friends and neither of us saying a word. But then as I was about to leave, he looked over at me and with a twinkle in his eye slowly said, in a deliberate, methodical, low tone of voice. "Slow down! Slow down! Life is too short! Enjoy it while you can! This is the Caribbean! Pick up some of the Caribbean ways! Try it! Slow down and enjoy!

You know, this was indeed a wise man. After taking a few moments to contemplate what he had said, I looked at him, took a hold of his hand and thanked him for his words of wisdom! Then I sat there another ten or fifteen minutes watching others walk by; hearing the surf in the back ground and the sound of a Caribbean Marimba Band off in the distance. Because of him I experienced the pleasure of the Caribbean and when I think of the Caribbean, I often think of this fine gentleman who taught me more than most about the importance of the life God gave us and living the moment; the moment we so often miss. Well after a leisurely stroll and a delightful meal, I returned to the hotel relaxed and ready for a good night's sleep.

The next morning I arose, all excited about the day's upcoming events. Little did I know how excited everyone else was and I soon discovered over breakfast, from several of the participants, that this gathering was sure to be a historical event. Apparently everyone was enthused. The excitement continued into the meeting and it was obvious that each of the Caribbean Nations was more than willing to do their part in this regional effort. They were overjoyed to have the presence and interest of the French, the Mexicans, the Canadians and the United States and we all cherished the advice and counsel of the Inter-American Institute for Cooperation on Agriculture and the World Health Organization's Food and Agriculture Organization.

It was fascinating to observe the enthusiasm demonstrated as each participant strongly endorsed the agreement; encouraged each of the countries to sign the agreement; and to participate fully so that we all could celebrate in five or ten years the completion of this program so critical to the future of our livestock industries. Oh what a day when we could celebrate the elimination of Amblyoma variegatum, the Tropical Bont Tick from their shores and the associated cattle diseases, Heartwater and Dermatophilosis.

Here I was on an all time high! I was filled with excitement and oh so ready to let my superiors know what had just been accomplished. But, alas, as is on occasion the case, what we think of as success can be so terribly short lived! Oh, boy! Little did I know what was facing me upon my return to Washington? I was only back in my office for a short while, when I received a call to report to the Administrator's Office (the top Brass so to speak). It was there that I was advised that the pesticide, Baytical, which was to be used in the Caribbean Program, was not approved for use in the United States.

It appears that the company (Bayer) producing the product, Baytical, was not interested in making it available to the American consumer. Apparently the cost of doing all the tests and protocols to meet our country's Food and Drug Agency's approval could never be repaid by the estimated U. S. sales projected for this product. This was based on the fact that Baytical is only used in the cattle industry if a herd owner has only one or two animals to be treated. As we all know, in the United States, this is rarely the case. In addition, it was brought to my attention that we in the Department, as a long standing policy would never be a party or signatory to any agreement that endorsed and encouraged the use of a product not approved for use in the United States. What a bummer!

So there I was from one moment filled with enthusiasm and then in the next moment filled with disappointment and despair. Nevertheless, I quickly reported the change in our position to each of the participants and reassured them that even though we could not be a party to the agreement, we would fully participate. We would identify introductions of the Tropical Bont Tick on each of our islands and would eliminate this Tick from all locations so identified, whether in Puerto Rico or the Virgin Islands. I must share that we were successful in eliminating the Tropical Bont Tick from Puerto Rico in the 1990s and now it appears we have been successful in eradicating an introduction in 2009 in St. Croix.

As you might be aware, we, in the U.S. are fortunate to have a research branch of government called the Agriculture Research Service (ARS). They have a remarkable history of finding solutions to not only agriculture issues, but also those of importance to Public Health. Well, one of the concerns in eliminating the Tropical Bont Tick was that on occasion, the tick will attach itself to any deer that may be passing by. This can make this problem more complex resulting in unfortunate delays.

Well, we can thank the researchers in the Agriculture Research Service for their creativity and innovative, scientific approaches to solving such problems for us. In the late 1990s, a group of researchers under the direction of Roger Drummond, PhD, designed a bait station that lured deer into a feeding apparatus that used rollers to apply a pesticide to the animals' head, ears, and neck as well as their back. Then, as the deer proceeded to groom themselves, they would transfer this product to other parts of their body. This resulted in the pesticide killing most, if not all of the ticks attached to their body and greatly reducing the population of these ticks in the environment.

As time progressed, another entomologist, J. Mathews Pound, PhD and his colleges further developed this device into a 4-poster Deer Treatment Bait Station that vastly improved its ability to reduce the prevalent tick populations. Then, according to a recent News release, Dr. Pound and his colleagues have now reformulated a broad-spectrum anti-parasitic medication produced by Pfizer called Doramectin into an injectable, time-release treatment. According to this news release, a single injection of the microspheres containing the anti-parasitic treatment greatly reduced the number of treatments needed and protected cattle for up to four months; killing the ticks; and saving the cattle ranchers/owners considerable time and expense. This treatment has apparently been tested with excellent results on the Island of St. Croix.

This is exciting news and will be useful in assuring the successful completion of this important program. The Tropical Bont Tick Program in the Caribbean is critical to protecting our country's cattle populations. It is important that we address this problem while it is limited to the Caribbean Islands and not wait until it becomes a problem for our valued livestock industries nationwide. While, it may seem that this program is taking way too long to complete, let me emphasize that working with animal diseases is not like many of our government programs such as building roads, buildings, etc. Rather, it is more like fighting a war, a war against disease. There are numerous variables and the complexity of each outbreak brings along with it the environmental differences, the commitment of the people, the availability of workable technology, and of course sufficient resources.

A Task Force Operation with sufficient expertise and the necessary resources can accomplish great things in a relatively short time. However, with limited resources, two things can happen. One, the problem persists at a constant rate and the public support dwindles because they believe nothing can be done. Or, the disease problem becomes less visible and the public support dwindles because the public believes the disease is not as severe a problem as the authorities and news media have made it out to be.

In this case, I believe the Caribbean Initiative has been successful in reducing the impact from that which one might expect. But let's not become lackadaisical and think everything is OK! Now is the time to give this program the extra push necessary and it is time for us to help our Caribbean neighbors finish the job. The timing is right, especially with the new tools and treatments available. It is time to get the job done and to get it done right. In the end we are protecting our Cattle Industries, saving resources, and maintaining a readily available, quality source of protein at a reasonable price.

In closing this chapter, the lessons learned include patience, living each moment to the fullest, and recognizing the value of supporting our brothers and sisters in the Caribbean as we should world-wide. As God looks at our lives and the way we approach each day, let us be thankful that we have each other and recognize the benefit of working together to achieve greatness. For only through this approach to life can we even begin to protect our valued animal and human resources so important to the future of our livelihood and that of all mankind!

CHAPTER 11

The Fly Factory

Eliminating "Screwworm" Flies is no simple feat. Even cowboys played a role. Enjoy the humor as I give my wife a tour and explain the workings of this "male only" facility.

This is one story I am sure you will find most unusual and unbelievable. Did you know the United States has cooperated with Mexico, Central American, and Panama in the elimination of a certain species of flies from the North American Continent? Did you know our government spends about Thirty-Two Million Dollars every year on these programs? And now, hear this! The species of fly that we are focusing on is Cochliomyia hominivorax, commonly called the Screwworm Fly. This fly is attracted to open flesh wounds on animals of all kinds including man. Now, as we have said, the Screwworm fly has been scientifically named Cochliomyia hominovorax. Of greater interest to me is that the name hominovorax is of

Latin derivation and it means, man-eating. How appropriate is that?

Once the fly lands on a cut or open wound, it will deposit between two hundred fifty and three hundred eggs. These develop into larvae that love to feed on live flesh. In many ways they resemble a wood screw being screwed into a piece of lumber. They enjoy every morsel of food as they rotate in a circular motion delving deeper into the bloody rich muscular tissue that helps them grow into fat and sassy little critters. Moreover, they are not particular whether they are feeding and thereby screwing into the live flesh of animals or for that matter a human being (man or woman). So, with that bit of information you can now understand why these nasty little flies have for years been called Screwworms and rightfully so!

After the larvae have finished feeding; they crawl to the edge of the animal; fall off; and burrow into the ground. It is then that they develop into the crusty pupa stage. This is when the fly dramatically changes in body structure through a process called metamorphosis. It is a non-feeding stage in which the larval changes into the adult form of a fly.

Now, in the eighteen hundreds the public only noticed that flies fed on dead material such as seen in garbage cans etc. Few, if any noticed that a large number of human deaths occurred as a result of Screwworm larvae feeding on a cut or open wound. Little did they notice that the feeding of these larvae created much larger wounds; making it difficult to sustain life. Moreover, they did not relate the feeding of larvae to their losses in livestock. From their perspective, such loses were due to a variety of conditions, diseases, predators and/or other environmental conditions. They were accepted as part of the consequences of raising animals in a rural environment. When larvae were seen in wounds, they would often clean the wound as best they could and then might, in some cases, consider using products like pine tar to help rid the wound of the feeding larvae.

To give you an idea of the impact of this fly on animal populations, it was reported in the nineteen fifties that annual losses in Florida wild deer populations were about twenty-five percent. We must remember that it didn't take a very large wound to attract the female fly. Even the umbilical cord of a new borne was a readily available site to lay eggs and was frequently used by the screwworm fly to her advantage. Often animals that did not die were still impacted in a negative way. This included weight loss, retardation in growth potential, a decrease in milk production, as well as a somewhat limited ability to produce healthy offspring. Then, there was the problem of hide depreciation due to the scars and holes received as a result of the feeding of the massive numbers of larvae.

Unbeknownst to many, the Screwworm Fly played a major role in our country's history. Very few people today can even relate to the historical or economically devastating aspects of this fly's story. In fact, the Screwworm played a major role in the story of the cowboy in the Wild West. I believe you would agree that when we think of the cowboy, we always think of the cattle drives as they brought cattle to greener pastures or drove them on foot to market. There is a lot of pride and joy as we think of the American cowboy and their life on the range. Movies and numerous books have enhanced this story with the inclusion of chuck wagons and covered wagons heading West as well as country songs sung around the campfire each evening.

In the nineteen fifties, Roy Rogers and his wife, Dale Evans, did much to bring these stories and the romanticism of the cowboy to the forefront as television and the movies took a hold of the American Public.

Well, a major part of the cowboy story that was not told was the role of the cowboy in keeping the cattle alive. Any animals with open cuts or wounds were susceptible to being attacked by the Screwworm Flies. With two hundred fifty to three hundred eggs being laid on open wounds by each of the adult female Screwworm Flies and the resulting hunger of the larval stage, it was only a matter of a few days and the larvae could have eaten a large portion of the animal's flesh. If the infested wound was not treated within a couple days with an insecticide, the animal would usually die and die from complications within about ten days or so.

Now you understand! This is why the cowboy's skills in roping cattle were so important. In fact it was critical to the cow or bull's survival. The cowboys had to check each animal on a daily basis for any possible cuts, abrasions, or open wounds that might be evident. He would then take his lasso off of the saddle, twirl it around a couple times and loop the lasso over the animal's head and/or with the help of another cowboy up and under their hind feet. This was done to topple the animal over so it could be restrained by quickly tying all four feet together. Once the animal was properly restrained, the cowboy would then apply an insecticide to the wounds observed, thereby assuring the destruction of any eggs and/or larvae that might be present.

Now I must emphasize that being a cowboy is not an easy task. For example, I remember visiting a checkpoint where all livestock had to be unloaded and inspected for possible wounds. During this particular visit, the inspectors noticed a wound on the shoulder of one of the bulls being transported to the area of Mexico that was free of this pest. The bull was moved to a large vacant pen, fully restrained and available for inspection. I climbed down from the high fence surrounding the pen and was soon inspecting and treating the wound with a powdered insecticide while pointing out the large number of larvae observed feeding. Suddenly, in the blink of an eye, the bull struggled with all of its strength and unraveled itself from the ropes. Before I knew what was happening, all of the cowboys were out of sight; scrambling up the sides of the enclosed pen, and there I was about to have a heart attack.

Yes, I did get my act together and barely made it up and over the pen’s metal enclosure in time. I can still remember the help given to me by the bull as he nudged me over the fence with his head and horns making contact as if to say "Don’t ever try that again, bud! Next time you might not be so lucky”. Such is the risks animal handlers and veterinarians are faced with on a regular basis.

Now let me share some of the background that led to the program of eliminating this serious pest from the United States, Mexico and Central America. In the mid-nineteen twenties, a Dr. Herman J. Muller noted that irradiation could sterilize male flies and make them incapable of producing offspring. Then in the 1930s and 1940s, Dr. Edward F. Knipling and Dr. Raymond C. Bushland of USDA's Agriculture Research Service identified ways to mass produce screwworm flies that could then be sterilized by exposing them to gamma radiation (Cobalt 60). Since the female screwworm flies only mate once, it was determined that with the use of this technology, this pest could eventually be eliminated from our country and the North American Continent.

When I came on board as the Director of International Programs (in the 1980's), the pest had successfully been eliminated from the United States and most of Mexico. I worked closely with my boss, Dr. John Atwell; the Director of Field Operations, Dr. Jim Novy, and Dr. Norvan Meyer, my predecessor and brilliant strategist in screwworm eradication technology, mass fly rearing techniques and field operations implementation.

The beauty of this program was the driving force lead by cattlemen who saw the value of this program and offered massive sums of money to get this program off the ground and moving in the right direction. They called themselves, The South West Animal Research Foundation or the acronym SWARF. They attended every meeting of significance and were a major influence in the success of the program throughout North America.

Ed Ketchum, a rancher in Oklahoma, Jerry Puckett, a banker, Bud Turner, a rancher, John Hays, Arizona State Legislator, Jack Hagler, Guillermo Osuna, Justo Dias, M. E. "Cotton" Meadows, P. H. Coates, C. G. Scruggs and their colleagues including Texas Congressman, Kika De La Garza all faced each challenge with optimism and support. They encouraged our colleagues in each country and each discipline whether it was research, field operations or mass production facility operations to be the best they could be.

Now, let me tell you a little about the fly production facilities. During my tenure, this facility was jointly run by the United States and Mexico. It was located in the southernmost State of Mexico, the State of Chiapas and was in the outskirts of the town of Tuxla Gutierrez, Mexico.

Air travel to this community was provided at an airport located on the only available area of flat land that also happened to be on top of a mountain. In other words, when a pilot was considering landing at this airport, he or she had to have their timing right to assure the wheels of the plane touched the ground immediately at the beginning of the runway on one side of the mountain and then had to quickly apply the brakes to assure the plane stopped before the runway ended on the other side of the mountain. This was just a little something to add a little excitement every time we planned a visit to this part of the world.

The fly factory itself was the size of two football fields and contained rooms with closely controlled environments to provide the necessary temperature and humidity for every stage of the fly's life cycle. At peak production this facility could produce about five hundred million sterile screwworm flies per week. That is no small number and you must realize that biological security had to be strict in that any fertile flies escaping could cause detrimental consequences for the local livestock populations.

Well one day, I took my wife to Tuxla Gutierrez and set up the arrangements to allow her to take a tour of this most unusual facility. Little did I know until after we arrived that she would be the first woman to enter this facility and have the grand tour? You see, in order to make this possible, they had to close the locker room and shower area at the entrance to all employees as Joanne and I entered the facility and changed into our coveralls. Also on leaving we put our coveralls in a hamper to be washed and took a shower (of course we were together) before putting our street clothes on and leaving. You see, we had to take a shower and change clothes in order to ensure that no fly eggs, or other stages of the flies' life cycle were present in our clothes or on our body upon leaving.

It was a very exciting time for Joanne and I am sure she will always cherish that experience. The skilled factory workers and their supervisors gave her the royal treatment and showed her all aspects of the operation. You see, only men worked in this facility and at that time we had three shifts with a total of about 1,200 to 1,500 employees.

The first section of this fly production plant had a very warm temperature and a high humidity to replicate the temperature and humidity found in an animal's body. In that room there were row upon row of trays. In these trays you would find a food product that was made of meat, cottage cheese and blood. This product replicated in part the live flesh the larval stage would normally feed on if they were feeding on a live animal.

Egg masses collected from another room where flies laid the eggs on wood boards (with an attractant applied) were added to each tray and the feeding process began. When the larvae had finished feeding, as was their nature, they would crawl to the edge of the trays and fall to a small canal of water running on the floor along the side of the stacked rows of trays. This would carry the larvae to a screened apparatus that would collect the larva for transfer to trays filled with sawdust. The sawdust trays with the larvae were then transferred to another room that was much cooler and dryer to replicate the conditions in the field when the larvae fall off of the animals and burrow into the ground. As in nature the larvae would then pupate and go through the necessary changes (metamorphosis) into an adult fly. At that point some of the pupae were placed in screened cages to become adult flies producing the eggs for the next generation of flies to be produced in this fly production facility.

One important consideration in this whole process was the possibility that mutations could occur from one generation of flies to another. When this did occur as it would from time to time, it would play havoc with the genetics of our factory made flies and interfere with their usefulness in the wild.

That is where our Agriculture Research Service Scientists were so important to the whole process. These scientists, such as Dr. H. C. Hofmann and his colleagues were specialists with extensive experience in Entomology. They knew more about the screwworm fly than you could ever imagine in that they were specialists in the nature and feeding habits of the screwworm Fly and its various stages of development. For instance, they were experts in the visual acuity of the adult fly produced, their wing span and the mechanisms that enhanced their ability to fly. They fully understood the important components of the factory produced sterile male Screwworm Fly's attraction to the wild native female flies as well as their aggressiveness in reaching the female flies before the wild native male species could reach them. These scientists were always working to produce a superior screwworm fly; making them available on a periodic basis for the production facility to assure the best, most aggressive sexually attractive flies were produced for eventual release into the wild.

In order to assure the sterility of the flies being produced, flies in the pupa stage were removed from the sawdust and placed in containers to be zapped with Gamma Radiation. This was done just at the point when the sexual organs had the most active cellular growth exceeding that of any of the fly's other tissues. As such, the Gamma Radiation would sterilize the sexual organs while not affecting the other body parts. As a result, they were effectively sterilized and unable to produce offspring after mating with a wild native female fly. Since the female Screwworm Fly only mated once; there won't be any offspring; and eventually with sufficient distribution of sterile flies on a weekly basis, the wild fly populations would cease to exist.

After the pupae were irradiated and sterilized with Gamma Radiation (Cobalt 60), they were placed in boxes the size of a box of Kleenex tissues. Inside this box a honey mixture was placed for them to feed on and several cardboard levels were placed for the flies to grasp on to as they emerged from the pupa stage, stretching and drying their wings. These containers were all constructed to have the environment and feed necessary to allow these flies to complete their maturation into fully functional adult flies preparing for their first flight and a mating opportunity. Then, at the proper moment in time, the boxes were loaded in a Piper Cub Airplane, flown over the area being tended to, and disbursed in a grid formation at a predetermined rate of automatic ejection out of an opening at the rear of the plane. Once the box was ejected and hit the blast of air going around the plane, the box would rip open, and the sterile factory produced flies would be freed to mate with the wild native fly population.

During these program activities, massive media campaigns were held nationwide in each country to encourage farmers to treat their livestock cuts, abrasions and wounds with an insecticide. They were encouraged to submit any larvae found in any of these wounds to a regional or national laboratory for identification. In addition, they were asked to report any larvae finds to their local inspectors for further surveillance and follow up.

If Screwworm Flies or Larvae were found and identified on a ranch or other location, it was immediately reported to the program's Field Operations Staff. The ground location where the Screwworm Larvae were found would then be identified with a white chalk like powder. This was in the form of a large circle or other marking that could easily be identified by a Screwworm Program Pilot flying overhead. The longitude and latitude for this location was also identified so immediate dispersal of sterile flies could be completed in the area and surrounding areas by the Program's Air Operations.

It was amazing how important this program was to the Cattlemen and Livestock Producers wherever we traveled in the southern United States, Mexico or Central America. As such, we tried our best to keep these individuals and their organizations appraised of the progress being made and how they could assist in the implementation of this important effort. Meetings with the local farmers and ranchers provided a great opportunity for us to receive information on how to improve our program implementation, making it better for the Livestock Producers and everyone concerned.

As part of this effort, there was one aspect in building international relationships that at first was rather uncomfortable for me and that was the way Mexican men approached each other, especially if they were good friends. As you may be aware, their tradition, in such situations, was that of giving each other an abrazo. Now as far as I could ascertain, that is a hug or embrace given between two men as a part of a greeting and/or parting of ways. In addition, it appeared that an abrazo was used as a form of celebration and/or acknowledgement when a speaker gave a speech highly regarded by the audience at hand. In that case, two or three men, accompanied by thundering applause, would immediately rise and approach the speaker with their arms outstretched, a smile on their face, and each presenting the speaker a short, but well deserved hand shake with a couple light slaps on the back, abrazo!

In order to clarify the point I would like to make relative to the use of an abrazo, we need to step back a minute and discuss some of the efforts I had made to learn to communicate effectively with my colleagues and friends in Latin America. Clearly I needed to learn the Spanish language and the sooner the better. I immediately enrolled in six weeks of intensive Spanish training in Antigua, Guatemala; lived with a family who knew no English; and worked daily with a professor to gain a working knowledge of the language.

After several months of practice, I started giving my talks in Mexico using my less than perfect, basic Spanish vocabulary. It was apparent that any and all of my attempts to speak in their native language were greatly appreciated. Then, whoa la, my day arrived. I can still remember that day most vividly. I was talking to a group of cattlemen and passionately expressing, in Spanish, my thoughts concerning the future of their program and the success it had achieved. I emphasized the outstanding working relationships we had with their livestock industry and finished by thanking them for clarifying some important issues that needed to be addressed at that time.

I must say that even though it was a complete surprise, I was indeed delighted when all of a sudden on finishing my speech several livestock owners came up and yes, gave me an abrazo! Oh, did it ever make my day. It was like we could finally, truly relate to each other and oh, yes even with the errors I may have made in my Spanish; my ideas and thoughts had been received, and we understood each other like never before. What an experience!

And what made it even more remarkable was that in my upbringing and the Puritan American view I had of men hugging or embracing, it was just not acceptable to touch another man, ever! In fact, in the town where I was born and raised, it was and, for all I know, still is verboten! So the first few times I was greeted with an abrazo, it was difficult for me. It took quite a while for me to understand and accept this custom. And it even took a much longer time for me to return the same as a sign of true respect and friendship. All I can imagine is that for some time they must have thought of me as very cold and not too friendly.

Well, to continue my story, one of the frameworks and keys to the success of this program was the necessity of having buy-in at the very highest levels of government. To accomplish this, we routinely held Commission meetings that included the Secretary and/or Assistant Secretary of Agriculture as well as all of the Program Directors from each of the participating Countries. Those in attendance included the technical/research staff as well as representatives from the livestock organizations who played a role in the establishment and funding of this program activity. This included members of the South West Animal Research Foundation and their President, an Oklahoma Cattleman, Mr. Ed Ketchum.

Now, as you are well aware, the Secretary and Assistant Secretaries of Agriculture are all political positions. For me, as a new member of the Administrator's Office, the political scene was an obstacle that was hard to overcome. Having advanced in the government through technical ranks, the discussing of program activities from a political point of view was most challenging to my psyche and frame of reference. From my vantage point, the answer the political appointees want to hear is not always the best answer from a technical point of view. As such, my position as the Director for International Programs taught me that there are several avenues that one must consider to accomplish program objectives and often the avenue of choice is not the most direct route. Nevertheless, if it has the support of the political appointees and will accomplish the objective, it is best to support their political agenda rather than lose the whole ball game.

What made this even more difficult; however was that the political agenda can often catch one off guard when you least expect it. It can drive a technocrat crazy and this is especially true when your career has not been faced with the level of political power and expectation often seen at such high levels.

While I could give several examples, one experience about drove me bananas while preparing for my first International Commissioner's Meeting. I can still remember being called into the Assistant Secretary's Office concerning this big occasion and being advised that he was disappointed that I had not presented him with Official

Invitations for his signature to be presented to the dignitaries being invited to attend. Furthermore, he was disappointed in the facilities we had selected for this meeting and expected much more from me in such arrangements and recommended that we find better accommodations for such an elite group.

Of course, I wanted to please him and quickly asked our staff to change the location of our next meeting; find a resort with better accommodations; and prepare formal invitations for the Assistant Secretary's signature. I was sure the Secretary's Office would be pleased and arrived at the resort satisfied with the arrangements made, the meeting's agenda, and the program points to be discussed and agreed upon.

Well, unfortunately, I was not prepared for the comments the Assistant Secretary had for me that evening. I soon learned that political individuals can quickly change direction. There is nothing, absolutely nothing that is sacred while working in the political arena. This became evident when I attended dinner that evening. It seemed like the Assistant Secretary couldn't wait to pull me aside and chew me out royally for wasting the taxpayer's money by holding this meeting in such a fancy resort. Sometimes one just cannot win, no matter how hard they try. I must say, however that wasn't the first and only error I have ever made, for there are many other examples. But, let's leave that for another time!

As part of my Screwworm Program responsibilities, it was important that I periodically visit the Fly Production Facility located in Tuxtla Gutierrez, Mexico. I learned much from the former Director, Dr. Norvan Meyer and remember his counsel that on visiting the Facility, I didn't have to know everything about the mechanics of production to be effective. As a result, I would follow his advice; trying to observe operations in every part of the facility. I would crawl behind various pieces of equipment; scan the entire roof top looking at the air-handling equipment, walk the entire grounds, inspect the sewage treatment facilities, the water tanks, etc., etc. I would use all my senses: my eyes, my ears, my nose and my sense of touch. If anything seemed unusual to me I would just ask a lot of questions and whoa, la, it was amazing how my actions were read by the various employees.

It quickly became evident that the employees, as is probably the case universally, always want their bosses to be proud of their work. When they saw me take an interest in their work it made them proud. But by the same token when I asked questions about a rusting machine part or leaking water or machines making a funny sound, they were honest about it and then worked ever so hard to improve everything, especially when they knew I was coming for another visit.

I was and still am proud of the work they did. At times, such as when there were vultures on the roof top and a foul smell from the sewage treatment plant, I knew they needed resources to fix the problem. Then, with a good listening ear and as on one occasion, attending their Union Meeting; we were able to resolve a lot of issues as a team and thereby accomplish our mission with much greater ease and efficiency.

Visiting the employees working on the scene always meant a lot to me. This was important in that those of us directing operations from top management can at times unintentionally affect employees in a negative way. As such, we need to be sensitive to their needs and how we can best motivate them to greatness; achieving our program objectives in a timely way!

One of my favorite stories concerning the Fly Production Facility still brings a smile to my face. This occurred about 1:00 am in the evening after touring the facility and visiting with the employees. As you might imagine, I was ready to hit the sack and have a good night's sleep. I parked my car at the rear of the motel and slowly walked down one of the hallways to my room. I put my key into the lock, unlocked the door, passed through the front sitting room, and entered the bedroom, trying to rip my clothes off as quickly as possible, ready for some badly needed shuteye.

When all of a sudden I heard the most panic stricken voice screaming at the top of her lungs! Oh, yes, it was a woman obviously scared out of her wits. Her scream brought me to attention and I didn't hesitate to argue about whose room I was in! I made a quick exit; suddenly realizing that I had gone down the wrong hallway and in fact had entered another person's room. I quickly got my bearings, flew down the correct hallway, opened the door to my room, and sat down trying to catch my breath while sorting this all out in my mind.

It soon became quite clear that if the lady complained to management, there was no way that I could come out of this unscathed. In Southern Mexico one would suddenly realize that there wasn't anyone that looked like me at six foot four, pale white skin and wearing a suit and tie. Just how difficult is it to figure out that I was the one and only gringo suspect that could ever be considered? As you can imagine, I did not sleep very well that evening and I was not the only one as I am sure that woman probably had a frightful night as well.

Now I must say that working with the Mexicans was most rewarding. They all worked hard, were very conscientious, had outstanding leadership abilities, and were technically sound in all of their operations, both in the production plant as well as in the field. It was a pleasure working with them.

As soon as the screwworm fly was eliminated from Mexico, it was time to extend the program to Central America and then finally to Panama. From an economical point of view, maintaining a screwworm barrier in Panama would cost about ten million dollars versus the cost of about thirty Million dollars in Mexico. At that time (1980s), we were saving the cattlemen in the United States and Mexico over one hundred thirty million dollars a year in potential losses. By extending the program to Panama the yearly costs for the program would be reduced and the cattlemen in Central America and Panama would receive added benefits to this already successful program.

Soon, Counselor John Golden, in charge of USDA's Office of General Counsel (legal guru), Larry Slagle, Director of the Office of Management and Budget for our Agency and I as part of a joint U. S.–Mexican Team traveled to begin negotiations between each of these countries, the United States and Mexico. We had a lot to offer and fortunately the negotiations went well.

Surprisingly the only areas of concern we faced at that time were more related to outside concerns and the troubled world we live in and not the negotiations at hand.

For instance, about two weeks after our meeting in Honduras, the building we held the negotiations in was blown up by terrorists who disagreed with their government on some issues of apparently great concern to them. Even though we never learned the reason for this attack, you can be sure it was rather unnerving to think it happened only two weeks after we were there meeting in that very building. So much for feeling safe and secure!

On another occasion, after a morning of successful negotiations, our friends in El Salvador pointed out the location, as we were eating our lunch, where several nuns were slaughtered by terrorists. This occurred a few weeks earlier as they were walking along a stone wall, just across the street from where we were sitting. So what has happened to the idea of resolving our differences in a peace loving way?

All of this is troubling when we consider the value of human life and the readiness in those times, as is still evident today, for individuals and/or groups, to perform such hideous acts to get their message out. The hatred and burning anger is hard for me to understand and yet for it to drive some individuals to such drastic measures must emphasize the need for better communication and understanding in this precious world we call planet earth.

Now let me end on a more positive note. Mexico is a beautiful country and I will never forget one trip I took to Mexico City. The air conditioning in the car was working, the scenery was breathtaking, and I was with two individuals I had the pleasure of working with. One was William "Bill" Sudlow and the other was Betty Liebe. It was an enjoyable trip and the highlight came as we were approaching some beautiful mountain peaks in the distance.

I will never forget what happened next. Bill Sudlow pulled the car to the side of the road and got out of the car without saying a word. He opened up the trunk and rummaged through his stuff before returning to the driver's seat. As he started driving down the road, he put a cassette into the car's tape player and I was thrilled as we all listened to Louis Armstrong as only he can sing, "What a Wonderful World"!

I am eternally grateful to have worked in this program with so many wonderful people (for example, Drs. Nazario Pineda-Varga, James Novy, Robert Reichard, James Mackley, and a brilliant friend and fellow, Raul Marroquin).

This experience has filled my heart with joy! It has helped me understand the beauty and value of each and every country's culture. More importantly it helped me realize that our hopes and dreams, especially for our families, are basically the same. Our international neighbors value hard work and their ethics in doing their life's work well are as ingrained in their being as it is in ours. And then, as I got to know each of these individuals, it became quite evident that their belief in God was as important to them as it is to me. This, of course, meant the world to me!

CHAPTER 12

A Boiling Black Kettle

Communication or the lack thereof can at times be problematic. Without telephones or cell phones, working with a native village in the Darien Jungle of Panama, can have unexpected consequences.

This is probably one of the most exciting and interesting experiences I have ever had as an International Veterinarian.

It was a beautiful day when I arrived in the Capital of Panama, Panama City. I was all excited about my trip to the Darien Jungle. I had never traveled to this part of the world and yet one of our most important Animal Health Programs was being carried out in the thick tropics of this jungle environment. We were concerned with the potential northern movement of a serious disease of cattle, sheep, goats and pigs called Foot-and-Mouth Disease. This disease was still prevalent in South America and by the same token, had fortunately been completely eliminated in all of North America.

Now, I had heard a lot about this jungle and knew, at least by some reports, that it was a thick impenetrable jungle that few if any would want to experience. According to some, it was not a place that anyone in their right mind would want to visit! And yet, from my perspective, we didn't need to jump to unfair conclusions especially when we consider that most of their experiences were limited to that of the military. Their sole purpose for being in Panama was to receive jungle combat training. So, their experiences were probably not the norm. Their stories were filled with terror including the fears of snakes, wild creatures and the presence of insects galore to make one's life miserable. And then, there were their impressions of the jungle environment and the need to have your hand on the person in front of you at all times to avoid getting lost and/or abandoned. And as if that wasn't enough, there was the ever present hot, humid, wet atmosphere at times making it difficult to breathe as well as the eerie sounds of the wild at all times, day or night. Then, of course, they would note that the most uncomfortable feeling was that of bugs crawling up their pant legs and/or all over your body as the case may be. Right! So who would want to go to the Darien Jungle? Who would ever think of someone even considering the possibility of moving domestic animals and especially those with some kind of terrible disease through this land? Well, you are right! I did!!

I arrived late in the afternoon and caught an early morning flight scheduled at 6:00 am from Panama City to the southernmost Province of Panama. The plane I was going on was a small Cessna like plane and didn't have the instrumentation needed to fly in cloudy situations. Soon, we were being asked to board. In this instance, the plane only had space for three passengers. Already, a lady, her son and daughter had made themselves comfortable in the passenger's compartment. That only left the Pilot and Co-Pilots seat. What am I to do? Then, before I knew what was going on, the Pilot jumped into his seat and asked me what I was waiting for? I am sure I must have given him a funny look. The next thing I knew I was climbing into the Co-Pilot's seat as he directed and yes, I prayed that no harm would come to me as a result of this foolish decision on my part.

Before long, we were heading down the runway and off into the wild blue yonder. The sky was clear and it was a beautiful day to be flying. Then as the flight continued, I noticed the sky becoming overcast and there was no way to see the land below. This created a most uncomfortable feeling in my stomach. Then the feeling worsened as the Pilot announced that the Capital of the Darien Province, the City of La Palma should be just below the cloud cover as he dived into the clouds at what seemed to be a very steep angle. My heart skipped a beat and my stomach seemed to rise and fall uncontrollably with a headache in the making and my nerves frazzled to no end. As we broke beneath the cloud cover, the Pilot had to adjust his flight pattern as we skimmed across the treetops brushing them with the body of the plane as we moved forward. The Pilot must have been a master at this and remained calm as if it didn't bother him one bit as he proceeded on course right for the dirt runway. A dirt runway and this is the Capital of Panama's Darien Province? Not only that, but there were several dogs running back and forth across the runway as the Pilot landed the aircraft and skidded to a halt with little or no trouble on his part.

Here I was trying to make sense of all this and trying to catch my breath when the Pilot said, "Sir, why don't you get out, stretch your legs and take a walking tour of the beautiful Capital City of La Palma. I asked him how long we would be there. He indicated that he would probably be ready to leave in about fifteen or twenty minutes. Nevertheless he suggested that I have a look around. So, I took advantage of this opportunity, strolled through and completely around the city, and returned in plenty of time for the plane's taxi down the so called runway and takeoff.

It wasn't long before we arrived at our destination. This time we had a grass runway, cleared of trees and brush, and just long enough for our plane to enter and land. At the end of the runway was a black pickup truck. My hope was that this truck was driven by the Inspector assigned to meet me and take me to our destination located a bit further down the road. But as luck would have it, the Inspector was no-where to be seen. As I found out later, there was a mix-up on the understanding of when I was to arrive and the Inspector had on his calendar that I was to arrive on the following day.

So there I was in the Darien Jungle, obviously unfamiliar territory where English is not spoken and no clue as to where to go from there. Luckily the truck was driven by a gentleman who had arrived to meet his wife and children and he graciously offered to take me to the only town within miles at the other end of the road/path connected to this runway. He apologized that he didn't have enough room for me in the cab of his truck, especially since it was filled with members of his family. He did offer, however that I was free to climb in the back of his pickup truck and apologized for the condition of the truck bed. I assured him that was fine and that I appreciated him doing this for me. He remarked that he was glad he could help and then in a somewhat casual manner noted that he hoped the trip to town would go well and that I would arrive safe in that there had been reports of a black Jaguar roaming the area and causing a bit of trouble. Oh, yes, that was all I needed to hear. "A wild black Jaguar was roaming the area and causing a bit of trouble." O, God, do I ever need thee now!!!

Well, the trip to town went without incident and the next thing I knew, I found the Inspector's home and we were on our way. Soon we arrived at our destination, an Outpost where one of the Inspectors lived with his family. Other members of our party had arrived by Jeep just a few hours earlier and the local Inspector's wife was in the process of fixing us dinner. After an enjoyable meal and conversation, we all decided to catch some fresh air, walking down Main Street of this quaint little town. It was like walking back in time.

The Street clearly appeared like that depicted in the Westerns I used to watch as a kid. I could almost visualize Mae West coming around the corner. The buildings were rustic and weather worn. In front of the buildings there was a boardwalk. In addition the men wore blue jeans with buckles on their belts and short sleeved denim shirts. Most of them had a holster with a six shooter belted to their waist. I could almost hear them saying, "Howdy Partner" and possibly even spitting tobacco juice to emphasize a point here and there in their conversation. I was getting into this whole experience in a big way! And then to make it even more authentic, there in the center of town was a Saloon. Sure enough, even the entrance had swinging doors, just like those seen in the movies. What happened? Had I somehow stepped in a time machine? Was I dreaming? O, well . . . .

The next morning we gathered at the riverside ready to paddle downstream to one of the interior Native Indian Villages. This was a moment to remember. All of their boats were shaped somewhat like canoes in that each of these boats had been hand carved (honed) out of the trunks of large trees growing in the jungle. I had never seen anything like it and some of them were big enough for three or four people. The hours of work that were entailed to make one of these vessels must have been tremendous.

Soon we were off and paddling with all of our might. After about an hour and one-half of paddling deep into the jungle we ported our boats/canoes and followed a well established path into the interior. The canopy of trees was massive, the undergrowth was dense, the sound of life was abundant and the colors, textures, and fragrant smells given off by the various plant species were overwhelming to the senses. This is truly one of America's richest wildernesses and yet if we are not careful, it could be destroyed. One could tell this path had been used for many generations in that it had been worn deep into the ground. The visual, the sounds and the smells were ever so refreshing and yet stimulating at the same time. It was far better than any ride at Disney World and yes, this was for real!

As the leader of the pack or at least the honor of doing so, it was a journey into the beauty of God's World as it was, it is, and it should be. I will always cherish the experience hoping that we as mankind can learn to be better stewards of this land we call home.

Having been given the honor of leading the pack, I was soon introduced to another experience I will cherish for all time. For at that instance a Jungle Native scared the "begebees" out of me. He jumped out of the thick jungle brush on to the path, a few yards out in front me. He was jumping up and down whooping and hollering with all his might. He was wearing a dark colored loin cloth. His arms, legs and face were painted black with designs some might describe as that of a warrior, a well trained warrior intent on doing some serious harm. You see, he carried a big shield in his left hand

and was jabbing with his right arm, in a flexed position, a pointed spear with an obviously freshly sharpened point; directed for my heart. For all I knew, he was probably highly skilled as a hunter and better prepared than any boy scout, having freshly applied a lethal prepared paste to assure the spears point would accomplish its intended purpose!

Was I scared? You bet I was! I was panic stricken! I knew he was not a happy man and he did not like my presence in this part of the world and especially my presence on land controlled by his tribe and his tribe only. His countenance and the look in his eye said it all. That stern, controlled stare daring me to take another step forward, was clear and forthright! No doubt about it! It was obvious he was committed to do whatever he had to do. That glare of intent said it all! From his perspective, unannounced strangers were not welcome and especially those whose attentions might be harmful to him and those he loved. You see, our visit had not been announced and as such was not well received!

As you may already realize, there are no phones or other means of communication to advise such tribal villages of an upcoming visit or for that matter the purpose of such a visit as ours. Furthermore, there was no way to call home to say good-by to my wife and family, life has been good,

I love you, and oh by the way I am about to be speared by an angry man and yes you won't see or hear from me again, my life is over, no time to explain! Punto! Oh, yes, all I could envision was a **Big Black Pot of Boiling Water** at the end of the path waiting for this agile (Young Buck) hunter's catch of the day. Who knows if they were cannibals or not? In my scheme of things to come, my life was over and if they could make a good soup out of their catch, so be it!

Well, for some reason my colleagues were screaming in Spanish for him to stop as they tried to explain the purpose of our visit! Was I ever relieved when I found out he knew Spanish or at least knew enough to understand what we were saying! Fortunately, his village had been visited by missionaries who had taught him and several others in his tribe the Spanish language. I will never forget the relief on the Native's face as he dropped his shield and spear; wiping the sweat from his brow while looking me directly in the eye; and saying, **"Wow, I bet I was more scared than you were"!** Oh, Boy! You know it! I didn't hesitate in the least and said with greater fervor and emotion, **"No sir, I know I was far more scared than you were or would ever be!**"

Just think of it. This young man had to have a lot of courage to face six of us on his own. As we were to later learn, he was the only male left in the village to protect all of the women and children. All of the rest of the men were out in the jungle hunting for food etc. to bring back to their families. Little did they expect outsiders paying them a visit and when this young man detected us coming their way for who knows what reason, he was willing to step up to the plate no matter how dangerous the situation. He faced his fears head on to protect the future of his village and those he loved. How many of us would have that kind of courage? Indeed I was impressed!

Later, the men, who were out hunting, arrived and we had an opportunity to discuss the purpose of our visit and to gain some information relative to any activity they may have observed on the river or in their territory. As I have noted before, our main interest was in preventing the northern migration of livestock and as a result, the possibility of Foot-and-Mouth Disease spreading out of Colombia and into Panama.

I must say that I wish I had a tape recorder with me in that after our discussions relative to the purpose of our trip, I was delighted when they described the different plants, roots etc. that they use for medical/healing purposes. I am a strong believer in the knowledge that can be gained from such individuals who through centuries of experience, from one generation to the next, have found natural treatments for a wide variety of human ailments. It is a tragic loss when such tribes disappear and no longer exist and their entire knowledge base is lost to future civilizations forever.

Well, later in the day, a middle aged lady came up to me and excitedly exclaimed as she looked up into my eyes, "You must be from the outside world"? Now you may wonder how she came to that conclusion. Well, you see almost everyone in that tribe was probably five feet or shorter. Also they were of dark skin and here I was six foot four inches tall and as pale skinned as anyone who has ever walked this earth. Yes, obviously I was from the outside world! She was thrilled to see us and for good reason. Her husband had recently invented something that she wanted me to see that would be of benefit to all of the women in the outside world.

Their home was just a short distance and it would mean so much to her if I would come to their home! Well, curiosity got the best of me and before long my colleagues and I were on our way. Now, I did get it right, didn't I? Didn't she say it was just a short distance? Now, let's not forget that they have no transportation and to get from point A to point B they have to walk. There is no other way! So for what they consider a short walk is Oh, My, a trek that takes forever and in a jungle it is as you can guess filled with all kinds of challenges.

After we arrived, she was a fine hostess in that she offered us a couple stumps to sit on and asked her husband to get some sugar cane and to squeeze it so we could have fresh sugar cane juice to drink, to refresh us. As you might imagine, I was surprised that they had sugar cane and secondly I was surprised when I noticed that they had a contraption that squeezed the juice out of the sugar cane stalks. One would probably classify this lady and her husband as technologically advanced, having picked up some of these ideas from visitors they had received in the past from the so called, outside world.

Finally, after catching our breath, the lady was ready to take me into her kitchen and to show me her husband's great invention. First of all, you need to understand that each kitchen had a fire pit on the ground that had several dry logs burning around three rather large sized stones. The tops of these stones had hand carved indentations creating a type of bowl. Each of these bowls was then used for the placement of the food that had to be cooked.

This was hard on the lady of the house in that cooking resulted in a lot of bending over. So as you can imagine, they would on occasion strain their backs and then have to live with a certain level of pain. In this case, the lady's husband cared deeply for his wife and was brilliant in inventing a new type of fire pit, designed and built with his own hands. You see, her husband created a new design, previously unknown, that raised the level of the fire pit and thus the cooking surface to waist height. It was ingenious and he and his wife were so proud of his invention. He did this by taking straight limbs from trees and with the use of vines assembled what we would call a table. He then put several inches of dirt on top of the table/stove and placed the three cooking stones strategically so a fire could be built around them.

Again, he was a genius and greatly improved the cooking arrangement without the "lady of the house" needing to bend over. I was delighted to see his invention and the excitement of his wife proudly demonstrating his creativity and care for her well being. In no way did I have the heart to tell her of the technology available to the rest of the world in stoves and ovens. It just made me so proud to see the God given importance of loving and caring for one another as God intended many centuries ago. As I was leaving, she made me promise to tell the women of the world of this great invention and as I share this story with all who will listen, I feel I am keeping that promise which to this day is one of the most precious and most meaningful promises I have ever made.

On the way back to our so called canoes, we stopped to again visit our newly made friends in the village and to wish them our best and to say our goodbyes. I will never forget the parting words of the Village Chief. As you may have already understood, but was new to me, all of the villagers dressed basically the same. Whether they were men or women, each of them only wore a loin cloth. As you can imagine this was quite different from what I was used to with my so called conservative heritage.

Well, for what reason, I do not know, the Village Chief pulled me aside just before we said our good-byes and wanted to apologize for one of the women in his village. You see all of the women were naked from the waist up except for one. And what that one wore looked like from my limited perspective, to be a brand new glistening white, Victoria Secret's sized D-Cup Strapped Bra. It stood out like a sore thumb.

For the Village Chief, it was disgusting and he saw no need for it! He said the missionaries brought them the Spanish language and talked of their God. Apparently none of that bothered him. But what he couldn't understand was their teaching that the human body was evil. It was just too much for him to accept that God would want us to cover women's breasts. He apologized over and over and explicitly hoped I would not be offended and that I would not think they had all accepted the thought that their bodies were something to be ashamed of. After all he said God made all things beautiful and to think otherwise was a slap in the face of God our creator of everything so beautiful. I assured him I was not offended and thanked him again for his hospitality and applauded the courage of the young man who one might say welcomed us to their village.

I learned a lot from this trip. I was impressed by the safety the Darien Jungle and the Panamanian Animal Health Inspectors provided in preventing the northern spread of Foot-and Mouth Disease. And more importantly, I learned some valuable truths about the importance of building relationships between our various cultures and differing ways of life.

With that thought in mind, I will always feel richly blessed to have had this experience and hope those I met on this trip feel as blessed as I do for the precious time we had together. Another trip I will never forget!

CHAPTER 13

Centered for Success!

Often national surveys can change the way we think. When one stops thinking in the traditional sense, new discoveries of great value and interest are realized.

In the late 1990s, I was assigned to Fort Collins, Colorado as the Acting Director of our Agency's "Center for Epidemiology and Animal Health". This Center has a reputation of looking at animal diseases from outside the traditional mind set and is known for viewing the science and art of epidemiology from a broad base of possibilities. In fact, because of this enlightened approach, this Center attracts and welcomes a dynamic diverse group of individuals. It is truly a "Center for Learning" and as some might consider, the "Learned"! The value of this institution is due to the enterprising, passionate coalitions/partnerships formed on site with world renowned professionals having expertise in a wide variety of disciplines. This may include pathology, virology, microbiology, statistics, economics, animal husbandry, epidemiology, as well as many other fields including individuals highly skilled in Public Health and/or survey design and analysis.

It was a pleasure working with these individuals as they took a fresh and unique look at many of the animal diseases we as a nation are currently faced with. Then, as if that wasn't a sufficient palette of skills and abilities, they were also well connected with the computerized world so important to compiling information of importance to diagnostics, international trade, and agriculture program policy and development.

For me, it was an honor to be able to assist them in identifying the resources and/or partnering organizations that would help them accomplish their goals and objectives. It was fascinating to see the wide variety of organizations and individuals with whom they would interact. This might include Commercial, State or Federal Institutions, Biologics Companies, Diagnostic Organizations, Academia and/or International Organizations as well as other individuals who might be helpful in their daily search for answers.

There was so much to do and the atmosphere was filled with creative energies and passions for excellence and knowledge that would keep one's brain buzzing from now until eternity. Each day was exciting to wake up to and as you might understand, I was one who wanted to meet all of their hopes and expectations for the future! And yet, as is easily understood, we, as a Federal Organization (which is no different than any other organization!) only had a certain level of resources available and thus it was necessary to focus our energies on those areas of greatest need and importance.

This necessitated a certain level of balance in our thinking to identify priorities that were critical to the disease entity or issue or flavor of the month for our nation's politicians while prioritizing those studies that had the best chance of providing the greatest benefit in the long term. This all required some flexibility while meeting the needs for the Animal Diseases negatively impacting our Nation's Livestock/Poultry industries or Public Health Initiatives at any moment in time.

When we considered the globalization of our world and the strategies for growth in our agriculture sector, we needed to consider the impact of our management practices and/or systems development packages on productivity. Furthermore, it was important that we consider any new methods of animal husbandry and/or disease control that could benefit the safety and health of our Livestock/Poultry Industries now and in the future.

Now, if this all sounds like a lot to manage and pull together, remember that we were not alone. It was the wonderful relationships we had with our colleagues in Academia, the Veterinary Profession (Practitioners), the various Livestock Organizations as well as a wide variety of other organizations that made each and every discovery so exciting. These colleagues may have had an interest in animal health, animal welfare, marketing, environmental preservation and/or possibly the symbiotic relationships of the various plants and animals that make up our planet called earth. Sometimes people forget that we need these types of relationships in order to keep our planet healthy and inviting, especially for those of us who cherish life and a life of abundance as is God's desire for us all.

An important part of this organization was a special unit that was responsible for nationally monitoring animal health. They had a systematic approach to surveying animal populations that incorporated a wide variety of questions/issues that would be most meaningful to the Livestock/Poultry Industries we served. The surveys were designed and based on the needs of the specific industry being studied. In fact the needs were, in most cases, identified by the livestock industry members themselves. This created a greater buy-in by the affected industries. It helped assure that those participating in the survey would take the time needed to fill out the data collection forms to the best of their ability. This would be beneficial in that we would then have the greatest chance of achieving the highest level of accuracy so important to our results/conclusions/findings.

As you might imagine, a lot of time was taken in the design of the survey forms to assure that there would be no confusion as to what each of the questions was asking for. Not only that, we also wanted to be sure that we would be able to validate our conclusions by the use of scientific proven methodologies. I must say the value of this approach was most evident and in my opinion, greatly improved the accuracy of our survey results. I admit, however, that I had no idea what all was involved in the development of such surveys until I worked with some of these individuals who could make such a difference in our survey results.

This Center works in many areas of Animal Health that are truly on the cutting edge both philosophically and scientifically. One such area was that of a disease of concern in cattle called, Johne's Disease. It was a disease that had gone for years as a disease entity of little significance. But, Whoa, La! How little we knew? Fortunately, more recently, the significance of this disease has taken on a life of its own as we have learned more, much more about the impact of this disease especially in the dairy industry. You see, Johne's Disease is a very slow acting disease. It takes years to reach its full potential. As such, we in the veterinary profession have unfortunately missed the significance of this disease for far too long. But then, thanks to the dairy industry, we are beginning to see the light and the importance of this little known disease.

As you may be aware, dairy cows can provide milk for many years and therefore, dairy farmers will generally keep their animals for a much longer period of time than beef herd owners. This has been beneficial in that it has provided us with more time in which to observe the impact of diseases, such as Johne's Disease, that are often missed in the early stages of the disease process.

Now, as a result of the observations of several Veterinary Scientists (especially in the Ohio State Veterinarian's Office, Cornell University and Pennsylvania State University), we have learned that the negative impact of these diseases is much broader than we had once thought. After more in-depth study we now have concluded that diseases such as Johne's Disease can cause extensive losses due to reduced overall growth, reduced milk production, let alone the serious intestinal problems associated with the disease.

What is interesting is as we have studied this disease, we find that the Medical Profession indicates that the causative agent, Mycobacterium avium subspecies paratuberculosis (MAP) may also play a role in a condition in humans called Crohn's Disease? Of further interest is the finding that Crohn's Disease demonstrates similar clinical signs and symptoms as Johne's Disease. Unfortunately, in humans the condition can become quite severe requiring surgical intervention to remove some of the damaged colon/intestine. The good news, however, according to many physicians, is that when the Mycobacterium agent is isolated, intensive treatment will often assure a patients' recovery and a dramatic improvement in their quality of life.

According to them, there may be several factors/disease agents that may result in a disease condition observed as Crohn's Disease. As such, could we be at our infancy in understanding such disease processes? Could much more be achieved if we in the Veterinary Professions worked more closely with our colleagues in the Medical Professions in diseases of this kind? Actually, I am pleased to note that the joint Veterinary/Medical initiatives called "One Health" are a step in that direction and will reap benefits for generations to come.

With that, I believe enough has been said about my concerns with the impact of this organism on human and/or animal life. Obviously, I don't know all the answers to such questions. And yet with the seriousness of the problems, I would like to see more research energy devoted to this issue and possible treatments that might be useful in Johne's Disease in animals as well as Crohn's Disease in humans. I believe in research and have found that when we devote our resources to some of the world's most difficult disease questions, we always seem to find answers and often answers that will surprise us and result in a benefit to mankind.

Another issue of concern to this Institution was that of the marketability of our livestock and livestock products worldwide. While the genetics, health and quality of our exports are of prime concern, it has often irritated me when the logistics of such transactions impede our negotiations as well as the international acceptance and transport of the animals/products en route. To me the use of electronic communication in the health certification process would address most of the concerns in this regard. While a lot of groundwork has been done, there is much that still needs to be done relative to the acceptance of electronic health certifications. While GlobalVetLink under the leadership of Dr. Kevin Maher has devoted a lot of energy to fostering acceptance of electronic animal health certification for interstate movements of livestock and poultry, it just blows my mind that this idea hasn't been accepted on the international front.

The benefits to electronic certification are immense and yet we seem to stick to the old cumbersome ways of paper shuffling, the use of mail, and expensive overnight parcels to finish our work each day. Maybe the Office of International Epizooties (OIE) in Paris, France should take this under their wing. As such, I would encourage the formation of a committee to develop an internationally acceptable Electronic Animal Health Certification procedure that would be available to the 150 plus or minus member countries.

The benefits internationally include:

- Shipment of animals in a timely manner.
- Better understanding of any specific health and/or other requirements needed.
- Less hassle at the port of destination.
- Less confusion by the Practicing Veterinarian and others involved in preparing the animals for export.
- Ability to have only one database held by a trusted International Organization

such as OIE to serve the world as a reference database.

- Better correlation between various aspects of the Export Certification Process. This would include laboratory test results, field test results, and health examinations by Veterinary Practitioners. It might also include other Certifications such as those relating to the animal's genetics and/or the Regional Animal Health Disease Status as required by the importing countries.

All of this can be implemented in stages. Just the efficiency of such operations through digital electronic communication would save millions if not hundreds of millions of dollars each year. The process alone would facilitate the availability of highly desirable genetic stock/animals and would greatly improve livestock productivity worldwide.

Now, I would like to turn our attention to another subject. While in Colorado, I also tried to take care of myself (not that it is all about me!) and made it a point to go to a near-by gym at the end of each work day. It was the type of gym that met my stiff criteria. It was a small gym with cardio, free weights and most importantly the price was at the cheapest end of the scale. It didn't need to be fancy and in fact was usually about as basic as they come. And yet it had everything I needed, was at a convenient location and the membership was always helpful as I tried to find new movements that would improve my health and give me renewed energy.

Well, about the third week of my stay in Fort Collins, a gigantic rain storm decided to come our way in the middle of the night. I have never seen so much rain and unfortunately it created a flood like I have never seen. In fact the trailer park located behind the gym I visited was just about totally washed away. As reported by the news media the following morning, several of the residents in that trailer park noted that in the middle of the night, their trailers were lifted up by a tidal wave of water and pushed quite some distance out into an open field. What a terrible sight to behold! Of all the people affected, it had to be those with limited income and just enough to pay for their home (a trailer) and the lot rental fees, but not enough for insurance.

Also, of all the buildings to be devastated by this storm on the Colorado State University Campus was the University's Library. Unfortunately the Library's basement was flooded and apparently this was the location for most of the reference books used by the students. What a tragic loss for all concerned. But as in most cases the community came forth and volunteers galore helped to save as many books as possible and to try to do all they could to help the multitude of individuals who had unfortunately lost their homes in this disaster.

Again, the lesson learned was that none of us are alone in this world. None of us can make it alone in this world. It takes all of us working together to live life to the fullest. We never know when we may have rough times. But once you have, you know the value of your friends and neighbors. Then there comes an even greater realization in that others care and will respond to your needs even when they have no idea who you are.

This is one of the wonderful results of God's creation and it is important that we realize this whether the need be individual, local, state, national or international in scope. When we are willing to give, it is always amazing to me what we receive in return.

CHAPTER 14

The Road to Timbuktu

What can we learn on the road to Timbuktu? Consider the rigors of obtaining manhood. Sharing our stories illuminated our different beliefs and basic life values!

Have you ever been to Timbuktu? Did you know that Timbuktu really exists? Or do you think it is just a term that in essence means a far off distant place? Yes, it is a term that is commonly used and for most people very little is known about this place. It is located in Western Africa, in a desolate location, the Sahara Desert. In some interpretations, Timbuktu means many small dunes.

To me, it has an interesting past. In the 15th and 16th centuries, Timbuktu was a bustling metropolis, a major trading center for that part of the world. It is located near the Niger River. Merchants from the far reaches of Northern Africa would often meet in Timbuktu to trade items they had in plentiful supply. This included food, cloth materials, ivory, gold, a rare but most desirable commodity, salt, as well as African native slaves. Originally numerous goat herds surrounded the city. But more recently as the Sahara Desert seems to have taken its toll, the town has diminished, the goat herds have disappeared, and the population has remained constant at about 32,000 people.

In addition, Timbuktu was known as a major center of learning. Many believe it had the first University in this part of the world. Numerous religious books were written in this place and for a period of time their scholars had an important impact on that part of the world, if not worldwide. While Timbuktu was a center for the Muslim faith, it was also an educational center for other subjects of interest such as astronomy and mathematics.

Well, I, too, have never been to Timbuktu, a city located in French West Africa in the Republic of Mali. And yet, I have traveled on the desolate road to Timbuktu and have several stories that should capture your attention and imagination. My story starts in the Capital City of Bamako, Republic of Mali. It is also located along the Niger River and today is considered the fastest growing city in all of Africa and apparently the sixth fastest growing city in the world.

The first item of business was to see an Animal Disease Diagnostic Laboratory the United States had helped build. After meeting with the Director, I was given a tour of the facility and noted several points that would be helpful in future projects of this nature. One, we, as Veterinarians or Veterinary Scientists, may know a lot about laboratory technology and laboratory tests and methodology. But, we know nothing about construction. Unfortunately what I observed was a deterioration of the structure that should not have occurred. As such, expertise in construction management is needed on site as the structure is being built.

In addition I was annoyed to find that since United States funding was used, all light fixtures in this building had to be purchased from a United States Company and shipped over to the Republic of Mali. This was unfortunate not only in the extra cost to the U.S. taxpayer for the shipment, but also the realization that there were no replacement light bulbs for these light fixtures to be found anywhere in all of Western Africa. Therefore, most of the structure was in the dark as one after another of the bulbs outlived their usefulness. You can be sure that was a high priority item on my list when I returned home to see that a supply of replacement light bulbs was shipped over as soon as possible. Furthermore, while measures were taken to assure a plentiful water supply from the near-by river, there was a problem in assuring that a constant source of electricity was available. This was an infrastructure problem of concern for the whole Country.

After visiting the laboratory, the U. S. Agricultural Attaché and I were on our way out into the countryside on the road to Timbuktu. The road for the most part followed the Niger River. This was understandable in that as we drove further into the Sahara Desert, the only plant life that was visible was along either side of this mighty river. From my perspective, the banks of the Niger were the only sites where agricultural production could exist. Their main crops included millet, rice, sorghum, and corn. Then, as for Livestock production, it was basically limited to herds of sheep, goats, and cattle.

Within a couple hours we were at our destination meeting with a local cattle owner. His home was a small green cinderblock building in close proximity to the road. In addition, there were several staked canopies protecting numerous women and children from the hot desert sun. Just outside the green cinderblock building was the owner, a gentleman in his forties with two of his elder sons.

Upon our arrival they immediately welcomed us and showed great hospitality in shaking our hands and nodding their heads while smiling broadly to show how happy they were to see us. The owner motioned to the area they were seated and we all sat comfortably on the ground in a circle. Having just arrived after a long ride, they wanted to offer us some fresh water to drink. What I was not prepared for, was how they approached us with their ladle full of water. First of all, you must realize that I had just been advised by our Attaché that for health reasons, I should, by no means and especially in the rural countryside, drink any of their water. So be it for health reasons, because before I knew it, one of the sons approached me from my blind side, my back, lowered a ladle of fresh water to my lips, tilted it to where I was drinking of this refreshing water, and thinking, "Oh well so much for that advice"! I nodded my thanks and finished drinking all that was provided. I noticed our U. S. Attaché did the same and felt, oh, sure, I was probably in safe hands.

We talked about many things including their lifestyle and the business of raising cattle. But one of the questions that will always stick in my mind was the owner's inquiry into my personal life. It was one of the first questions asked and that was, "How many wives did I have?" Now that is a question I had never been asked before. I believe in our society it is assumed we all have just one. But I took his question seriously and answered with a smile, "Just one sir, just one." With that, he shook his head in a negative way while looking disappointed. So I asked, "Well, Sir, how many wives do you have?" He immediately sat straight up with his chest puffed up and his shoulders pulled back and said while smiling broadly and nodding in a most approving and proud matter, "I have sixteen wives!!!" With that I answered hoping to share some western humor and a smile, "Well Sir, for me, one is all I can handle." Well, again he looked down as if in great disappointment and from my perspective seemed to say under his breath, "You poor, poor man!"

So then I asked a follow up question that stimulated my interest having seen all the women and children under the canopies nearby. "Well, Sir, may I ask how many children do you have?" Again he sat erect; smiled proudly; and announced that he had sixty three children!!! Then, after a few moments of hesitation and with a sparkle in his eyes; he asked how many children I had? Without a moment's hesitation, I smiled proudly and answered, "Sir, I have four children, three girls and a boy." He looked at me in disbelief and again shook his head in a negative way as if to say you poor, poor, poor man! Of course, as you noticed, I just had to throw in another "poor" for added emphasis!

Well after explaining our marital customs in the United States, he seemed to understand and the conversation continued as he explained their way of life and who knows, this may have been a way to justify why they had so many wives. He began by noting that a young boy can become a man at about the age of thirteen. The father takes his son on a long walk to a distant part of their land. It is far enough away and strange enough territory that the father knows the boy will not be able to find his way back home. The boy also knows that he must not try to find his way home. He must survive on his own in this wilderness for a period of one year after which his father will return to bring him back to the family fold. The boy is left alone to survive the year without any tools or hunting equipment provided.

In order to be accepted back home, he must learn to survive on his own. As the boy is growing up, his father shares stories of how he survived as well as those stories of his father, etc. back for several generations. So this was a big step for the young boy and an important year to prove to his family that he was a man. Now there is one more thing I haven't shared with you and that was that within that year the thirteen year old boy had to prove his manhood by killing a lion and upon his father's return, show proof of his having accomplished that by producing a trophy of sorts (possibly the lion's ears). As the story unfolded, the father noted that most of the boys do not survive. He emphasized, however, the importance of the boy to manhood ritual to the future of their society and their family as a whole. This ritual assured their survival giving them strength, determination and fortitude for generations to come. Although he never said that this created quite an imbalance in their male to female ratio, it all seemed to come together and I now better understood how one could possibly justify having numerous wives.

As you might imagine, it was quite another thing when I shared this story with my wife, Joanne. I will never forget her looking me straight in the eye while pointing her finger and jabbing me in the chest and saying. "Well, buster, if we lived in that culture, all I can say is you had better be sure that I was your number one wife, got it?" And as you would assume, my answer was a lovingly, "Yes, dear, you know that you will always be number one!!!"

Soon it was time for lunch and the proud father of sixteen wives asked us to accompany him into his home, the green cinder block building. It was a small home about the size of a small bedroom with a chest on one side wall and a single bed with springs and a mattress along another wall. We sat in a circle and one of the wives brought in a small tub of water for us to wash our right hand. Yes our right hand only. As my friend and Agriculture Attaché explained only the right hand is used for eating. The left hand is used for other purposes, generally for sanitary measures associated with rear hind end (toilet) cleanliness so to speak if you understand what I am saying. So being the honored guest I washed/rinsed my right hand in this bowl of water so generously provided and waited to see what would follow.

Within a few minutes, allowing the hand to air dry, another one of his wives came in with a huge, a really huge bowl of rice. The Attaché after explaining to me their custom, helped me out by demonstrating how they gather the rice with their right hand rolling it up in their palm to what might look like a rice hot dog and then slowly partaking of the food from the heal of your hand up to the area of your palm next to your thumb. The only place I had ever eaten, in a similar manner, with my hands was in a traditional restaurant in the Philippines. And so, as might be expected, the customs were somewhat strange to behold and to participate in. As I was finishing my first hand full of rice, I suddenly realized that this was the only rice prepared and that it was prepared for not only each of us, but also his sixteen wives and sixty three children. Suddenly I was not hungry in the least and while trying to be courteous, ate only a little more and then refused any further offerings of rice and thanked the host graciously for the meal.

After the meal, the host indicated he wanted to treat me in a special way by having me participate in their Tea Ceremony. I was indeed honored as he took a small pot and after adding a few tea leaves, poured in a little water. As I remember it, he had a small heating unit about the size of a small kerosene lamp to heat this pot, steeping the tea from the tea leaves provided. After the water had boiled for a spell, he poured some of the tea into individual demitasse cups for us to enjoy. During the whole process, the Tea Ceremony was a celebration of sorts! The ceremony was one of recognition, honor, and respect. The conversation was lively and filled with laughter and joy! To be with the host and his sons who had achieved manhood (thereby being allowed to be a part of this inner circle) was special, indeed! While we were enjoying the tea, the host poured a little more water into the pot and again let what tea remained in the tea leaves steep out and then refilled each of our small cups with the fragrant and tasty tea. This ritual was repeated several times until it was clear that all of the tea leaves had been used up and no further steeping of tea would occur.

As this ritual was about to end, the host asked if I was tired from the day's journey and would I like to use his bed for an afternoon nap. I thanked him kindly and noted that we needed to return to Bamako, their Capital and that I so appreciated his generosity, hospitality as well as his sharing of his knowledge and experience in raising cattle and how he maintained such a healthy, productive herd.

We parted our ways; having learned more about the diversity of our world, its customs and ideas for the future. It was interesting to note how mankind has addressed the many and varied environments and living conditions while living a full and wonderful God-given life. Another experience I shall never forget.

CHAPTER 15

The Maasai People

To the Maasai, God gave them all of the cattle on earth. This can be problematic. There is much that can be learned, especially in regard to their understanding of the environment and how to protect it.

My story starts in 1983 with a trip to Nairobi, Kenya to welcome Dr. Christopher Groocock, to our Agency's first International Office in the Continent of Africa. This Post was created to cover our interests in Animal and Plant Health in Africa, Eastern Europe and the Middle East.

My first stop was in the Capital City of Addis Ababa, Federal Democratic Republic of Ethiopia. Unfortunately, this country has had a history of civil wars, draught and famine. Nevertheless, it has always accepted refugees from other countries and I understand that even continues to this day. Ethiopia is probably one of the fastest growing economies in all of Africa and has archeological sites depicting some of the earliest remains of mankind. I was impressed by their genuine kindness, honesty, and beauty.

They were committed to protecting their environment and expressed pride in a recent project that achieved great success. Their awareness of nature and their skills in using their observations to their advantage just blew my mind! In this instance they recognized the important role trees play in their environment and especially how their presence relates to the amount of rainfall received. While trees are known for their ability to remove carbon dioxide and add oxygen to the air; they also give off an abundance of water vapor. They witnessed a cooling effect not only due to the shade provided, but also because of the large amount of water vapor discharged into the surrounding area on a daily basis. This contributed to their cloud formation and as a result the amount of rainfall received. So you might ask where do trees find water? Apparently many species of trees have root systems that not only anchor the tree to the ground, but also grow to greater depths attracted to any underground streams or water found nearby.

Therefore, in order to increase the amount of rain, these astute Ethiopians decided to plant a lot, I mean and emphasize the word "Lot" of trees in an area of their country marginally affected by draught. Then, for the best part; according to the information relayed to me, their observations were correct in that rainfall in that area dramatically increased especially after the trees had matured and grown in size. To me, this was remarkable and an important find that needs to be shared worldwide. The planting of trees is obviously the key to providing the rain needed to increase productivity of marginal land thereby benefiting the lives of so many worldwide.

Well, soon I was in Nairobi, Kenya. I met Dr. Groocock and we were on our way to the East African Veterinary Organization Research Laboratory located just on the outskirts of Nairobi in Muguga, Kenya. This laboratory is well known. It is where a Dr. Walter Plowright began his historic discovery in the 1950s of an effective tissue culture vaccine to protect cattle from Rinderpest. Apparently, at that time, some of his colleagues joked that there was no way to eradicate this disease even with this amazing vaccine. From their standpoint there was an insurmountable obstacle and that was another host for this disease, the wild, cantankerous wildebeest. No-one, absolutely no-one on earth could get near enough, let alone vaccinate those wild critters! Then, as they soon found out, Dr. Plowright proved them wrong and personally wrestled them down, one by one, and got them vaccinated as was required to eliminate this disease from the continent.

To understand the seriousness of this disease, we need to note that Rinderpest in the 1760s caused such havoc that the Human Medical Profession decided to train individuals to be specialists in fighting and controlling this troubling disease of cattle. This led to the development of the Science of Veterinary Medicine and the first Veterinary College being established in Lyons, France the very next year. Then, much later, in 1865 this disease was of such concern to the government of England that they decided to create another first, a Veterinary Services Unit within their Federal Government. When Rinderpest spread to Belgium in 1920, it became obvious that a multinational approach to the control of this disease needed to be established. Within a year an international meeting of Veterinary Scientists was held in Paris and as a result of this meeting, the World Organization for Animal Health (Office International des Epizooties) was established in 1924 and headquartered in Paris, France.

And now, the Veterinary Profession is elated in that in May 2011, the World Organization for Animal Health (OIE) announced that the world is finally free of this destructive disease called Rinderpest. Isn't it wonderful and amazing that the disease that was the impetus for the beginning of Veterinary Medicine is the first animal disease to be totally eradicated from the world! What is interesting is that the last outbreak of Rinderpest was, of all places, in Kenya in 2001. Since then, no cases of this disease have been diagnosed anywhere in the world.

Well, the next day Dr. Groocock and I continued our tour and visited the International Center of Insect Physiology and Ecology (ICIPE) located in a suburb of Nairobi called Kasarani. The Director there was most hospitable and took the time to explain the purpose of their mission and to answer any questions we might have had. A lot of their work is centered on the control of the Tsetse Fly that carries pathogenic Trypanosomes that cause problems such as Sleeping Sickness in Humans and Nagana in animals. It was interesting to understand that while their focus was to control such harmful entities on the human and animal populations, they wanted to find methodologies of control that could be used without undo cost or burden to the general public. They were also interested in finding methods that were environmentally safe to use on a daily basis without a negative impact in any way on the environment in general. I must say that I applaud this philosophy of operation and hope all of us will be more supportive of organizations that consider the importance of this philosophy in the future.

Now the next morning I was all excited because we were heading out to the Rift Valley and Lake Nakuru, the home of a million or more pink Flamingos. What a beautiful sight to behold. There were thousands of pink flamingos to be seen. The setting was perfect. I was mesmerized by their presence, not only along the shoreline, but also in the air. Their colorful pink bodies calmed the senses as they competed with a palette of colors including an aqua blue lake surface and white puffs of clouds against a light blue sky. What a joy!

But now, let's talk about the valley, itself. As you may know, the Rift Valley is a huge valley with gigantic cliffs on either side. These cliffs were formed by the tectonic movement of the earth's plates (separation of the surface of the earth) creating a geological rift or fault. It is a spectacle to behold.

Unfortunately it is also the site of a devastating disease called Rift Valley Fever. The animals affected by this disease include cattle, buffalo, sheep, goats, camels, mice, rats, puppies, kittens, wild ruminants and oh no, it also affects humans. It was first described by a Drs. Montgomery and Stordy in Kenya in 1912-13. The virus, however, wasn't isolated until about 1931. The disease usually appears after an abnormally high rainfall (similar in some respects to Vesicular Stomatitis).

In livestock the first wave of infection is basically 100% abortions. It is spread by several species of mosquitoes including the Aedes and Culex Mosquitoes. In 1977-78 several million people were affected and several thousand died. It was a serious epidemic. In 1998 an epidemic of Rift Valley Fever killed over four hundred people in Kenya. In general, most of the cases of this serious disease seem to have occurred in or near the Rift Valley. How can that be? While we have learned much in the last seventy years, there is still much that we don't know about the reservoirs and epidemiological spread of this disease. Again, we have so much to learn!

Now, if we consider this valley and the extent of this shift of tectonic plates we can see a relatively close succession of Rift Valleys from as far north as Turkey (possibly thought by some to be the origin of the Garden of Eden) along the Sea of Galilee, Israel, Euphrates River and Red Sea, through Ethiopia, Kenya and down to Southern Africa. Apparently many geologists claim this Rift may be as long as 3,700 miles. Some refer to this area as the Cradle of Civilization. In fact, in the areas of Ethiopia and Kenya there are many Early and Middle Stone Age Archeological Finds pointing to the earliest remnants of civilization and the presence of human remains.

There are many stories including that of the Queen of Sheba (from Ethiopia). Apparently she visited one of the richest and wisest men of history, King Solomon. You may remember King Solomon (960 to 922 BC) in that he is the one that built the first Jewish Temple (in Israel) housing the sacred Ark as previously carried by the followers of Moses during the Jewish exodus from Egypt. At that time there was extensive trade between their two countries and the Jewish belief in one God from the beginning of time was reaffirmed in the land of Sheba (Ethiopia/Southern part of the Red Sea). It is also of interest in that the Ethiopian Orthodox Church currently claims they have the Ark of the Covenant in one of their churches. It is, according to them, located in the Holy of Holies in the Church of our Lady Mary of Zion in Axum, Ethiopia.

According to ancient scripture, the Ark of the Covenant contained God's Law (the Ten Commandments) as inscribed on stone tablets; Aaron's Sapphire Rod (Representing the power of God) and a Jar of Manna (Representing the daily provision of God). This is noteworthy in that the Ark of the Covenant, while known to have been in the first Temple in Jerusalem, was not in the second temple of Jerusalem. As a result, if this is the original Ark of the Covenant, it must have been transferred around the time of the destruction of the first Temple by the Babylonians and taken to the southern part of their territory (in or near what we now consider Ethiopia). Furthermore, it is interesting to note that Ethiopia is one of the first countries (in the fourth century) to have established Christianity as their State Religion.

All of this is quite meaningful to me in that the people in Ethiopia as well as the Maasai people of Kenya are basically loving, caring, devout God loving people who have renounced slavery even while their trading partners in other parts of Africa supported slavery and allowed it to continue. I do believe that with their strong Jewish roots from King Solomon and the passage of their oral stories, they knew the suffering of the Israeli people under slavery in Egypt and were strong proponents of preventing slavery from ever occurring under their so called, "Watch". I also so appreciate their oral tradition and belief in one God, Creator of this world. While the Maasai people practice several Jewish traditions such as circumcision, they are Christians. They have a strong belief in the creation of Jesus as one being, not part God and part man, but rather God in Human form as accomplished through the immaculate conception of Mary, mother of Jesus.

Whether you believe this or not, to me this along with my personal experience is overwhelming proof that the stories of the

Bible are true evidence of God's presence in our world; God's role as the Originator/ Creator of our world; and God's wish for us to love Him with all of our heart, soul, mind, and strength while loving all of our fellow men (men and women) as ourselves. For what it is worth, as a trained Veterinarian in Veterinary Science, viewing the complexity of this world, I cannot understand how people can even begin to doubt that our world was created by our one and only triune God; the Father, the Son and the Holy Ghost.

Sometimes I think the evolutionists go way too far with theories based on their faulty belief system. It is aggravating to read their assumptions and reference points without any consideration for the complexity, biodiversity and strict atmospheric, biological tolerances that are so critical to life. When we consider the statistical probability of the world being created by random events, the probability of such occurring is, in my realm of beliefs, zero. Even the formation of some of the simplest molecules by random selection and/or events, let alone the formation of complex systems, enzymes, or hormones and the miracle of life would be preposterous. Sometime when I am really in a foul mood, I even question what scientific data the evolutionists base their radiocarbon dating processes on? Is this process loaded with assumptions that no one can really rely on? Even they admit that the atmospheric levels of carbon 14 are not constant.

So, with that, let's continue with our story! Soon we were on our way to Voi, Kenya. As we approached that part of the country we were in an area inhabited by the Nomadic Maasai people. Historically, it has been reported that the Maasai originated in the southern part of the Nile River. We arrived late in the afternoon and as we drove into town, there was an elderly lady sitting by herself on the side of the road at one of the intersections. As we pulled to a stop to check for traffic, this lady caught my eye and before I knew it, she was up and approaching our car. She was dressed in a traditional Maasai dress and smiled as she greeted us in the Swahili Language. I was most fortunate in that Dr. Groocock was familiar with the Swahili Language. He was able to translate and to share her greeting, welcoming us to the Town of Voi. Apparently she noticed that we were strangers to that area and wanted us to feel welcomed and to know that they were happy to have us visit.

Then, I was caught off guard and somewhat confused as she showed me a beautiful bracelet she was wearing on her wrist. It appeared to have been handmade of brass wire and several gorgeous stones/jewels. According to Dr. Groocock, she wanted to give me this beautiful bracelet as a gift to welcome me to their land and to remind me of the hospitality of their people. I had difficulty accepting her gift and refused, thinking that this was probably the most precious thing she owned. To take that would be inappropriate. Dr. Groocock encouraged me to accept the gift, but in my heart, I just couldn't do it. So I thanked her and soon we were on our way.

As we were driving along later in the day, I expressed my surprise that anyone would be so generous. It was then that Dr. Groocock explained that in the Maasai culture, the welcoming of strangers is an important custom. In fact, if one sees a stranger and wants to truly make them feel welcome, they are to give them a gift and that gift must be the best of what they have. Apparently they also believe that if the stranger accepts their gift, their life will be blessed with much goodness. However if the gift is refused, their life will be filled with much sorrow and/or difficulty. Oh Boy, I did it again. By not knowing the custom, I blew it and messed up another life for which I had no such intention. It was too late by then and unfortunately what happened, happened!

The Maasai are an interesting group of people who, according to their tradition, believe the Creator established them as the owner and caretakers of all of the world's cattle. Apparently, they have been known to take cattle from other tribes with the belief that they are only repossessing that which is rightfully their own. In fact, while visiting one of the Maasai elders; I was asked with a smile on his face, whether I was taking good care of their cattle in America. I responded with a broad smile on my face, that indeed I was and that he could rest assured that all of the cattle in the United States were well cared for. He nodded and said that he and his people were most appreciative in that the United States was a long distance away and that it might be a while before they could make the trip.

The hard work ethic of the Maasai people was most evident. The young boys are responsible for the care of their cattle as they feed on the Savannah grasses. In the evening, they bring the cattle into the family corral to assure they are protected from the wild animals, lions, etc. The adult men are responsible for the gathering of food and the building of the family corral (fencing made of thorny acacia trees). And the women are responsible for the gathering of the milk, the preparing of the meals and the building of their homes, thatched buildings (built/made by hand). The building of their homes is a laborious task including the framing of the buildings with tree limbs; the thatching of grasses around the framework; and then covering the grass with cattle manure and either human and/or cattle urine. This process is necessary to assure the entire structure is waterproof and thus provides a safe, warm but crowded hut structure for their family to live in. All of this is important to their survival and that of their livestock (mostly cattle and possibly some goats and/or sheep).

While in Voi, we stayed at a local resort. I was intrigued by the beauty of the animals and was looking forward to seeing more of them early the next morning. Apparently, as was their custom, they would gather at the local watering hole to bathe and refresh their thirst as a new day began. What fun, the possibility of seeing them was exciting indeed! So the next day I arose early in the morning before sunrise hoping to see as many of the animals as possible. However what I wasn't ready for was the presence of a tall Maasai Warrior dressed in his rich, draped, red clothing with yellow designs. Apparently he was assigned to assure my protection during the night and in no way was he about to let me leave the Resort facility at that time of day.

The only word I knew in Swahili was "Jambo", a shortened Swahili version of a greeting used by tourists which is translated as "Hello". Now as you probably realize, there isn't much that can be said when the only word we both understood was "Jambo".

However, it must have been very clear that this usage of "Jambo" was not only a greeting of "Hello", but in effect was referencing a problem recently affecting us both.

Finally when the English speaking staff arrived, I explained my disappointment in not being able to go to the local watering hole. It was frustrating to have this Maasai Warrior interfering with my plans. I probably exhibited a bit of anger in that this was the only morning that I would have had such an opportunity. Was I ever surprised when the Resort Manager advised that I should thank this man for saving my life! You see, the watering hole is a very dangerous place early in the morning and one is placing their life in grave danger when they are present while the animals are gathering at the break of day.

Well after a hearty breakfast we were off and I must say we were able to observe numerous animals in the wild. It was an honor and privilege to see them in that they were in outstanding condition, full of life and the healthiest I have ever seen. The giraffes would come right up to our jeep while the zebras and wildebeest were running in the distance. Once a herd of elephants decided to cross the road in front of us and of course we let them have the right of way. The herd included all ages and the care of the young was most notable. On one occasion we saw a pride of lions shaded under a tree and one would hardly guess how dangerous they could be as they rested peacefully with their cubs under the noon day sun. A little while later we came upon a Cape Water Buffalo standing in the middle of the road. Of course we stopped! The look on his face as he turned to check us out made it quite clear that we in no way should try to mess with him. His glance in retrospect said it all, "Don't even try to come any closer. Don't even try it! Bud!" So we stopped and waited and waited until he proved he was the boss and moved on.

Later we saw hippopotamuses bathing in a river and I learned that you do not want to mess with them either. If you have never witnessed the life style of the Common/ River Hippopotamus, let me explain. They are aggressive, dangerous and unpredictable. In other words, you only observe them from a distance. They usually weigh about four thousand pounds as adults. They can be found in slow moving rivers in the day time and come out at night when it is cooler to look for green pastures. They are social among their own kind and are often found in groups of about forty animals with one bull and the rest cows or young calves. Bulls are known to fight to their death to have their own Harem. What is unfortunate is that the local farmers have been killing them off. From the farmer's point of view, the Hippos are competing with their livelihood and as such, destroying the crops they have planted along the only fertile land that can be irrigated and that is along the river plain.

What a rich environment of animal life! Oh to be able to preserve this for future generations to enjoy. Even the majestic Kilimanjaro Mountain in the distance seemed to emphasize the importance of our God given responsibility to preserve the multitude of resources God has given us to enjoy. I believe the Maasai (as well as the American Indians) understand, better than we, the importance of having symbiotic relationships on planet earth. Even more importantly, we need to learn how to live in sync with our animal and plant life while preserving the quality of our water, and soil so critical to our survival. Once we recognize the importance of these life sustaining principles, we will become a true partner in the majesty of life. Together, with God's presence in our lives, the masterpiece of life can and will flourish; exceeding all of our dreams and expectations! To all of that, I can only say, "Hallelujah" and "Amen"!

CHAPTER 16

Land of the Drug Lords

Sometimes veterinarians work in dangerous places. In this case, the U.S. Embassy required a few attitude changes before we could accomplish the mission at hand.

As part of our effort to prevent the northern spread of certain animal diseases of economic importance, various animal disease control possibilities were discussed with our counterparts in the South American Country of Colombia. More specifically, we were interested in a disease of cattle called, Foot-and-Mouth Disease. At that time, all of North America was and has continued to be free of this disease. Since this disease was still prevalent throughout South America, we in the United States were concerned about any possible spread and especially any spread into our part of the world.

This disease has caused serious economic consequences in every country within which it has occurred. It is feared by countries free of the disease and is a highly volatile political disease as well. One case of this disease in a country, previously free of this disease, results in massive embargoes being imposed by numerous countries effectively cancelling all future shipments of cattle, sheep, goats, hogs, etc. as well as their meat and byproducts. It causes negative economic consequences for the country affected and takes years to rebuild.

After much discussion, an agreement, on how to prevent the northern spread of this destructive disease, was finally reached by the Colombian Officials and my predecessor's (Dr. Norvan Meyer's) Animal Health Team, including the highly skilled leadership of Dr. John Wyss, the U.S. Co-Director in this special activity. We agreed that the expansion of a National Park to include all of the Colombian side of the Colombian-Panamanian Border would be most helpful. The key provision of this agreement was that no domestic livestock would be allowed within the area identified as the National Park. Surely this would prove to be of benefit in minimizing any risk of Livestock Diseases and especially Foot-and-Mouth Disease moving into Panama, Central America and as a result all of North America. Then, to further strengthen the agreement, a well defined area adjacent to the National Park and within the interior of Colombia was identified within which to jointly implement an extensive Foot-and-Mouth Disease Surveillance, Control, and Eradication Program that would be mutually beneficial to us all. With these provisions, an International Agreement was formulated and signed by the United States of America and Colombia.

The success of this program in controlling and eradicating Foot-and-Mouth Disease was phenomenal! Starting in the 1970s, Colombia had, in less than five years, not only contained the disease; basically eradicating the disease from the area, but had also increased productivity of their livestock herds in that area by over 200 per cent. This included increased weight gains and reduced losses due to disease including diseases other than Foot-and-Mouth Disease. This, in my estimation, should be a model for Animal Disease Control Programs worldwide! As demonstrated in Colombia, the program's bio-security measures, as implemented at their markets and on their farms, so limited the spread of disease that they not only dramatically increased productivity, but also profitability beyond all expectations. And, to the surprise of many, this all occurred within a relatively short period of time.

I have even heard, on several occasions, the benefits of such an animal disease control program as extolled by the very industries affected. According to them, they are able to observe significant increases in productivity and in their opinion; this was due to the program controls that reduced spread of other debilitating diseases of concern. Apparently, a five to ten percent increase in productivity is often recognized. This is so important in demonstrating that there is still much that can be done to improve Animal Health or even Public Health, especially when we consider those diseases reported in the media and of concern to the public as well.

This includes a wide variety of diseases and especially those disease agents that are frequently referenced, such as Salmonella and E. coli. What is unfortunate in most cases is that such disease situations can and should be prevented. Premise sanitation as mentioned in earlier chapters can make a big difference. This is true for all Livestock-Poultry-Animal-Human Diseases. As a case in point, let's consider the disease of Salmonella in poultry:

- If poultry manure is piled next to the hen house and not hauled away, we are asking for problems.
- If manure is not hauled away regularly from under the chicken coops and pest control for Dung Beetles etc. is not completed on a regular basis to control infestations, we are asking for problems.

- If we have no rodent control and the buildings are not rodent proof, we are asking for problems.
- If we transfer equipment or egg and poultry crates between farms without adequate cleaning and disinfection, we are asking for trouble.

In reality, if chickens are raised in healthy, sanitary conditions, the eggs have a natural barrier to the entry of disease especially if the eggs are properly washed and sanitized. These precautions should prevent any diseases of human concern to arrive at the grocery store. In such situations, it is my belief that the only way an egg can be contaminated is if the chicken laying the egg is sickened with, for example, a Salmonella infection. That, however, should be quickly recognized by the egg producer, especially if there is reduced egg production, ruffled feathers, general poor conditioning, and an increase in death loss.

In such instances, I believe the owners have a moral obligation and responsibility to hold the eggs produced until the diagnostic work necessary to identify the problem is done. This is important in preventing any subsequent Public Health consequences that could or most likely would occur. In well maintained facilities with sound disease control procedures in place, such occurrences are extremely rare if they occur at all.

While I have had extensive experience personally with swine and poultry diseases, the same sanitation problems can be significant in all livestock operations. As a Veterinarian, I can often sense the amount of difficulty I might have in arriving at a definitive diagnosis by observing the premise sanitation upon my arrival. If sanitation is poor, I will find the process of arriving at a diagnosis to be far more complex, often involving several entities that may be bacterial, viral, nutritional, parasitic, and in some cases toxic in nature.

In such instances the owner may want a quick fix; when in reality the resolution of the problem may be more complex than anticipated. It may and often does require the implementation of the basics of sound animal husbandry before much can be accomplished. That is why National Animal Disease Control Programs can, to the uninitiated, be quite challenging and frustrating at first. But when we see the results of the entire industry working together to improve biosecurity and basic animal husbandry-disease control, it is amazing not only at the productivity gains that can be achieved by each owner, but also by the industry as a whole. We all win in such circumstances.

Now in this instance the gains achieved in the control of Foot-and-Mouth Disease in Northern Colombia were quite significant. Their successes motivated other farming groups outside the area to be a part of the program. As a result tremendous success has been achieved throughout Colombia and in fact all of South America. This is not to say that it was all accomplished easily. For one reason, the northern part of Colombia, essentially near Medellin, Colombia has had a reputation of having been controlled in many respects by drug cartels. It is sad, but true that Medellin has had the reputation of being the most violent city in the world. While the country and area is trying to curtail the violence and drug cartel activity, it is unfortunate to observe the heightened level of resistance, to these efforts, taking place as well as the continuing trend of increased crime.

In our work with the Colombian Government, it was our hope that the joint efforts of the Cooperative United States Colombian Program could be successful on several fronts. Not only that it would free the area of Foot-and-Mouth Disease, but that it would also be helpful in reducing other animal diseases as well as increasing farm productivity and the growth of successful farming operations in the vicinity.

It was clear that a side benefit of our program activities was that of encouraging farmers to consider the benefits of raising livestock while discouraging them from growing plants that would produce the drugs needed for international export. When farmers can expect a higher standard of living for their efforts in meeting the production needs of illicit drugs, they will most likely choose that form of agriculture rather than producing traditional agriculture products or livestock. You know the almighty dollar will often win out, right? So where do most of these drugs go. Yes you are so right, right here in the United States. Why is that so?

- Do we value the almighty dollar more than our own lives or our kid's lives?
- Is our culture valuing material things more than relationships and taking care of our Heart, Mind and Soul?
- Is success, pressure to be popular, and living in luxury more important than being healthy and enjoying the simpler things in life?
- Are we pushing ourselves and our kids to value being workaholics?
- Are our expectations driving us and our kids to failure and dependence on drugs to feel good?
- Are we pushing ourselves and everyone around us to do more and as a result not take care of ourselves, lack exercise, eat quick fat saturated meals, not

get enough sleep, feel stressed out, become depressed and with poor judgment become hooked on drugs that take on a life of their own?

When are we going to learn that we cannot do everything on our own?

When are we going to recognize that we need each other for support and that we need God and a balanced life to maximize our creative energy?

When are we going to begin valuing the positive aspects and knowledge each of us brings to this world?

When are we going to enrich our lives with the refreshing feelings of having a symbiotic relationship with the world (humans, plants and animals) we live with?

Then and only then, life can be one amazing adventure of celebration and joy! Hey America, lets' get with it and recognize that which our forefathers valued! That is the value of all human life and the richness of diversity to our very existence. As such we can demolish the need for the artificial highs of drugs that are so temporary and devastating and we can then live life as it was meant to be and should be for time eternal.

Well, you may wonder how we were ever able to work with the livestock owners in an area of such heightened terror and violence. With my strong belief in God, I am sure that God was helpful every step of the way!

As you might expect, the United States Embassy wanted to learn everything about the drug activities in the areas we and our Colombian Counterparts were working. We, in the United States Department of Agriculture, however, made it quite clear that we could not wear two hats. We could not assist in the control and eradication of Foot-and-Mouth Disease and also be undercover agents providing information on the activities relative to drug production. We went into this Cooperative Program with that understanding and those who worked in the Medellin Area focused on the work at hand. As far as we were concerned, we had no interest in what was going on relative to drug trafficking and the drug cartels. The workings of this cooperative effort remained focused and as a result achieved tremendous success!

Another point in this story that I would like to discuss is that in the Colombian Capital of Bogotá, there were several research facilities highly regarded by the international community. In fact, there was a Foot-and-Mouth Disease Vaccine Facility well known for their research and production of a quality vaccine. The vaccine produced by this facility was of the highest quality and known for its effectiveness in reducing the incidence of this disease in areas previously known to have had a high prevalence of this disease. As such, this facility turned out to be a critical component of the success of this important program.

Another factor that helped immensely was a meeting held in the early 1980s in Rio de Janeiro, Brazil. This was a meeting sponsored by the Pan American Health Organization to identify how each of the countries of South America could better work together to control this economically devastating disease. It was a meeting of Veterinary Epidemiologists representing each country in the South American Continent. The meeting was well received in that it provided an opportunity for each country to share of their expertise and perspective in working with this disease, Foot-and-Mouth Disease. It was a powerful meeting of the minds and proved to be the critical point in establishing the strategies that ultimately have, for the first time, achieved dramatic reductions in clinical Foot-and-Mouth Disease throughout South America.

You see, through the discussions and deliberations of these highly skilled epidemiologists (experts in how disease spreads), they suddenly realized that much of the previous failures in each of their countries was their lack of understanding as to what the cattle production role of each country was in the whole scheme of things. They didn't realize until they had gathered together that some of the South American Countries only specialized in the raising of mother cows. Their offspring would often go to another country where the calves would be raised until they were old enough to be shipped to another country to be fed out as steers for meat production. Other countries might specialize in Dairy Production, etc., etc.

Once they understood the movement of animals and how these movements impacted the spread of disease, they recognized the importance of which countries to focus on first (i.e. eliminate the disease from the mother cow countries first, then the calf countries, etc.). Then, in addition, they learned the importance of strict disease control procedures, the issuing of movement permits, health inspections, routine testing and/or the vaccination programs necessary to further safeguard the previous accomplishments made. Suddenly they were all working from the same page and supporting each other in the requirements so necessary to achieving their objectives.

While it is still taking some time to accomplish that which they had hoped to achieve (that of eradicating, yes, eliminating the presence of Foot-and-Mouth Disease in all of South America), it is amazing how far they have come and how close they are at this time to achieving that objective. As difficult as Foot-and-Mouth Disease is to control, they have made amazing progress and it won't be long before they achieve their goal of not having to deal with or struggle with this terrible disease.

Now just so you understand a little more about me and don't get the false impression about me, I would like to share a short tale about my first trip to Bogota, Colombia. I was excited as usual and especially excited to be able to view first hand some of the activities surrounding our Cooperative Program as well as to meet some of the key figures both from the government perspective as well as from the industry perspective.

While my itinerary indicated that I was to arrive in Bogota about 9:30 in the evening; airline delays, such as is often the case, had me arriving at about 3:00 am the following morning. As you can imagine I was exhausted and even though the United States Embassy had asked me to call upon my arrival, all I wanted to do was go to my hotel, check in and get some ZZZZZ's. So I caught a taxi and before long was comfortably catching some well deserved ZZZZZ's at the hotel where arrangements had been made.

I arose about 9:00 am, had a healthy breakfast and was anxious to get on the road. So I called the Foot-and-Mouth Disease

Vaccine Production facility; noted I arrived early that morning; and wondered whether I could come over at that time for a visit. Of course they were most hospitable and I quickly caught a cab arriving shortly thereafter. The meeting went well and I learned much about their operations, their future plans and some of their recent research findings. I was thrilled to have this opportunity to meet with them and then decided I had better contact the U. S. Embassy so they would know that I had arrived and to inquire whether they could have someone pick me up and bring me to the Embassy for further consultations.

As soon as their vehicle arrived, I was transported to the front door of the U. S. Embassy. Still being relatively new to Embassy protocol, it disturbed me when the Embassy Vehicle arrived and I found that it was a bullet proof vehicle. Not only that, but there was a Security Person in the front passengers' seat with a machine gun in his hands. Apparently he was assigned to protect me. Frankly I would have felt safer in a taxi and it was embarrassing when the Security Person got out first and quickly glanced in all directions flailing the gun before allowing me to enter and/or exit. I never considered myself a threat to anyone and didn't see why anyone would want to harm me. I put up with it, to my discomfort, and didn't cherish it one bit considering all the attention created by such procedures.

Well, little did I know the trouble I was in for when I arrived at the Embassy? I was immediately called to the Ambassadors' Office and chewed out royally for not contacting them upon arrival and for using a taxi instead of the Embassy Security Services for my transport to the Hotel and then to the Vaccine Production facility. In fact, the Ambassador indicated I was to spend that entire afternoon being personally briefed by their security personnel and that I must follow their security procedures exactly as required. He indicated that if he heard of even one more infraction, I would never, ever be able to come to Colombia again. Wow, I had no idea the seriousness of the situation. There was no way that I would do anything to disappoint the Embassy personnel and especially this Ambassador. The Foot-and-Mouth Disease Program in Colombia was too important to our National Security and in no way did I ever want to be prevented from visiting this part of the world again.

Nevertheless, in spite of my transgressions, the Agriculture Attaché and the Ambassador were most accommodating in helping us accomplish all that needed to be done and to facilitate the numerous government and industry contacts so important to this program and its success. And yes, I was most appreciative of their facilitating our program activities and as you might imagine, I did everything possible to be a "Good Boy", a real "Good Boy" from that point on!

CHAPTER 17

"Mustang" Challenge

For those who love horses, this is a story you will enjoy. The dynamics between veteran cowboys, Dr. Temple Grandin and myself will both amaze and enthrall you.

While horses are known to have existed in the Americas in ancient history, it is believed that the ice age took its toll and eliminated all such populations in this part of the world. As a result, there were no horses in the Americas until 1493 when Columbus, on his second voyage to the Americas, decided to bring horses from Spain to the West Indies. Then, it was not until 1519 before horses were again transported to the Americas and this time it was by Hernan Cortes, a Spanish explorer, as he brought horses from the Iberian Peninsula (Spain) to Mexico. As some of these horses escaped and/or were captured by the Indians, they eventually became established as Feral Horses or as we have more commonly called them, Wild Mustangs.

The term Mustang comes from the Mexican Spanish word Mestengo which is derived from the Spanish word, Mesteno which means Stray Livestock Animal. The American Indians found these horses to be of great advantage in transporting them from one place to another and therefore, valued their presence in their lives. They bred them for certain traits of endurance and speed and weeded out those that did not meet their needs. They recognized that they could rapidly double a population in a very short period of time and used them extensively in their somewhat nomadic culture.

Since all of our Mustangs have come from domesticated horses, the Mustangs often have a wide variety of horses in their genetic makeup. This can include any horses that escaped to the wild and include Arabians, Thoroughbreds, and in some cases heavy boned Draft Horses. Some horse enthusiasts even note that the American Quarter Horse, so popular in the west, came about from such mixtures in the wild.

Unfortunately there has been a lot of controversy centered on the Wild (Feral) Mustangs. Some people, in certain horse circles, think they are inferior to the scientific breeding accomplished by Registered Breed Organizations. Others believe and agree that in some instances they may be smaller. However, they note that this may be due in part to the fact that in the wild they forage more roughage and as a result receive less than the most desirable nutrition for optimal growth. Nevertheless, they believe that due to the tough environmental conditions within which Mustangs have had to live; any weaknesses, they might have had, are bred out. They are convinced that the Wild Mustangs carry the genetic traits of hardiness, durability, and endurance so important to the future of any and all horse breeds. They argue that while such horses can usually survive in less desirable forage areas, they can also travel fifty miles or more in a day's time to obtain water. Other livestock such as cattle, sheep and goats would not be able to survive in such conditions.

This does not mean that all is or has been well for this majestic breed. You see, livestock owners and especially the cattlemen who use the western range land have a concern that is most troublesome. From their perspective the Wild Mustangs overgraze and destroy much of the plant life so important to their raising of cattle. As such, there has been a continuing battle between the cattlemen and those who cherish the Wild Mustangs as a prime example of Americana and the Wild West.

In 1959, after much debate, the United States Congress passed a law protecting the Wild Mustangs. This was called the Wild Horse Anne Act and was passed to prohibit the use of motor vehicles in the hunting and indiscriminate harvesting of wild horses and burros for commercial purposes. This Act was named after a tireless, persistent Nevada woman, Velma B. Johnston who took on the name of Wild Horse Anne for her effective activism and lobbying efforts. Then, in 1971, after even more debate, Congress passed another law entitled the Wild Free-Roaming Horse and Burro Act. This time, the lobbyists and their supporters who so value the presence of the Wild Mustangs were elated when the United States Congress recognized Mustangs as:

> **"Living symbols of the historic and pioneer spirit of the West, which continue to contribute to the diversity of life forms within the Nation and enrich the lives of the American People."**

This Act provided protections for certain previously established herds of Wild (Feral) Horses and Burros. As a result, the Bureau of Land Management of the Department of Interior and the Forest Service of the United States Department of Agriculture were given the regulatory authority to oversee the protection and management of the Wild Mustang populations that were located on the public lands they already managed. Since most if not all

Wild Mustangs are located on public land managed by the Bureau, they have in essence been given primary authority. As such they have done much to protect the Wild Mustang populations and at the same time protect the fragile environment within which they roam. While some rough estimates in the early 1900s noted a population of around 2 million Wild Mustangs in the Northwest; the Bureau of Land Management now indicates that they manage a herd of approximately 33,700 with over half of them in the State of Nevada.

Unfortunately, in the 1980s, there was a lot of controversy over how the Wild Mustangs were being handled by the Bureau employees. As a result they were faced with way too many court cases. Most of these cases were centered on the methods they used to gather horses from the wild as well as the methods used in shipping and breaking (gentling) the horses for sale to the general public. The battles in the courts were sometimes ugly and with the public outcry for more humane methods of handling, the Bureau of Land Management came to our office asking whether our Veterinary Services Unit would be willing to provide advice and counsel.

We, of course, quickly agreed to do just that. The Bureau of Land Management was given the responsibility by Congress for administering the Act and we were in no way to be the decision makers. We noted that we would only provide advice and counsel relative to their operations and especially those aspects relative to humane care. In all other aspects of veterinary care, they were to use private Veterinarians specializing in the practice of equine (horse) medicine for their routine health examinations, vaccinations, treatments, etc. The only time our Veterinarians on site might get involved in such activities would be in an emergency situation that would need immediate attention.

After gaining a general overview of the Bureau's operations it became clear that what they needed most was the expertise of an Animal Behaviorist, Dr. Temple Grandin of Colorado State University. She was well known internationally as one who understood animal behavior better than anyone else. It was our thinking that she could provide the advice and counsel needed to facilitate the process of handling these Wild Mustangs during the Bureau of Land Management's periodic roundups, transport and care to various locations as well as in their various holding facilities.

For those of you who have never been on a Wild Mustang Roundup, it is something to behold. The first time I witnessed a roundup, it involved more activity and personnel than I could have ever imagined. First of all, the Bureau of Land Management analyzes the various locations where the

Wild Mustangs are located. They then complete a census of the population and assess the surrounding land area as to the capacity of horses it can provide for. In other words, how many horses can live on the land without unreasonable damage to the native plant flora? Once they determine the number of horses the land can support, they then identify the number that need to be removed. They also consider the normal reproductive cycles and as a result, plan for periodic roundups as needed in the future.

In addition, each and every roundup requires the identification of a location in the vicinity of the Wild Mustangs' habitat that will provide the best possibility of leading the horses into a corral and their capture. This ideal site might be in a narrow valley or along a steep hill. The location is even more desirable if they can identify an open space between relatively heavily wooded or bushy environs that lead to the end of a valley that might be somewhat wooded and yet provide space enough for the horses to enter.

Then, a crew from the local prison is brought in to set up the fencing needed. In the best of circumstances this fencing is usually installed along either side of a somewhat narrow valley in a V shape formation leading into a temporary corral made of the same fencing material. At the entrance to the corral, a large gate is built that can be quickly drawn across the opening thereby confining the horses once they have entered the enclosed space. All of this is camouflaged by tying shrub material/branches to the fencing from the beginning of the V shaped entrance to the gate and throughout the corral area.

Then a couple days before the big event, volunteers who are Mustang Enthusiasts arrive to assist in the roundup. You would think you were in the old Wild West. Many of the volunteers know the Mustangs quite well and have participated in all of the roundups at that location for many years. In fact, most of the volunteers plan their annual vacations around the roundup and have even photographed each of the horses; have given them names; and know which horse sired each new foal/colt, the year the foal/colt was born, and even which mare gave it birth.

There is excitement in the air. They bring their campers, their tents and their horses. It is an event they all cherish and from the smiles on their faces, you know this is a special occasion and that each and every one of them enjoys being a part of it! They have a chuck wagon and a cook/chef with huge black iron skillets and kettles to cook their sausage and eggs in the morning or beef stew in the evening. There are bonfires and much singing and rejoicing with someone always available to play a medley or two on their guitar as the sun settles into the western horizon. After a couple days of briefings, they know what their role will be and they are ready for the roundup to begin.

Since the roundup I attended was in the later part of the twentieth century, a helicopter was used to bring the Mustangs from the far reaches of their territory to the valley where the corral was located. As you might imagine, everyone was patiently waiting for the sound of the helicopter blades and the arrival of the majestic steeds surrounded by their devoted mares and offspring. As the horses neared the V shaped entrance, a "Judas" horse, owned by the Bureau and trained to lead the horses into the corral was released. Since the Mustangs were somewhat disoriented and disturbed due to the somewhat strange surroundings and the presence of the noisy blades of the helicopter, they believed the "Judas" horse knew where to go and followed it into the corral and their capture.

As the Wild Mustangs entered the valley and the V shaped entrance to the corral, the volunteers on horseback would come up behind them from a distance on each side shouting and waving bush/tree branches. In addition, volunteers on each side of the fence stood up, as the horses passed their location, yelling and waving branches thereby further disorienting while encouraging the horses to follow the "Judas" horse into the Corral. Now as the horses entered the corral there were three men hidden in the brush along one end of the gate. When the last of the Mustangs had entered the corral these men quickly grabbed the rope attached to the gate and swiftly closed the gate with all of their strength and might. The first part of the roundup had been accomplished!

Then it was time to sort out which horses would remain on the range and which ones would be loaded up on trailers for movement to one or more of the Bureau's holding facilities. To me, the involvement of the Mustang Enthusiasts was a positive step taken by the Bureau of Land Management. The volunteers especially appreciated having input in the selection of which horses should remain on the range. Their reasoning was thoughtful and through the dialog that occurred, I felt confident that the best decisions were made for all concerned.

Well after sharing with Dr. Grandin the concerns expressed by the Bureau and their desire to obtain professional help in improving their roundup and handling procedures, she graciously agreed to work with them to assure humane procedures would be used. I was thankful for her interest and support and my heart celebrated when she indicated she was able to free up her time for the next roundup and was ready to go.

Well I wish I could say that everything went well. But unfortunately it did not! In fact, after the first day's activities, Dr Grandin was furious. It appears the cowboys who were hired by the Bureau belittled and taunted Dr. Grandin to no end. They felt they were the experts and that she didn't know what she was talking about. They figured they had more experience working with horses than she did (in many cases the cowboys had worked with horses for thirty or more years) and they in no way where going to honor any of her directions or requests.

I can still remember that evening when she called. She was angry and insistent that she would go to the papers and the media and expose them and their lack of concern to the world. After much discussion and understanding what she was faced with; I asked her if she would give them one more chance. I indicated that the treatment she received was inappropriate and that a person with her expertise and knowledge in animal behavior should not have to face such insults and lack of respect. I noted that I would like to have the opportunity to show them that her methods of operation were correct and that if correctly implemented would greatly improve their operations and the handling of our national treasure, the Wild Mustang breed.

I also noted that I was willing to call their superiors in Washington, DC and ask them to call their people on site and order them to give her twenty four hours of respect and dignity. In addition, they were to obey every direction or suggestion given by her, to not harass or say anything of a negative nature, and to do everything possible to comply with her every wish. Then after twenty-four hours, they could decide whether there was any improvement in their operations and whether they wished to continue with her services.

Finally we both calmed down and Dr. Grandin in her gracious manner agreed. So I immediately called my contact in Washington, DC and emphasized that Dr. Grandin was the most knowledgeable Animal Behaviorist in the World and that I had the greatest confidence in her. In addition, I was confident that if they would do as I suggested; giving her every opportunity to succeed (without any hassles); they would see that her knowledge of animal behavior was second to none. Fortunately, the Bureau's National Coordinator agreed and asked me to call Dr. Temple Grandin, apologizing on their behalf and indicating that for twenty-four hours she would receive their full cooperation.

The next day seemed to drag on forever. I never heard a word and my hope and prayer was that everything was going well and that

Dr. Grandin was able to do that which she does so well. That evening my phone rang and it was a call from Dr. Grandin. She explained that the day's activities went very well and that she was most appreciative of the cooperation received. Then, later that evening I got a call from my Washington, DC contact and he was pleased with the reports he had received from the field. He said that by using Dr. Grandin's techniques they were able to reduce the time necessary to process and transport the horses by one-third. Furthermore, he noted that there was no fighting amongst the stallions as was usual in the past. The horses seemed far less stressed, and in fact, appeared to be more willing to load up on the trucks than ever before. It was obvious he and the Bureau were happy with the results and thankful for her willingness to work with them even after the most difficult time she had with their cowboys on the previous day.

Later, I learned of some of the insights Dr. Temple Grandin had provided that proved to be beneficial to their Wild Mustang Program Operations. For instance, it was noted that on the range, Wild Mustangs are extremely territorial with each Stallion marking his territory with piles of manure. Within this territory each stallion usually has six to eight mares and their foals/ colts. As might be suspected, each stallion is very protective of his piece of land and even more protective of his mares and their offspring, his family.

In previous roundups, the stallions and mares were separated and mixed with other stallions or mares indiscriminately. This, as you might imagine, caused the stallions to become quite angry and physically aggressive challenging other stallions with their mouths open, their noses flaring and attacking each other with all intent of doing harm and/or not cooperating while trying to do everything possible to get their family back together. So apparently with Dr. Grandin's advice and counsel, the stallions were kept with their harem and apart from the other harems. As a result, the Bureau's roundup went remarkably well with an atmosphere of calm and peacefulness that from all reports had never been achieved before.

Another recommendation that was made by Dr. Temple Grandin was the importance of understanding that the loading of horses on trailers should not be forced upon them. For you see, after being in the wild and considering the recent circumstances and events, the Wild Mustangs are leery of just about anything, including everything going on and everything around them. In fact, the horse trailers, in their eyes, are very strange looking and therefore it takes time for them to check them out and to feel comfortable that they will not get hurt in the process.

So instead of forcing the horses to enter the trailers by beating them and/or using other devices such as cattle prods that give an electric shock, it was found that they were more likely to cooperate if they were slowly eased up to the back of the trailer giving them time to check it out. Then, gently, yes, ever so gently, the cowboys would encourage the Mustangs to slowly move forward. All that was necessary according to Dr. Grandin was softly spoken encouragement and a slow motion of their arms, as if to say, in my interpretation, "Don't Worry, Be Happy". (This is, of course, an expression made famous and sung by the one and only, Bobby McFerrin.) And to everyone's disbelief, the so called, Wild Mustangs settled down; established a trust with the cowboys working the roundup; and with little coaxing, gently stepped up into this strange piece of equipment often referred to by us and from their point of view, strangely so, a horse trailer. Then, as the horses already loaded on the trailer further adjusted to their surroundings, the cowboys would encourage the next group of horses to move forward and before you knew it, the trailer was loaded.

Now, another area of responsibility for the Bureau of Land Management was the gentling of the horses before they were put up for auction to the general public. To assist in this process, the Bureau trained and utilized inmates at the State Penitentiary in Colorado Springs, Colorado. The response of the inmates was encouraging and it soon became apparent that this was a program the inmates so hoped to be a part of. In preparing the inmates for this activity, one of the first things they learned was that training/gentling of the Wild Mustangs is not achieved by force or harsh treatment. They learned that horses are naturally very social animals. While they may temporarily fear strange objects, their social nature soon takes over, stimulating their curiosity, the foreign object is thoroughly checked out, and before you know it, their fear subsides and the horse no longer fears its presence.

When I say they are very social animals that includes their curiosity and desire to be close to us as human beings. In the gentling process it was emphasized that each horse has an area of about thirty feet that to them can be an area of concern. Outside this area they usually have few if any concerns. Therefore, in order to gain the trust and acceptance of the horse, especially a Wild Mustang, you needed to approach them slowly, carefully observing their reaction as you enter their 30 foot circle of trust. I cannot emphasize enough that you could only enter their circle of trust if you did so calmly and yes, ever so slowly. As long as the horse was looking at you and/or had its ears in a relaxed position you could keep moving toward them, quietly and carefully in a slow calm manner. But the instant the horse showed signs of fear or questionable trust, such as pulling its ears back and/or snorting, you had to immediately, calmly and slowly retreat toward the outside of the thirty foot perimeter. In some instances you may have even had to turn around and/or look in another direction as you moved away. Then when you noticed the horse in a relaxed mode with its ears forward, looking in your direction, you could again approach the horse, as before, in a slow calm manner. This often needed to be repeated several times.

Nevertheless, if this procedure was implemented as outlined, you would often be surprised in that the horse, even a Wild Mustang would often within fifteen or twenty minutes be walking right up to you and allowing you to gently pat their neck or side. And if you were really lucky, you would have a friend for life. As long as you continued to work with the horse on a regular basis and preferably on a daily basis; maintaining their trust and respect; and treating them with loving kindness at all times; I can assure you that you would be blessed with a trusted friend and companion for life.

It is amazing how much can be accomplished by using training methods that are similar to the biblical statement of treating others as you would like to be treated. It is the best advice I can give to someone who would like to learn equestrian skills along with their new companion, a horse that will truly give them years of enjoyment.

What was interesting with this particular Program at the State Penitentiary was that it has been reported that the inmates that have participated in this program have received pride in their new accomplishment. They have learned the importance of respect for all of life. As a result with their new life skills, they have only on the rarest of occasions, found themselves back in trouble after their release from the prison environment. What more can we ask for? What a fantastic program! How often do you find a program that teaches not only how to value and respect a creature such as a horse while applying the same teachable moments of valuing and respecting ourselves? To this we must applaud not only the Bureau, but also the Colorado State Prison system as well!

Again, I must relate that this was an experience I will always cherish. To me, it emphasized the importance of treating our world's animal populations with the honor and respect they so rightfully deserve. And from my perspective and hopefully yours, this is the least we can do, especially when we consider the level of pleasure and joy we receive from them today, tomorrow and for that matter, each and every day!

CHAPTER 18

"Mad Cow" Disease

Have you noticed how the media can scare the wits out of each and every one of us? In response, how can we protect the public's concerns while serving the needs of our valued livestock industries?

"Mad Cow Disease", the Media term for a disease in cattle called, Bovine Spongiform Encephalopathy, is in medical terminology considered a Transmissible Spongiform Encephalopathy. It is in many ways similar to Scrapie in Sheep and Creutzfeld-Jacob Disease in Humans. In fact some scientists believe that the disease in cattle originated from infected animal by-products added to their feed. In such incidences, they believe that the by-products may have contained infected material from Scrapie infected sheep. Also, as you are probably aware, there seems to be a rather high probability that the people infected with a variant form of Creutzfeld-Jacob Disease had, in fact, been eating beef from cattle infected with this disease. This finding is further validated in that the highest incidence of the new Variant Creutzfeld-Jacob Disease in humans has been closely related to those countries that have had the highest incidence of "Mad Cow" Disease diagnosed in their cattle herds.

In response to this close correlation, several countries forbid the inclusion of certain products from ruminants (cattle, sheep, goats, etc.) in cattle feed. Their main concern was with the products that were of neurological origin (brain, spinal cord, and other nerve tissue) which seem to have a greater chance of harboring the infectious agent should this disease be present.

From a historical perspective, the usual form of Creutzfeld-Jacob Disease in people seems to have had a direct correlation with those human societies that practiced cannibalism. What is confusing, however, is that there have been cases of Creutzfeld-Jacob-like diseases since the early 1900s as well as possible Bovine Spongiform Encephalopathy-like diseases reported on rare occasions. Could it be that the increased feeding of cattle and sheep byproducts to cattle, as a protein source, resulted in the high incidence of Mad Cow Disease in the United Kingdom and as a result the increase of Creutzfeld-Jacob-like disease in mankind?

Now I should point out that the infectious agents that cause these types of infections are quite stable and very hard to destroy. In fact high temperatures including incineration alone will not inactivate/kill the causative agent in infective/diseased material.

While scientific observation directly correlates these diseases with misshapen protein and vacuoles in the brain, spinal cord, and nervous tissue; other scientists have postulated that the observed misshapen protein may be the result of some other, maybe virus-like infectious material. So, who is right? For some time, it has been accepted by most that these misshapen proteins named Prions are the infectious material/agent. So for now that is considered to be fact! Or is it?

One thing I have learned is that while observation is critical to the learning process and the eventual accumulation of new knowledge; the minute I believe I know everything and have the absolute facts, I am wrong, wrong, wrong! I see life as a process of uninterrupted, continual learning. I have repeatedly witnessed scientists in my profession describe something as absolute fact and then with additional discoveries have it totally discounted and dismissed years later. We as human beings are not perfect. In my mind, only God, our Creator is perfect.

So, from my perspective, I would seriously question that we have all of our facts in a row and believe that there is more to this than meets the eye. As I look at the Universe, I have come to the realization that science is finding the expanse of our universe to be greater and greater beyond imagination. This is especially true as new technologies are invented, identified, and utilized. In my belief system there is no end to the Universe. Yes, for some that may be hard to explain. That is unless you are ready to accept that there is a God and from my perspective, no doubt about it!

But by the same token I have found and firmly believe that it is equally evident that there is no end as to how small the minute parts of our universe can be! I believe there are much smaller entities than we can imagine or even hypothesize in this day and age. To do otherwise limits our thinking and the possibilities for investigative research in the future. So, I applaud those who think out of the box and who through creativity and thoughtful thinking look for new dimensions we have never thought of or have begun to realize.

Well, we can be thankful that the incidence of "Mad Cow" Disease has dramatically dropped since the mid 1980s. In fact the incidence has gone from several thousand cases mainly in the United Kingdom down to only a very few. In most countries, where it was present, only one or zilch cases have been diagnosed within the past year or so.

Now, in its heyday, the media had the disease blown up to scare the living daylights out of each and every one of us. In fact there were surveys done in the early 2000s indicating that the diagnosis of one case of Bovine Spongiform Encephalopathy (Mad Cow Disease), originating in the United State, would cause half of our population to totally stop eating beef. That just blows my mind. Yes, even though there is a close correlation between the incidence of Mad Cow Disease in a country and that of the new variant Creutzfeld-Jacobs Disease, both of which is certain death and no known cure, I still cannot understand the panic one case could potentially cause.

Even with all of the thousands of cases of Mad Cow Disease in cattle in the United Kingdom and Western Europe, there were only about 200 to 400 human cases of variant Creutzfeld-Jacob Disease (depending on who you talk to) worldwide. Now that may sound horrific. However, if we consider the general population dynamics of human disease, it really isn't that bad. In fact, if we look, for example, at the number of deaths caused by influenza in the United States, we would find that we average about 30,000 deaths each year. So where should our priorities be? Should we let our media (television, radio, and newspapers) who like scary headlines versus true reporting determine how we think? Or should we insist on better journalism that can help us achieve a higher level of greatness and as a result serve our God and our fellow man worldwide in a more meaningful way?

Well, as all of this Madness was saturating our TV screens and newspapers, we had a scare in Vermont that made the news media and seemed to almost get out of control. You see, we had a flock of sheep in Vermont that was diagnosed with a variant type of Transmissible Spongiform Encephalopathy. It was different from the Scrapie form usually seen in sheep and in some ways had some similarities, based on the tests run, to that of Bovine Spongiform Encephalopathy. Not only were these samples run at our National Veterinary Services Laboratories in Ames, Iowa, but they were also run and rerun at a private laboratory on Long Island. In addition, samples were sent to the World Reference Laboratory for such diseases in Pirbright, England.

With similar results, the decision was made that the United States Federal Government must seize and destroy this flock of sheep immediately. While the owners would be paid fair market value, they were not happy and voiced a lot of resistance and of course won the hearts of the media with multiple stories of the value of these sheep and how they were like members of their family.

Now I can relate to all of that especially since my wife's parents raised Shropshire Sheep and each of them were dearly loved not only by Joanne's parents but also by each of their kids and grandkids, including my four children, Amory, Julie, Richard and Anna. In fact every summer, my kids would look forward to going to Grandma and Grandpa's house to train the sheep for the County Fair and then my wife and I would watch with pride as they with their cousins showed these "Prize" sheep hoping for a ribbon or two to show all of their friends back home.

Well not only was there a lot of grief expressed by the owners, but there was a lot of discussion amongst my colleagues and our colleagues in Europe as to the best way to dispose of the infected sheep so as to not perpetuate any infection or contamination that might be present. It was clear that any further delay or exhibiting of indecisiveness would make matters worse especially with the news media loving every moment of the controversy or hesitation on our part.

So after discussing the situation with the Laboratory Chiefs at our National Laboratories in Ames, Iowa; I, as the Laboratories' Director, advised my boss that we at the Laboratory would be glad to receive the animals and that we, as a Diagnostic Center, had the best expertise to properly dispose of the carcasses after the sheep are destroyed. We believed that to be true because, as the National Veterinary Services Laboratory, we were a diagnostic center for animal disease and as such, often had to deal with the final disposal of highly pathogenic laboratory specimens that were frequently submitted for our evaluation and/or diagnostic purview.

So arrangements were made. A team of USDA Employees were to arrive at the affected Vermont farm at day break. They were to load the sheep on tractor trailers made for hauling animals and to immediately leave with all of the sheep, feed and waste manure for our facility in Ames, Iowa. It was interesting in that, as soon as the news media got wind of this, they were hovering over the property and apparently filmed the entire process including the loading of the sheep into the tractor-trailers/ semitrailers. Then, in order to get the full scoop, the news media was again present as the tractor trailers crossed into Iowa from the State of Illinois. They loaded their gear onto helicopters giving a blow by blow account as the sheep traveled the interstate. And then, as one might suspect, they hovered over our National Laboratory Facilities as the sheep were unloaded into buildings prepared for their arrival.

In addition, as the trucks were pulling through our front gates there was a group of individuals from "People for the Ethical Treatment of Animals" (PETA) holding large signs and picketing our premises. They were advocating the life of a vegetarian and discouraging the inhumane slaughtering of animals for the pleasure of eating meat. Then about noon I remember looking out of my office window and not believing what was going on. For just before lunch time, a group of Iowa State University students arrived; set up charcoal grills; and were offering the folks from PETA freshly grilled Hot Dogs with any condiments they desired to tie them over till dinner that evening. As you can imagine, the news media was there and enjoyed every moment filling the evening news with all kinds of stories and interviews from both points of view.

Well, in short order, the sheep were unloaded into the buildings prepared for their arrival, they were immediately destroyed, bagged in large, sturdy, plastic bags, and placed in refrigerator trucks until such time as we could handle them in the disposal process. This was not an easy process and the methodology implemented was that of using a newly developed piece of equipment that not only cooked the carcasses but also completely broke down all tissue (muscle, nervous, glandular, etc.) into a slurry-like liquid. The process included the use of potassium hydroxide and as a result totally denatured all protein including any of the misshapen protein called Prions. The equipment could only handle a few carcasses at a time and took several hours to completely process the carcasses rendering them into safe, non-infective products that could be readily disposed of.

Now I wish I could say that everything went smoothly from this point on. But then as you know, life just isn't set up to work that way. As usual there can always be human error. Of course it is hard to admit that and so, as is often the case; we try to find a way to blame the equipment or whatever. In this case I received a panic call from one of our engineers that the new equipment we were using to process these carcasses had just exploded and that there was carcass material everywhere. I couldn't believe or rather I didn't want to believe what I was hearing.

Thank God, my first concern was for our employees. After all, the splattering (explosion) of the highly corrosive Basic pH material could play havoc; creating serious burns all over an individual's body. When I was advised that two of our employees had received some spattering of the material on their arms, I rushed to the scene worrying to no end for what may have happened to them. When I arrived, I was pleased to find that they had already gone to the emergency room for treatment and found out later that they would be fine. What a relief, no program or project is worth injury or harm to any of our employees. In my view, the most valuable resource any company or firm can have is their employees.

Then after getting the mess cleaned up, the engineers reported that the automatic controls to prevent such catastrophes were the problem and were not functioning properly. Before we would allow them to Fire Up the equipment again, we asked that they run several tests to be sure the safety controls would work this time and would work as planned. After much discussion and several adjustments, I was convinced it was safe to proceed. Thankfully no further problems were encountered.

Once the carcasses were processed, the final product, a liquid, was no longer infective. As such, the liquid could be safely disposed of as any other waste product into our drains leading to the local Sewage Treatment Plant. After consultation with our local Sewage Treatment Plant authorities, as was our usual custom, we soon realized that our laboratory was able to process these carcasses much more rapidly than the local sewage treatment plant was able to receive, handle and process the final non-infectious product. They advised that they could only process this material at a given rate and we, of course, agreed, as we should, to their terms.

Therefore, we decided to store the final liquefied product as processed in tanker trucks until it could be released into our drains and properly disposed of. We had high hopes and believed that the tanker trucks would only be needed for a few days or up to a week or so. But as is so often the case, our best made plans were delayed and in fact it was several weeks before the last of this material was disposed of and our participation in this project complete. What an experience!

All I can say is that we all agreed that the decision to depopulate this flock of sheep was correct in protecting our livestock industries from any potential harm that might or could have resulted from any possible spread of this disease entity. With the recent Mad Cow experiences of our friends in Europe, we did not want to take any chances. The potential risks were too high and any chance of failure was totally unacceptable. In spite of the tragedy to all concerned and especially the owners, it was better to error, if indeed there was an error, on the side of safety and protecting our livestock industry and especially the health and well being of mankind.

As always we did everything possible to ensure that we were in compliance with the local, State, and Federal Ordinances, Laws, and Regulations. In reality, such situations are often difficult to deal with and the impact on the owners of the animals is devastating to say the least. My heart goes out to each and every one of them and I know that it is an unpleasant task for all involved. Sometimes I feel that fighting disease (whether human or animal disease or infectious to both) is like being in a war zone! The battles are quite complex and not easily resolved. The war against disease impacts a wide expanse of humankind and involves strategies, battle lines and committed troops to achieve success. And that often takes time, resources, and persistence by all who are involved. From my perspective, disease is an enemy that on occasion must be faced head on and in such instances is an unfortunate and truly tragic experience for all!

CHAPTER 19

Fishing for Salmon and Carp

The latest field of endeavor, for the veterinarian, is that of aquaculture. But then, how can we help an industry for which we have had limited or no experience?

Now when you think of Veterinarians, do any of you truly think that they can treat all animals whether they are on land or in the sea? If we are honest, we will soon realize that there is no one who knows everything about every animal classified in the animal kingdom. In fact, when I think of my veterinary education (well, not quite ancient history), I have trouble remembering if any of our instructors even mentioned fish, oysters, whales, etc. It was truly a specialty that had to be pursued after graduation. In fact, at that time, any expertise in veterinary aquaculture was rare indeed.

Even in the early 2000s, aquaculture was hardly ever discussed. If my recollections are correct, I didn't even consider the possibility of veterinarians working with fish diseases, let alone other forms of aquaculture, until the mid to late 1990s. In fact, I do believe the first time I even thought about fish and aquaculture was during a meeting of the United States Animal Health Association. It was at about that time when they recognized the need for and decided to establish an Aquaculture Committee as part of their annual meeting and proceedings.

The first time I attended one of their committee meetings, the discussions were both informative and inspiring. I was impressed by the membership's motivating, creative spirit and energy. It was obvious, at that time, that this could be one of the world's fastest growing animal production industries to be found.

Then, with the beginning of the 21st Century, it came to my attention that the aquaculture industries were seeking advice and counsel. They were concerned with two serious and deadly fish diseases that had just been identified in the United States. One was Infectious Salmon Anemia as identified in Salmon raised off the coast of Maine in Cobscook and Passamaquoddy Bays and the other was Spring Viremia of Carp as identified in Koi produced in ponds in Virginia and North Carolina. In both cases the aquaculture Industries were familiar with the expertise Veterinarians had in population animal disease control and eradication. As such, they looked to the Offices of the State Veterinarians, the Universities and our organization, the Animal and Plant Health Inspection Service, Veterinary Services for guidance and assistance.

I remember the first time these diseases were brought to my attention. Even though we had never worked with any aquatic species, I could see the reasoning for their looking to us for guidance. Obviously aquaculture was a relatively new form of production agriculture and as such they were impressed with the numerous accomplishments we had made jointly, with a diverse group of individuals and organizations. This was a whole new adventure and I strongly encouraged our Federal Area Veterinarians in Charge to assist the States and the Aquaculture Industry in any way possible. It was exciting to say the least.

In the case of Infectious Salmon Anemia (not infectious to humans), it was the very first time our Agency, The Animal and Plant Health Inspection Service, developed an Aquatic Animal Health Program. In fact, it was also the very first time indemnity was offered to producers of aquatic animals that needed to be destroyed because of disease. One of our best Veterinarians, Dr. Steve Ellis along with the Area Veterinarian in Charge, Dr. Bill Smith actively worked in concert with a wide group of individuals interested in solving this complex and challenging problem. This included officials from the Maine Department of Agriculture and Natural Resources, as well as the Director and other key officials in their Animal Disease Laboratory System. They worked with members of the Maine Aquaculture Association, the Salmon Industry and a wide variety of other professionals. It was amazing to see their accomplishments, especially when you consider that the causative agent, a virus, was first isolated only a relatively few years previously by Norwegian Scientists in 1984.

There was little known about this disease, its reservoirs of infection, or how it spread. And yet, with the support of the affected Salmon Industry, it is amazing what they have discovered and learned in a relatively short period of time.

With the help of one of my assistants, Dr Ulysses Lane and our Agency's newly established National Coordinator for Aquaculture, Dr. Otis Miller, we were able to make initial contact with our colleagues in Canada and soon we were all working as a team.

Now, in order to understand our undertakings more fully, it might be useful to discuss a few tidbits about the Salmon Industry and the program initiatives that were implemented to control Infectious Salmon Anemia in this area at that time.

In this instance, Salmon were raised in coastal salt water in large netted pens. Both the Canadian and the United States pens were within relatively close range. So, if one pen was found to be infected with Infectious Salmon Anemia; in a relatively short period of time, this disease could spread rapidly to any or all of the other pens.

At first we didn't have a clear understanding of how the disease spread. To help us in that regard, a new test using Polymerase Chain Reaction techniques was developed and implemented. This test could rapidly detect minute amounts of the virus in a water sample and thus gave a relatively early warning of the potential for disease in the vicinity.

Other areas of concern included the identifying of potential risk factors for disease spread. For example, one individual noted that if the industry was interested in feeding young Salmon (Smolts) moist feed containing herring, it could be a problem. And why was that problematic? Well, unfortunately, as was soon learned, herring can be infected with this nasty virus without showing clinical signs. Now, with that bit of information, it was clearly understood that the feeding of herring could be a problem, a really big problem!

Now, for those of you who are not familiar with the term, Smolt, let me explain.

According to Webster's dictionary, a Smolt is, "A young Salmon at the stage at which it migrates from fresh water to the sea (salt water)". This, is amazing, to say the least. As you probably know, fresh water fish generally cannot live in salt water and salt water fish generally cannot live in fresh water. Since Salmon are able to live in both, it must be another miracle of life. While some scientists indicate this is possibly due to the ability of the Salmon's kidneys to balance the body's level of salt at all times, the question of how this mechanism is initiated and accomplished appears, in my way of thinking, to be another mystery of life. While some scientists may emphasize that they know the hormones, the cell changes, and the physiology and that it doesn't seem any more mysterious than any other part of biology, to me it is another exemplary example of the creativity of God and the miracle of life. And now back to our story!

Once the disease was diagnosed in the area, the primary goal was to eliminate any further spread by removing all known infected populations from the sea as soon as possible. If there was any evidence of illness and/or death observed in a netted pen of Salmon, diagnostic tests were immediately run; and if the presence of the Infectious Salmon Anemia virus was identified, the entire pen of Farmed Salmon was removed from the sea and destroyed. This was done in that the local industry after looking at several options considered it to be the most workable methodology (at least at that time) for treating and/or protecting other pens of Salmon from Infection.

To facilitate program compliance, the Salmon Industry did have indemnity payments available. This was especially helpful in reducing the financial burden on those who had to destroy their infected Salmon in order to prevent further disease spread.

Individuals who participated in the harvesting of Salmon, whether as part of the normal production cycle or during emergency removal of infected populations, worked long, strenuous hours in an environment that included bitter cold seas. As the netting and the enclosed Salmon were being hauled onto the fishing boats, there was always the possibility of injury, falling over-board and/or succumbing to the frigid air and/or water. It was a difficult task that could rapidly induce fatigue. To the uninitiated, the sudden confrontation of unexpected employment/equipment risks could quickly turn into dangerous, life threatening moments that needed immediate medical attention and support.

As such, safety was always a primary concern. In order to mitigate the inherent dangers involved, each participant was outfitted with a suit that would keep them warm as well as protect them from the harm of the frigid water should they fall overboard! It was reassuring to know that in such instances, this suit was designed to keep their entire body afloat until such time as they could be rescued. While it was difficult to work under the constraints of such bulky clothing, I repeatedly heard that it was welcomed by all as a necessary safeguard.

Well, not only did the infected Salmon need to be safely disposed of; but in addition, all of the equipment and the netting had to be carefully cleaned and sanitized, another laborious and difficult task.

Since this was a serious disease, causing lethargy, protruding eyes, bleeding of the kidneys and other organs, extensive precautions were taken to prevent any residue virus from infecting any new Salmon that might be introduced to the same site at a later date.

For instance, strict bio-security measures were implemented by the industry to prevent any cross contamination of pens by cages, netting, equipment and/or personnel that had not been properly cleaned and sanitized. Furthermore, the pens were left vacant for an extended period of time before being repopulated with new fish.

In addition, pest control measures were utilized. Such procedures were implemented in order to minimize the risk of potential carriers of disease such as sea lice. Yes, even marine life deal with those pesky critters! Now, to be honest, I do need to point out that sea lice are not lice as we land dwellers usually think them to be. According to Dr. Andrew Goodwin, an aquaculture specialist, sea lice are parasitic copepods (crustacean, not arachnids) and are only referred to as "Lice" based on their appearance.

It may be interesting to note at this point that Sea Lice are Planktonic. Now, even though I had no idea what that meant, I am sure that those of you who are linguists probably know that Plankton is derived from a Greek word that means errant, wanderer or drifter. As such, this fits the description of sea lice perfectly. For you see, sea lice, as part of their survival strategies, are well known for their ability to drift with the sea tides and/or currents. Then, when the sea lice come upon a fish such as Salmon; they will usually attach to their gills and feed off of the mucous and surface tissue. Thus if they are infected with the Infectious Salmon Anemia virus, whoa la, the Salmon becomes infected too.

Now, apparently, one or two uninfected sea lice feeding on an Adult Salmon will usually do no noticeable damage. But apparently it is a different story when Juvenile Salmon/Smolts are first introduced to a production agriculture pen. In such cases, they will often succumb to just one sea louse attaching to their gills. Now consider a heavy concentration of Salmon being raised in the confines of a pen and before you know it; you have a haven for sea lice to reproduce rapidly. Then, without the implementation of some kind of sea lice pest control measures, you have a catastrophe!

As for the future of the Salmon Industry, it is encouraging to note that the Salmon Industry and Aquaculture Scholars continue to work on developing improved vaccines for use in protecting farmed salmon from this serious disease. Supposedly there are some issues with the varying times it takes for the Salmon to develop adequate immunity, but hopefully with additional research into immune enhancers as part of the adjuvant or production processes, better immunizing techniques will be developed. I should note that this is often an issue in the development and use of vaccines for all species of animals including that of Homosapiens, mankind.

I do believe the Salmon Industry; jointly with their academic colleagues have learned much along the way. That doesn't mean that all is well. Unfortunately, as with so many components of the agriculture production industries, they are still faced with a variety of issues relative to the environment, population density, economics, and government bureaucracy. Unfortunately, there is much work that needs to be done to improve their chances for survival in the United States and in the mean time, the small business producers are put out of business and the larger business operations are struggling to survive.

Now, let's talk about the second disease that was, at that time, of such concern to our Nation's Aquaculture Industry, Spring Viremia of Carp. In many countries the Common Carp has historically been prepared for and enjoyed at the dinner table. More recently, it has been selectively bred as an ornamental fish and enjoyed in garden ponds, pools, and/or streams. In such cases, fish enthusiasts have identified them as Koi. While this disease has frequently been identified in the Middle East, Russia, and Europe, it was a new entity in the United States of America. In this instance it was a serious problem for the Koi Industries in both North Carolina and Virginia.

I can still remember the discussions I had with my colleague, Dr. Terry Taylor, our organization's Area Veterinarian in Charge for the State of Virginia. According to him, the Koi producers were having unusual death loss and were looking for professional expertise to help them rid their ponds of this terrible disease. Unfortunately we had no expertise with Spring Viremia of Carp, let alone any diseases of interest to aquaculturists. But, with the interests of the affected industries in getting our organization involved, we agreed to assign some of our staff members, our talented Epidemiological Investigators as well as some of our field staff to try to come up with answers that might be helpful to this relatively new struggling Industry.

Well, we did extensive research, contacted numerous fish experts and learned that infected Koi shed the virus in both their feces and urine. We also learned to our dismay that the virus is easily spread in the water from one fish to another. And then, we found that the disease could be carried from one fish to another by Carp Lice (There, again, we have to deal with those lousy lice.) and by Leeches. If that wasn't enough, we also learned that Spring Viremia of Carp could survive for some time in mud even after the mud had dried up. So, you see, it was not an easy fix.

Finally after much discussion with the owners of the affected ponds and our colleagues (the State Departments of Natural Resources, Fish and Wildlife personnel, as well as various scientists and laboratory personnel); we all agreed the best and probably only workable solution was to depopulate the ponds and dispose of the fish by burial. Then we would need to drain the affected ponds and have the bottom of the ponds treated with Lime. This would change the pH of the remaining mud; hopefully killing any virus before refilling the ponds with water and restocking them with fish.

Then the question was raised as to what treatments should be used on the water in the ponds before the ponds were drained? Before I could blink twice, our discussion was focusing on the possible use of ultraviolet light. This was being considered in that it is known that ultraviolet light can kill the virus with proper time controlled application. So then the question was raised as to whether we should set up a system of channels with ultraviolet lights including controlled water flow before we would even consider draining it into the nearby stream?

Before I knew it, the screws were being tightened and in my mind the owner was beginning to panic. So, we all decided to gather (have another meeting) and after much reflection I opened my big mouth and made another suggestion that kept me up for several nights. I noted that I truly understood the concern for the virus's presence in the water. However, it was my understanding that every time there was any significant amount of rain; the ponds had already overflowed through screened drain pipes to the nearby streams on a regular basis. Also I was advised that regular sampling of the water and fish in these streams never resulted in an isolation of the virus.

Therefore, in my opinion, it was time to address the concerns of these Koi Producers, help them free their ponds of this terrible disease, and let them get these ponds back in the business of raising Koi, a truly beautiful, ornament fish that is enjoyed by families the world over.

And so the decision was jointly made! In addition, our staff would delay no longer and would help the Koi Producer get back on track, so to speak. We would do that by helping them clean out their ponds, removing all of the fish, immediately disposing of them by burial, draining the ponds without any treatment, and then treating the bottom of their ponds with Lime. Then, and only then, after their ponds have been vacated for 60 days (according to my recollection); they could refill their ponds and get these ponds back into business by restocking them with their favorite fish, Koi.

We knew there was a risk in taking this approach. However, I felt it was a calculated risk with a very low probability of failure. I felt that as the water from these ponds was drained, the water so drained would be diluted to quite an extent, especially after it reached the stream and mingled with the stream's constant current/water flow. Furthermore, based on the information available; the risks were ever so small in that even with the numerous overflows of the affected pond water into the streams during each rainfall, there was no indication of the disease/virus being present in the water and/or fish inhabiting the streams' environment.

As such, it was my firm conviction that a monument to mankind was not needed in order to assure the world that the draining of this water into these streams could be done safely. It was important, however, (and I felt strongly about this) to support the thinking of the Department of Natural Resources to mitigate any possible consequences by fine screening the water leaving the pond; reducing the amount of debris/organic material entering the stream, and thereby hoping to eliminate any potential problems in the future.

In addition, our Nation's Scientists and Researchers indicated that a change in pH using the Lime would, in their opinion, surely kill any virus remaining in the mud. They further noted that all scientific studies completed to date had indicated that the virus could only be isolated for 42 days in mud and no longer; even without any treatment applied.

So the decision was made! Fortunately the job was completed within a few months and in spite of the reports I received of repeated follow-up testing in the ponds and local streams, the virus had, at least, not been isolated from the time of the depopulation until that of my retirement in January of 2004.

In my mind, the Infectious Salmon Anemia and Spring Viremia of Carp programs were the driving force to our profession acknowledging the importance and value of the Aquaculture Industries.

It has been a pleasure observing the Veterinary Profession as it has become more excited about Aquaculture Medicine. And of course, it is rewarding to realize that when scientists, laboratory researchers and field professionals of diverse backgrounds work together sharing of their knowledge and expertise, much can be accomplished and with that job satisfaction that brings abundant joy!

CHAPTER 20

Future Strategies!

Strategies to bring inventors, scientists and theorists to greater heights of productivity are identified. The importance of crossing new frontiers is emphasized.

As we have discussed previously, I believe there is no end to the knowledge spectrum or in other words no end to what mankind can learn about this magnificent world God has created.

I am a firm believer in thinking outside our current belief systems and while using the experiences and/or observations of life; expanding our realm of thinking to include our dreams. For it is through our dreams we can seek new pathways to discovery through research and through that discovery we have the greatest chance of improving our lives and that of the world we live in. So let's get started.

In my future world I see much greater use of solar panels to harvest one of our greatest resources, solar energy. I see, as some have proposed and developed, greater use of solar panels on roofs, siding and in our roads and sidewalks utilizing hardened glass strong enough to withstand tremendous wear and tear. I see the development of major improvements in efficiency and design of solar collecting systems as is already becoming apparent.

With this advancement in technology, I envision improvements and greater use of electromagnetic propulsion systems. I see them replacing the gasoline engine and being solely relied upon for travel whether it is on land, seas, in the air or in outer space.

I see greater use of electric trains and vehicles that can operate on their own; traveling in sequence on highways without the need for drivers and/or policemen to assure that we are driving safely.

I believe we will be utilizing the land more effectively and efficiently. We will live in smaller units in high rise apartments/ condominiums and live in symbiotic relationships with all of our plants and animals as I believe God intended.

I also believe that any given acre of land can, at the same time, produce multiple flowering plants, bushes and trees while providing a wide variety of mammals, birds, and reptiles for us to enjoy. The land can and will greatly increase in productivity with this multiplicity of use as already witnessed by researchers at the Land

Institute near Salina, Kansas. They have already shown that the planting of multiple plants on the same land as livestock can produce at least the same equivalent of grain as we currently produce utilizing the rotation of one crop at a time. This approach adds to the efficiency of land use by adding the availability of animal protein while eliminating the need for fertilizers, a limited resource.

Such plantings better utilize the moisture available during heavy rains while also being productive during periods of relative drought. This is due to the individual characteristics of each plant. Some are good at holding surface water during periods of heavy rain and others have deep root systems assuring the availability of water during periods of drought.

Furthermore, it is apparent that the stems and fibrous material from these plants are great for replenishing the nutrients we need in our soil as is the fertilizer received from animal urine and feces.

If you have ever talked with a Soils Scientist, you will be well aware that trees love the waste from animals including human waste. As such when the fecal material is delivered to the land; the trees seize the opportunity and flourish with a noticeable increase in growth thereby producing extensively more wood/lumber than many have ever thought possible.

Some individuals even suggest that if we used more trees and bushes along the sides of our rivers and streams, water contamination would be greatly reduced; our lakes, rivers, and oceans would be more pristine. As such, it would seem to me that our relationship with our aquatic friends would also be greatly improved.

Along this line of thinking one man's junk is another man's treasure. This is also true with the wastes from our homes and/or industries. In Europe and especially in the Netherlands the Industries are rewarded for finding another industry that can put their waste products to good use. This saves in the cost of disposal as well as the transport or purchase of the chemicals/materials needed by a member of another industry.

In addition there has been research on how to use the wastes from our homes that are gathered in refuse pits/dumps. While we have moved in the direction of recycling metals, glass, etc. and the idea of green buildings and furnishings (reuse of the old wood, furniture, etc.), we are a long way from realizing the true treasure to be found in every trash pit/dump. Apparently there are ways to separate the Treasured Garbage into many different components and then selling it to the various industries needing these components including some highly valued chemicals as Raw Materials. So, again, let's get started!

Now what can we do in the realm of Animal Health and Public Health?

As you know, clean water and clean air are important to our health and well being. And yet, we seem to disregard this truism, with no sense of guilt, as we continue to pollute both at an astounding rate. We seem to have little regard for the amount of water we use on a daily basis and figure it will always be there as we spend our money freely for chemically treated water as well as the tremendous cost of treating water and our sewage at sewage treatment plants.

Have we regressed from the days when we had cisterns (large tanks/cement walled and floored structures in our basements or outside) to collect rainwater for our use in our clothes washers, toilets and for watering our lawns and plants? Could the runoff from roads be stored and used by our industries, public parks, government and commercial buildings to maintain their beautiful lawns and gardens? What about carwashes and the power washing of buildings to keep mold from destroying the exteriors of our buildings?

Again, how about the idea of using trees to clean up the runoff before it reaches our rivers? What about the ability of trees to clean our air and provide moisture to our air? Can we expand our thinking and allow trees to do more than provide shade and shelter for us and so many animal species?

Then in the area of diagnostics, could we put our electromagnetic microscopes to better use? Could we use the broad spectrum of electromagnetic waves to learn more about disease causing agents and their impact on the various tissues of our bodies?

Yes, electron microscopic technology has aggressively improved our ability to observe small cellular structures from the point of 2,000,000 times magnification a few years ago to over 50,000,000 times magnification today. Nevertheless, can we better utilize the differing electromagnetic lenses, combination wavelength electromagnetic/ electron microscopy techniques, and/or tissue preparation techniques? Would this provide us with either a direct or indirect indication of smaller agents that might be considered infective and/or disease causing?

What new technologies can be used for disease detection? There has been work on the development of a wide variety of diagnostic tests, some of which can take air samples and identify whether certain diseases might be present. I could even envision our ability to have equipment in our bathroom that could take air samples or samples of the water in our toilet to identify certain diseases when we feel under the weather. Such testing with immediate results could make a big difference on our getting ahead of a disease before it gets ahead of us.

Another area that probably needs our attention is the scientific validation of the various diagnostic tests we are currently using. As you may have already understood, none of the tests used in Animal Health and Public Health are 100 per cent accurate. In fact there are always a certain percentage of the diagnostic samples that are tested positive that in reality are not positive and a certain percent of those diagnostic samples that test negative that are truly not negative. This in fact can be quite problematic.

Yes the chances of the test results being correct can be increased by running several different kinds of tests and seeing if the results are compatible. Unfortunately most of the diagnostic tests used in human and animal medicine have not been validated by known scientific methodology. As a result, wrong treatments may be used, some of which can impact our health in a negative direction. As is so often the case, the tests we use in our laboratories have gained acceptance as being accurate based on past practices and not scientific validation. It is an area that needs a lot of work and the results of such verification could be surprising; showing that some other test or combination of tests could be far more accurate and as a result more beneficial.

Another arena that bothers me is our reliance on vaccines and their role in immune response. Unfortunately there have been findings, especially in the poultry industry, that immune systems sometimes can only tolerate so much. In some instances, our immune systems rebel and our bodies will react negatively. It is true that most of our vaccines provide beneficial responses in the majority of cases. But remember such vaccines are often developed in Eggs, Bovine Calf Serum or other foreign cell cultures that might in some individuals create side effects or possible problematic immune reactions in different parts of their bodies. Then there is the use of vaccine adjuvants to preserve and/or enhance the immune response. Even though efficacy and safety tests are completed on each batch of vaccine, I believe more studies need to be done relative to the administration of multiple vaccines with a variety of different adjuvants over a period of time.

It seems that we should consider that vaccines while usually beneficial could in certain situations create responses that may be quite troublesome. This could be in our intestines, our circulatory system, our nervous system or in most any of our body's systems.

While vaccines have provided great successes such as the elimination of smallpox, I do think we need to be careful.

We need to consider when vaccines may be necessary. We should not use a Shotgun approach of treating everyone with every vaccine known to mankind whether they are at risk or not.

There is also a need for more research in diseases considered to be autoimmune. I may be wrong but I often wonder whether we at times call diseases autoimmune because we have not identified a single causative agent? Could it be that we are only observing the clinical response? Could it, in some cases, be a clinical sign instigated by different causative agents? It appears that we would prefer having just one causative agent for a given set of clinical signs. But for those of us that have been involved in Investigative Diagnostics, it soon becomes clear that clinical signs are not definitive. They are only sign posts that help us narrow the list of diseases most probably involved.

Then there is the need for more research in the possible disease agents, nutritional factors, stress factors, or other causative factors for the rapid proliferation of cells as witnessed in cancerous tumors. If we find that near-by lymph glands need to be removed when we are surgically removing a cancerous tumor, does it not make sense that the causative agent could possibly be found in the lymphatic system? Maybe our efforts would be more fruitful if we spend more of our energy studying our lymphatic systems and/or our giant filter, the liver.

Then there is the question of neurological diseases and functions. Unfortunately the use of drugs for Attention Deficit Syndrome or Autism Type Diseases at times seems to be more troublesome than we would like. Often these individuals are the most brilliant individuals on earth. Are we considering other options when we approach the issue of hyperactivity or excessive firing of the nerve endings? Are we stifling creativity in some instances with the drugs we use?

Is it not true that in many of these cases, the individuals may not have sufficient insulating fat along their neurons? Then because of this lack of insulation, their bodies produce excessive firing of the neurons as a result of their body's receptors receiving the usual stimuli of sight, sound or touch. Is that why these individuals often see more detail, complain of loud noises, and/or do not like to be touched or hugged? Could research find a way to help these individuals better insulate their nerve endings? Could stress have an impact on this thinning of the insulation layer?

So let's talk about the effects of stress and/or the products of stress such as epinephrine or cortisol on our nervous system or our bodies in general? It seems we understand so little in this regard. If stress causes the release of epinephrine and the production of cortisol, what is the impact of these on our health especially if we do not exert the energy and physical response activity that nature originally intended for us when we were in emergency situations? Is exercise not just good for our physical health, but also essential for our nervous system's health? What is the impact of stress on our animal populations? Would there be more weight gain and/or levels of productivity if environmental stress factors could be reduced? Maybe all is well, but would more research in this arena be beneficial in the understanding of the impact of stress on our lives as well as that of our friends in the animal kingdom?

As I have spent more time studying my area of interest, Foreign Animal Diseases, it seems that we just might learn a little bit more by spending more time observing nature and trying to utilize more of nature's secrets relative to animal health and production.

So often the problems we are struggling with seem to be related to our ignoring some of the God given principles that lead to a long healthy productive life. Instead of our highly competitive workaholic push to extremes, should we not learn that rest is also important? We often talk of a balanced life and did not God indicate that after six days of work, we should rest on the seventh? Have we studied enough about the role of rest and sleep in our lives? Why do we need sleep at least physiologically? Why do we feel tired? What causes the tired feeling? We understand to some extent why muscles become fatigued. But do we really understand fatigue and why some people need less sleep than others. Is there a biochemical reason for feeling tired and why is deep sleep more important than light sleep? What does sleep accomplish? Why can't we function without sleep?

Maybe only God knows the answer, but I believe we in the Medical Professions are still in the dark ages of understanding some of the most basic concepts of life. With a willingness to keep our minds open, our ability to share the reality of life as experienced in different parts of the world, and with God's help, much can be accomplished!

For some, the thoughts I have expressed may not be worth considering. But if they stimulate your creative juices, do take that first step! For it is through the implementation of our passions that new ideas develop. With new ideas, new frontiers of knowledge are conquered. And then, as a civilized society, we can all enjoy the fruits of our labors and celebrate the beauty of a future as bright as a new found star!

EPILOGUE

Our relationships with animals may have not been fully understood. And yet, hopefully, we now appreciate the important role they play in our lives. And as a result, our passion for life will blossom for time eternal.

In addressing the needs for agriculture, including hunger, the importance of livestock in our world becomes apparent. Not only are livestock a source of nutrition, including high quality protein, but they are also important in improving our quality of life.

For many years we have recognized the need for animal proteins in our diet. The importance of this need is further clarified when we compare the percentage of essential amino acids we can obtain from eating animal protein with the essential amino acids we must have on a daily basis in our food as human beings to be healthy.

In each instance, the animal proteins have always scored high. Hen eggs, beef, lamb, and fish contain all of the amino acids identified as essential for human health and as a result have amino acid scores of 100 percent. Poultry meat has a score of 99 percent and cow's milk has a score of 96 percent. In contrast, plant proteins rarely score higher than 75 percent with most scoring between 50 and 65 percent.

The studies completed by Dr. R. E. McDowell and his colleagues at Cornell University, Ithaca, New York have illustrated the impact dairy cows can have on human protein supplies. He noted that from the grain of a small maize farm of two hectares (measurement of land) humans obtain about 23,470 Megacalories of energy and 246 Kilograms (weight) of protein. If, however, the grain from one hectare of land is consumed by humans and the grain and residue from the second hectare of land is fed to cows, the total energy available as human food drops to 21,491 Megacalories (only 8.4 percent loss), but the total protein available rises to 653 Kilograms, an increase of 165 percent.

Livestock provide a food reserve that is efficient and minimizes problems of waste and food preservation. They are a form of cash reserve. They serve as living banks of stored capital that can be used for either financing on-farm agricultural investments or for emergencies during periods of economic depression. They are considered by many as measures of security and community esteem.

It is important to note that outside the developed world, up to 90 percent of the power for crop production, irrigation, harvesting, and transportation is still derived from animals. They are a source of wool, hair, hides, and skins. Their wastes are often used for fertilizer, methane gas production, feed supplementation, and as heating fuel.

While the need for livestock is readily accepted, those officials with control over developmental funds often do not realize the benefits that might be achieved through the implementation of effective Animal Disease Control Programs. An important aspect of animal disease control that needs to be mentioned is that of the management of the zoonotic diseases such as brucellosis and tuberculosis. An example that is in serious need of worldwide attention at this time is the zoonotic disease caused by Brucella melitensis, a disease of sheep and goats that causes a disease called Undulant Fever in man. With sheep and goats living in very close proximity to the dwellings of most people in the developing world, this disease needs immediate attention!

In those instances where Veterinarians have worked with the livestock producers and industries in the control and eradication of such costly diseases, a direct correlation in improved human health has been found. Losses from disease are a needless loss. When technically sound disease control procedures have been used in conjunction with technically sound management practices, the production potential of the livestock populations at risk have been maximized.

While disease eradication is considered by some to be too costly for developing countries, I believe that many of these countries should consider, at least for some diseases, the benefits of Disease Eradication. Remember that the cost of Disease Control Programs continue on into perpetuity, while the cost of Disease Eradication is a one-time cost.

This cost is relatively insignificant if one considers the magnitude of benefits received year after year. Besides the realization that there is a reduction from the losses due to the disease in question, there is often a general improvement of animal health, as well as improved management, nutrition, and understanding of how to prevent the spread of diseases in general. The use of sound quarantine procedures and sound epidemiological principles increases. Veterinary diagnostic methods become standardized and the industry gains by immediately focusing their limited resources on the causes of their losses rather than the continued costly use of broad spectrum Shotgun treatments that in most cases are only a temporary fix.

We have only begun to develop the potential for livestock production. With apparent general acceptance that over 60 percent of our world's landmass is suitable for pasture, the production of livestock becomes all the more important.

While the cost of animal disease in terms of our human health and wellbeing is astronomical, some still argue that disease control will disturb the balance of nature. They believe that livestock have been the scourge of the earth, and as a result of overgrazing; erosion has occurred and the very source of agriculture production and food supply has been destroyed.

If we listen to integrated agriculturists such as Dr. Albert Sollod of Tufts University or Dr. Michael Coughenour of Colorado State University, we can appreciate that livestock is a benefit rather than a scourge to the human population and environment in general. In fact, some consider herders of livestock to be the cornerstones of stability, providing a sustainable level of productivity.

For example, in Kenya, the Turkana people are able to use their livestock in a remarkably efficient manner. Milk composes 80 percent of their livestock-derived diet, which itself composes 76 percent of their total diet. More than half of their milk comes from camels, which eat mostly woody plants that are relatively abundant, even during a drought. The animals eat whatever is plentiful at any given time and place without inducing discernible degrading of the ecosystem.

A major challenge facing agricultural development is that of identifying production systems that will increase food production while maintaining the valued forest and fertile soils of our world. For any who have traveled to the jungles of Latin America, Africa, or parts of Asia, it is obvious that it is man who is stripping the jungles for the valued hardwoods and destroying the rich habitat for countless irreplaceable plant and animal species.

What, then, can we, as Animal Health Specialists, do in this regard? In many of the developing countries of the world, a herd of 100 cows will only produce 40 calves a year. If an effective Animal Disease Control Program could be implemented, one might consider the possibility of doubling the calf crops in these herds. The farmer could then have the same level of production with only 50 cows. Consider further that with an effective Animal Disease Control Program, the number of calves that would reach maturity would be greatly increased. The result would be improved feed efficiency and less but higher quality animals on any given section of land.

We, in animal health, have some basic homework to carry out with our governmental policy makers. We need to accept that we often use inappropriate indicators to measure the success of livestock related projects in developing countries. Production and income criteria often ignore indicators such as environmental conditions, social, political, and cultural variables. Factors, such as resource degradation, may be in conflict with maximizing production and income.

If economic measures are used as indicators of success, they may be misleading; for example, return per unit of land is a commonly used indicator. However, animals usually involve marginal land with low opportunity costs. If we turn to labor as an indicator, it too is often misleading since animal care, especially in the developing countries, is often performed by children and older family members which, like low quality land, have a lower opportunity cost.

It is apparent that more care must be given to the selection of indicators of success. These indicators should include social, political, environmental, as well as the economic factors and should view livestock projects as a system and not as a commodity.

As we view the current world situation, only a small percentage of domestic animals are competing with humans for resources. The vast majority, quite to the contrary, exists symbiotically and provides man with a significant means of deriving life-sustaining products. In addition to converting products, inedible to human beings, into high quality protein, animals provide countless non-food uses which are essential contributions to the existence of mankind.

At this point, we may be unable to place a monetary value on contributions by animals through non-food services, such as animal traction, but these certainly equal or exceed the value of meat, milk, and eggs. This is especially the case in developing countries. We need to recognize the impact we can have on the future of this world. Animal Health strengthens Public Health. Animal Health improves Animal Production and thereby provides economic stability. The benefits of Animal Health Programs are realized by a broad section of the populace, especially in regard to rural development. The benefits of such programs are great and lasting.

Together, working with specialists from a wide variety of disciplines, we can accomplish much. If we consider the quality of life we would like for our children, we need to recognize that to a great extent it depends on the future health of our valued livestock populations. And in that regard, the availability of healthy, productive livestock depends on that which we can and are willing to do!

CPSIA information can be obtained at www.ICGtesting.com
Printed in the USA
LVOW13s0053310713

345427LV00001B/1/P